MW01596206

No Tokens Issue 5

A BIANNUALLY PUBLISHED JOURNAL CELEBRATING
WORK THAT IS FELT IN THE SPINE.

SUBSCRIPTIONS
$25 for 1 year
www.notokensjournal.com/subscribe

CONTACT
notokensjournal.com
notokensjournal@gmail.com

PRINTING
Brilliant Graphics

DESIGN
Department International

INSIDE COVER ART
Cindy Bernard © 2008.
Silent Key: Deleted Entities 1925–1996

SPRING / SUMMER 2016

ISBN 978–0–692–56118–8

COPYRIGHT © 2016 NO TOKENS JOURNAL

All rights reserved. No part of this publication may be reproduced, distributed, or transmitted in any form or by any means, including photocopying, recording, or other electronic or mechanical methods, without the prior written permission of No Tokens, except in the case of brief quotations embodied in critical reviews and certain other noncommercial uses permitted by copyright law. For permission requests, write to No Tokens, addressed "Attention: Permissions," at the email address above.

Masthead

Editor-in-Chief .... T Kira Madden

Senior Editor .... Molly Tolsky

Fiction Editors .... Leah Schnelbach

Samantha Turk

Assistant Fiction Editor .... Annabel Graham

Poetry Editors .... Hannah Beresford

Lauren Hilger

Non-Fiction Editor .... Rowan Hisayo Buchanan

Editorial Assistants .... Justine Champine

Carina del Valle Schorske

PR and Marketing Director .... Ursula Villarreal-Moura

Editorial Intern .... Suhasini Yeeda

Magazine Art Direction .... Department International

Contents

LETTERS

NON-FICTION

ARTWORK

RECEIVED
DIRECTORY
SEP 24 1944
SEO.

AIR MA

Em Oh You Eye See

MICHAEL SHARICK

I WAS OVER AT Duke's place feeding the dog and delivering his smokes, which he's not supposed to have, and Karen calls, right at Duke's house, she calls, for me. She asks if I can please drive to the airport and pick up the Robinson family; they're on their way home from Disney World, and someone from Make-a-Wish forgot to book them a ride.

"They're not consumers?" Karen says. Fifteen years she's been hospice director and still can't make her voice go from ask to tell. "There's the mother and three kids. One of the kids is sick, but I don't know which one or sick with what, but it's Make-a-Wish, so you can bet sick pretty awful bad."

I ask her how she knows where I am.

"Also," she says, "the Robinsons don't know how they're getting home, so you'll have to make a sign."

I say she must be kidding me.

She says, "We're giving you mileage on this one."

I say I'll make the sign.

You know me, I'd've put on a black suit and little cap, but there isn't time to make the flight, so I go in my Carhartts and what you see here. Turns out limo drivers don't wear black unless it's a tracksuit, anyway.

So but I don't have to wait long, and the Robinsons are easy to spot. The mother is like all the women around here, over and underweight at the same time. She wears the grey Reeboks and sweatpants and a t-shirt with an airbrushed howling wolf she probably got at the fair ten years ago that barely covers her gut, and did she wear it all over Orlando, probably yes. The two kids are called Bobby and Jane, this I find out later, and they're yellow-haired twins, and they both have that space grin you get from breeding too long in the same zip code. They bother me, these kids. The foreheads are too high, the cheeks sink into the face, and little brown rings hover around the eyes. I'm thinking maybe it's hunger, but they just came from an all-expense paid vacation. Also, and this just makes it too perfect, they wear matching Mickey and Minnie Mouse ear hats.

And there's one other person, an older daughter, Annelise. She's maybe twenty, twenty-one. Yes, she's attractive, but not in any way I like. She carries a green pocketbook and drags two Wilson duffel bags behind her, their only luggage, which is good because I didn't even think of trunk space.

I hold my sign and sort of raise my eyebrows like this in a way that is supposed to say, "I'm friendly, ride with me." The Robinsons walk right on past. Or no, "walk" is the wrong word. Mrs. Robinson sort of hobbles. Bobby and Jane bounce and bound like rabbits with missing legs. Annelise has a limp like a young person should never have, dragging those duffels. I second-guess my sign.

I'll skip ahead a bit and just say that it takes a good fifteen minutes to sort out with airport security who I am and who the Robinsons are but eventually we're all in the car and on the road, and it's a few miles before I realize I shouldn't have grabbed for the duffels without introducing myself first. "You don't *look* like a limo driver," says airport security. I'm telling you, I saw those other signs, and mine was the best.

We're on the interstate and I make the mistake of asking about their trip, because why shouldn't I try and make conversation, it's an hour back to Prospect Falls, and between you and me I want to know which kid is dying. Mrs. Robinson is in the back with Bobby and Jane, Annelise up front with me. She is supposed to know where we're going.

"They changed the sheets every *day,*" says Mrs. Robinson. This woman, I swear, has had the same pair of glasses a good eight years. I can see the scratch and smudge from the rear-view mirror. She goes on about the hotel, the soaps in the bathroom, a towel for *each* of them new and clean every day, the blower-fan thing in the window, the breakfast that was totally free and no-strings-attached, the cushy armchairs in the lobby, all those pillows on the beds.

"The pillow was bigger than my brother," says Jane.

But how was the vacation, I want to know.

"I'm saying," says Mrs. Robinson.

I check the odometer, which I reset leaving the airport. We've driven eight miles. Fifty-one to go. These people never stayed in a hotel before. If they hadn't just come from Florida I'd swear that spot on the highway was the furthest they'd ever been from home. The odometer is up to twenty before anyone even mentions Disney.

"The pirate ride," says Bobby. "But it's not like the movie.

Also Buzz Lightyear."

In the rearview I ask Jane if she went to Cinderella's castle. She frowns and looks at her mother as if to say, did I?

Mrs. Robinson answers, "Janey had her heart set on the Ferris wheel. But can you believe they don't have one? That whole big place and no Ferris wheel. We always go to the fair, but we missed it this year and no Ferris Disney Wheel."

"I'm sorry about that," I say, and I think it could be Jane, the sick one.

This whole time Annelise hasn't said word one. She sits, arms folded, forehead pressed up on the passenger window, smudging and breathing. I take a curve too fast on purpose just to see if she'll move. Thirty miles, we're off the interstate now and on the county roads. I have no idea where the Robinsons live and Annelise is supposed to say where to turn.

"How about you," I say, a little softer, so she'll know I'm speaking to her.

"She's not talking," Mrs. Robinson says. "We're in a fight."

I know about fights, so I switch on the radio and we just drive. Trace Adkins and Carrie Underwood and Luke Bryan and Craig Morgan. Nobody tells me what they like but I'm a good guesser.

Eight miles to town and Annelise still says nada. I'm starting to wonder if maybe she's mute or damaged. Bobby and Jane have had enough of new country and they chant the Mouseketeer theme song. Em I see, Kay-ee why, Em oh you I see. Mrs. Robinson tries to talk over them.

"And the hotel people, so friendly. Always want to shake your hand. After a few days I guess we got to know them and they weren't so friendly, no more handshakes, you know people when you know them."

I say that I guess so.

"What?" says Mrs. Robinson.

I say that I said that I guessed so.

"Mickey Mouse!" shout Bobby and Jane.

"Guess so what?" says Mrs. Robinson.

"Donald Duck!" I shout, and the kids explode all over the back seat, and that's when I realize I'm the only one in the car wearing a seatbelt which is totally unacceptable how could I be so careless and where's the best place to pull off and make damn sure everyone is buckled the heck up and I just barely hear above the noise that Annelise is *talking*, something about her photograph, she can't believe they left it behind.

"Well it's not my fault," says the mother. "The door locked behind us and we gave them back the cards that open the door."

I say they could've just asked at the front desk, that they left something in the room and the maid would let them back in.

No one says a word.

"Alright," I say. "Where do you people live?"

It isn't far, just a half-mile off Blackberry Road. It's getting dark by this point and when I stop and Mrs. Robinson lights up, her cigarette looks like a firefly. The kids don't even *think* about the bags and run straight in the trailer, which, the trailer's north end's up on cinder blocks and that's totally unsafe. But I haul the duffels out of the trunk and go to shake Mrs. Robinson's hand and she says, "*Oh* no, we *know* each other now," and Annelise doesn't move. Mrs. Robinson hitches up the grass, leaves the bags. I wait and count to ten. Annelise doesn't budge. I walk back around to the driver side. The trailer's vinyl siding is missing just to the left of the front door, leaving exposed insulation, not at all stormproof.

I try and make my face like *time to go*, but I don't know from girls.

"I don't live here," Annelise says.

"No?" I say.

"I'm over on 16, past Bravermann's."

"On 16?"

"Do you mind a lot?"

"That's the other side of the reservoir!"

Bobby runs out of the trailer and screams, "Mister Whiskers had kittens all over my bed!"

I get in the car and put it in drive.

By the time I get to her road it's all dark, and I can't see the house and have to turn up the driveway. If I say the house creeps into view, do you know what I mean? It's like the house drives up to me. It's not even a house; it's an RV trailer. The lawn is littered with rusted metal and hunks of plastic and old tires. Annelise unbuckles her seatbelt.

"Thanks for the ride," she says.

She starts to walk up the grass and stops. I notice for the first time her clothes, a black tank top and black jeans. She turns back to me.

"Just so you know," she says, "the trip was all paid for already. Only Mamma wasn't supposed to go."

"Right," I say. I don't know what she means. Then I say the dumb thing. "You need anything else?"

"Actually," she says. "I don't have a car and can't get to the dump. Toss something for me?"

Now I'm taking out her trash, perfect. But I nod and say okay. She jogs around the side of the RV and a motion sensor floodlight kicks on, and it is *bright*, and I'm blind for a second. But then the lawn comes into focus. It's not really just garbage everywhere. It's toys.

Annelise appears again, towing something by one handle, limping like she did at the airport. I know what it is before I can see it, just by the sound the rubber makes dragging in the dirt. I get out of the car.

"Thanks," she says. I place the kid's bicycle in the trunk, gently push the lid till it clicks.

"I just don't need it around anymore," she says.

"No," I say. "You don't."

End of Season

DIANA KEREN LEE

people disappoint me
the cues they have missed
deliberately, the calls
and what makes me think
I am so perfect
as the ice melts in my drink
quick to pick apart
a sentence, what you meant

oh, to be stuck in honey
nothing but a bug
am I just too impatient
for people to change
the earth to be saved

evening wrings the blood from its shirt
horizon pink with grief
the color of the inside of a slab
of beef when it's medium rare

admit it: most of the day was drivel
and you waited to cook it through

VIA AEREA

Some Days

TOCHUKWU EMMANUEL OKAFOR

THERE ARE FIVE OF us in the car: Chima, Musa, Boye, Mary, and me. Boye is our driver. His stubby fingers circle the steering wheel, and he goes, "Vrooom. Vrooom." His eyes tear through the windshield, into the meat-coloured yard with an avocado tree standing in the middle, like they are about to jump out of their sockets anytime soon. Like he truly believes he is driving. "Vrooom. Vrooom," he goes again like a mad dog—his teeth clenched, his back straightened.

Mary sits in front, beside Boye. She has the look of a newly married wife whose husband has just bought a brand new Jeep. But she is only eight or so. Her left palm rests on her thigh, where there are four big holes on her yellow-gold skirt. And this makes me wonder: Does she leave her clothes for rats to feast on? Not that I'm angry about being cheated out of my turn to drive or for any other thing; the truth is, most of her skirts appear the same—faded, with holes the size of fish eyes. Her plastered smiles annoy me. They annoy me so much I don't know when I say, "Boye, it's my turn to drive."

Chima is the first person to speak after what seems like a long pause, a long pause which makes me look as though I had only spoken to myself, the way madmen do. You see, Chima's tongue can cut right through your skin like a sharp knife, even if you are as fat as those cows his father sells at Abule market. So it doesn't surprise me when he says, "Shut up your mouth." But it stings, like a fresh nosebleed. I am twelve and the oldest among them. Chima is nine. Perhaps he is like his mother, who wakes the whole street with her shouts at her mother-in-law every morning because the poor woman wets her bed daily. Disrespect and anger run in their blood.

"But it's his turn," Musa says in a voice so thin it can pass for a rat's scratch. Maybe he is afraid of what Chima will name him today. Yesterday, it was shit-eater. Last Sunday, after the football match between Spain and Portugal, it was *anu ohia*, the meaning only Chima and I understand. *Anu ohia* made Musa cry as he ran home, like a baby hungry for his mother's milk. Now Musa sits beside me, close to the window at the back. I watch his trembling hand curl around the door handle. I think he is scared of Chima hitting him. After all, who knows what other bad things run in Chima's blood?

"I see you ate too much tuwo. And it has given you strong

power, bah?" Chima says, jerking back and front as though the car is actually moving, bumping along potholes. "If you open your dirty mouth again this afternoon, your father who looks thinner than aziza will not recognize you again." I've always thought of Musa's father as broom-thin, but I never knew it would make my heart stop when said out loud—especially from someone like Chima. He begins to cheer Boye who, by now, waves to other invisible drivers and honks the horn that never blares.

"Children, it's okay. Daddy will soon get tired of driving."

I'd like to call Mary a big fool. Who is Boye that she should call him Daddy? I'm beginning to dislike this game. In fact, I'm beginning to dislike Mary. Her right elbow leans against the open window, collecting cobwebs and smelly dust. Look at her—how dirty! Musa must have been right about her when he told me she sometimes skips her morning baths. But then, I wonder how Musa gets to know the kind of things he knows. Like whose sixteen-year-old daughter was kicked out of the house for getting pregnant. And whose son slept in a cell for robbing Mama Atinuke's supermarket. Musa is like my younger sister in the village—they know too much for their age.

Boye is getting tired. This, I know. His voice is thinning out. His grip on the steering wheel is like a year old baby holding a big torch in one hand. His straightened back relaxes in slow curves against the back of his seat. Me, I never let my back rest on that seat. Who knows what sleeps inside of those ugly-looking holes oozing stained brown-yellow foam? Bugs? Cockroaches? Rats? Who knows?

Boye gives up. "Make anoda person come drive."

Boye sounds like a broken radio—cracked, way too throaty for a boy his age. It's not his fault his English is as bad as a rotting egg. His father doesn't send him to school; instead, the poor man leaves him in his mechanic shop to tend to petty car issues. Most days, his father is never around in the shop, so Boye has his father's unpaid apprentices as companions, as friends. Musa once told me he had seen those boys—Boye's father's apprentices—smoking wee-wee. And Boye was right there in their midst. He said he saw Boye breathe in air from the wee-wee before coughing out his intestines like an asthmatic patient suffering an attack. Then Boye tried again, sucking in smoke as if he was sipping sweet kunu, exhaling, smiling, laughing, his friends welcoming him into a hallowed club of wee-wee smokers. Again, I wonder how Musa knew this, how he was afforded the chance to see all that. But his story rings true. If you've ever seen a wee-wee smoker—with his blackened, dry lips and dark lines under his eyes and fingers—you would believe Musa. Boye looks like a wee-wee smoker, or is it just my eyes?

Chima climbs out of the car soon after Boye does. I follow, too. Boye's palms no longer look like a person's palms. They are pitch black with an oily sheen, like the generator man who spends half of his day messing with machine parts in the name of generator repairs. He rubs his palms up and down and sideways on the front of his shirt, and this does not surprise me: One day, he is going to be a mechanic, like his father. While Boye takes the middle seat in the back, Chima reaches for the front door.

"What do you think you are doing?" I ask Chima and aim for the door handle.

"What does it look like?" says Chima, whose hand is now underneath mine. "Are you getting blind like your mother? Or is the smoke from the puff-puff she sells spoiling your eyes?"

In this life, there are two things I don't joke about: my mother and my books. And for the rubbish Chima just spat out, I must make him take it back and chew, and I won't mind if he chokes on it the same way I sometimes choke on my saliva.

"You dare not talk about my mother in that manner. Say you are sorry."

"Sorry? Is the smoke now getting to your brain and frying your senses, too? *Anu ohia.*"

I withdraw my right arm and punch Chima in the face. He squeals, almost sounding like amplified clucks of a rooster on heat. He rushes at me, trying to pull me off the ground. I land him a hard blow in the back and two on his head. His might—even his senses— is not as sharp as his tongue after all. He picks a stone the size of my fist and shoots at me. I duck faster than an eye blink. He misses, for the stone drops at the foot of an abandoned refrigerator just near the rusty metal gate. I make use of this opportunity to finish him off. I strike him twice in his sides and then draw back my hand to give him a hard slap across the face. He is too sore to cry. He whimpers and runs away, tripping as he runs.

Boye goes after Chima. Musa sits there in the car, looking ahead as if something special has caught his interest, but beneath his straight face, I know he is happy to see Chima all beaten up like a sack of threshed corn. I climb into the driver's seat. "Ooomph, ooomph," goes my wheezy breath. I feel for my left thigh where Chima bit me with his teeth. A round throbbing welt grazes my fingers. Mary is looking away. Her husband is gone, gone like her own father Chima sometimes laughed about. She should be happy, you know. Chima taunts her like the other children he plays with. But I'd still like to tell her she's a big fool; she stood up for Boye even when his time to drive was through.

"Are you okay?" Musa still whispers his words, even when the almighty bully of a Chima is gone.

I ignore him. I ignore the swelling pain in my thigh. I ignore the thought of a bug or a cockroach sneaking up my back when I recline fully in the driver's seat. A drop of water falls on my hair. I look up. It is raining, and I don't even know when it started. More drops of rainwater and late-afternoon sunlight trickle through the rust-eaten roof of the car. I shut my eyes tight, allowing the wetness on my hair, on my worn clothes, on my rubber wristwatch that forever ticks 12 even when it is only a few minutes after five. And when I open them, Musa and Mary are no longer in the car. I circle my fingers around the steering wheel and go, "Vrooom, vrooom," quite louder than the *tap-tap-tap* angry pelting of rain.

I return home just before the sun begins its departure. The house is empty. I change into a set of new clothes—half of Spiderman's face on my t-shirt is gone, and my pair of green shorts has a hole in each leg, round enough to fit two of my fingers. But I don't mind, it's getting dark outside and besides, who cares to look my way? People around here go about their lives minding their own business. I grab a handful of newspapers from the pile Mother's friend gave us the other day and hurry outside.

If you stand close to the middle of Idowu street—it's a popular street in Lagos, a famous Nollywood actor was once robbed there—and look ahead as if to read the words on the only billboard on that street, you will see black whorls of spicy smoke rising and disappearing into the sky high above. The smoke is from Mother's shop. Although it's not really a shop, Mother and I like to call it so. At least, that is what the men from the local government office call it, and we even pay for it. Her shop is just a small space in a corner, near an open gutter, with only a table and a fireplace. But because she has stayed there for over three years, the ground of her shop is no longer leveled. Heaps of charcoal and ash have compressed and hardened into a rough black rock, the shape of a mound. Early one afternoon, a few months back, the men from the local government office tried evicting Mother from her shop. That same day, the chairman of the local government visited us there. I remember Mother squeezed five hundred naira note into his palms, and, later that evening, after the day's sales, I found him leaving our one-room apartment, his face heavy with smiles, as if he had won an American visa lottery. I don't know what Mother must have given or said to him, but all I know is this: We stopped receiving eviction threats from the local government office.

Mother is frying another set of puff-puff by the time I arrive. She has sliced the yams and cut the potatoes into fingerlike shapes, and steam is escaping the pot of freshly prepared pepper stew. The paper she uses to wrap puff-puff for customers is almost finished, but when she sees me with newspapers bundled under my armpit, she looks happy.

"Godspower, it's good that you brought additional paper so neither of us needs to return home," she says. "How are you? Did you eat the food I kept for you? Has your father returned?"

Mother is like that, asking questions like a runner racing to the finish line. She never waits to hear your reply after one question. But it surprises me that she asks after Father. She hardly does. Father and Mother are like oil and water. Mother thinks Father is a lazy man who sits around beer parlours waiting for a free drink. Every night, before Mother leaves in tight clothes for her other work, she tells me to study hard and not to be like Father. I don't know how I'm going to tell her that I haven't read a thing today, that I have been fighting and driving the car in Musa's compound.

"I'm fine," I say, attending to the next customer who wants fifty naira worth of puff-puff. "I didn't know you kept food for me. I hurried here as soon as I returned home." But I avoid mentioning Father.

"Help me with the gallon of groundnut oil by your leg." I pass her the gallon. "Will you eat puff-puff, my son? You must be hungry. Or do you prefer to buy boiled rice? The woman selling food is still around. Let me buy some bread. Will you like bread?"

"Mother, I'm fine."

Evening is getting darker, and there are more customers than ever before. Is it the fried yams and potatoes Mother now sells that attracts them? Or is it the new big umbrella, poised over the centre of the table, with a bright yellow bulb dangling from its middle? Whatever the source of attraction is, I don't care. I'm only feeling happy that we'll top our sales today.

But my happiness is pruned short, an hour or so later, when Chima appears out of nowhere with his mother, both of them carrying wooden faces. My heart takes a quick somersault, my throat dries up, and my eyes begin to ache.

"Good evening, Mama Chima," says Mother.

"What is good about this evening, eh, Nne Godspower?" Chima's mother doesn't know, but her voice sounds like a parrot's, even in her visible fury. Mrs. Parrot, this woman.

"Ah. Mama Chima, my good friend. *O gini neme?* What is the problem?" Mother tries to pacify Mrs. Parrot with her gestures and her Igbo, but the woman is so angry I think she doesn't hear a word Mother says.

"You are acting as if you don't know. Look at my boy. Take a close look at Chima's body. What has my boy done to your son that your son wants to kill him? What I have done to you people?"

Mother looks at me through narrowed eyes as if they had those metal-cutting lasers I see on television in Musa's house, as if she wants to rip me apart and feed my parts to Mrs. Parrot so as to calm her down. Some customers simply stare at us, folding their arms to see what happens next; others leave because they are tired of waiting. The yam slices frying in the hot oil start to burn.

I begin, "Mother, it is Chima who looked for trouble first. It was my turn to drive, not his. But he insulted me and you, Mother. He said the smoke from your puff-puff is making me stupid. He said—"

Tochukwu Emmanuel Okafor

Mother slaps me with the hand she used a while ago to touch the oil and yam slices and salt. She pulls me by my ear and drags me around in front of Mrs. Parrot. She slaps me. Again and again. Mrs. Parrot is still not satisfied. She jumps all over the place as though Mother has not punished me enough. Maybe she will stop if Mother lifts the frying pan off the fire and empties its contents on me. Out of the corner of my eyes, I see Chima laughing behind his mother, a silent wicked laughter. He is making many faces at me. This is the kind of night I wish will pass like it never existed.

"Tell Chima you are sorry," Mother says.

I say I'm sorry as if I'm talking to myself.

"Louder. And on your knees."

I obey as instructed.

I catch the tears in my eyes, hoping to release them when Mrs. Parrot and her son are long gone. Mother insists on giving Chima some puff-puff, but Mrs. Parrot rejects the offer. She asks after Father, comments about the killings by Boko Haram in the north, asks Mother about the outcome of the last Christian Mothers' meeting, mentions so-and-so, says such-and-such—and before she is done talking like the parrot she is, hot tears pour down both sides of my cheeks like a dam tired of being caged. Chima sees me crying, bends as if to pick a fallen object, but actually, what he does is laugh at me, that same wicked laughter. After a few minutes, Mrs. Parrot bids Mother goodnight and scurries off with her son the way they came.

"This is how you want to repay me after everything?" Mother says. "Do you want to end up like your father? Am I not trying my best to make sure you get the best of everything? Is Chima your mate, or even your size, that you engage in a fight with him?" A long silence falls between us. "Get up from there. Let's go home."

Mother must have been packing up when Mrs. Parrot was chit-chatting away. I want to ask Mother when she bought the umbrella. I want to ask her who had offered to connect the electric bulb for us. But all I do is hang my head low like a guilty offender of the law. Now, all I feel is hunger and shame and desire for revenge in equal amounts. All this seems to vanish when I see Father. He is sitting outside on a low wooden stool, a bottle of Chelsea dry gin in one hand. I greet him. But he only nods his head, sleepily, like a person head-dancing to an inner music. Mother walks ahead, straight into the room, undresses, ties a wrapper around her bosom, grabs a bucket, and heads to the bathroom, which is a tiny aluminum-roofed room standing in the backyard, attached to the wall. She waits her turn.

Father lifts himself out of the stool, supporting his weight with his free hand on the unpainted wall. He wobbles into the candle-lit room where I sit in a corner picking at my cold meal. He turns the radio on and dances to the *scratch-scratch* sounds of the radio. Is this man alright upstairs?

"Dance with me," Father says to me.

I turn my back to him, acting as if I didn't hear him. An hour or so later, Mother is in the room. She is getting ready to leave for her other job. This other job, if you ask me what it is, I will tell you I don't know. But what I know is this: She returns from this job as early as Mrs. Parrot's shouts at her mother-in-law begin in the morning. When she returns, some parts of her face have the faded version of her lipstick, and her breath is heavy with the smell of alcohol and cigarettes, and there are black smudges under her eyes like Boye's. Maybe she cries too much in this, her other job. Maybe this other job requires her to fight, because when she comes back, her hair looks like it has never seen a brush, and her clothes are rumpled in many areas of her body, and she comes back very, very tired. I don't know. But I think Father knows, which is why he allows her to do this night job.

"Dance with me," Father says to Mother.

Mother is putting on the brown leather high heels I took to the cobbler for mending two days ago. Her legs have outgrown them, and I don't know why she still struggles to wear them. She doesn't even walk well in them. Won't her manager complain about this? Or perhaps her manager never notices, because whenever she is ready to leave for her night job, a Jeep is already waiting to pick her up. Again, I wonder why she never lets her driver into our house. There are many things about Mother's night job that baffle me, and if I don't stop thinking about them, one day my head will swell and burst like a nylon filled with too much water.

"Papa Godspower, I don't have time for this or any of your games. I'm already late for work," Mother says.

"Which work? You think I don't know where you hang out

every night." Father is spraying spittle on Mother as he talks, but she doesn't seem to care, or is she becoming like Mary? Most times, I think Mother is like Mary—she sneezes on her wrapper, and when she does it on her palm, she rubs the mucus between her palms until it dissolves.

Father is holding onto Mother's tight clothes now. He doesn't want her to leave for her night job. And while the two of them go at each other, raising their voices to see whose is the louder, I sneak outside, into a windy moonless night. I hear Mother calling Father names like useless man and *onye iberibe*, and telling Father how he is the reason they decided to keep only me in the city and my sister in the village. I hear the *kram-kram* breaking of bottles on the walls of our one-room apartment, and the dull thumps of heavy objects falling. I am running almost blindly into the night, past the parked Jeep waiting for Mother, to the car I know how to drive, to watch the blank sky through the rust-eaten roof, to sleep there, and to forget that some days, some nights, are ever like this.

Hour

KELLE GROOM

Ow wah the black haired man behind the case of meat
said, laughed, face in profile. A sentence I can't remember.
In his dark cap, nose rounding, dark round laugh,
I saw my uncle Dean who died a few towns up the Cape
last Spring. Wept wide empty aisles of things on sale,
past natural foods, quietly mouthing *Ow wah, Ow wah,*
with Dean's intonation, hard on the Ow. I want to go back to
the meat counter man, Say *something else.* Afraid my greed,
will drive Dean out, & only the meat man will appear,
changed back to who he was & Dean who I've loved my whole
life who loved me my whole life will be gone. At the checkout
counter at the hardware store a bald man holds a yellow tape
measure around his skull. *Are you measuring your head?* I ask.
For a costume, he said. I nod. James appears, tells me a shortcut,
disappears. After I walk by the paint cans & plastic boxes,
James returns, said the shortcut's no good. It's even longer,
with walls of snow. I walk the edge of Conwell, a truck unsteady
& fast pushes toward me & another man while we slosh
through melting ice, gray snow shoved to our left in hedges.
It's not easy, he calls over his tan coat, animal back. I'll go
back to the meat counter at the Stop & Shop. *Ow wah Ow wah*
I'll call like wild animals do, black ducks on the water.
Between us, glass, red meat & white fat, puckered yellow
chickens look cold, in need of a blanket, everything cut & named.

Royal Mail
Oxford
Mail Centre
11.12.02
05:45 pm
23010057

Ruben

SHELLY ORIA AND NELLY REIFLER

00131/0000

WE WERE FEEDING THAT rat for three weeks straight before it uttered a word.

"Messiah," Lonny said after two weeks and a day, "you're full of crap. We're doing everything you said, the tamarind basmati, the glazed bacon, the popsicles, and nada. Not a word. All it does is run around and squeak. I got a bad stomachache, my woman's pissed off, and I don't know if you're shitting me or what."

"Patience," Messiah said. Messiah usually spoke in single words.

The fog, with its peculiar, dull orange tint, rolled in and pressed against our windows. Every morning was foggy in those days, the world outside our apartment obscured.

When the end of the third week was approaching, we took up Cuban cooking. "If those plantains don't do the job," Lonny said, "I don't know what will." He didn't mean to imply we might give up.

The first word was *more*. Lonny was not excited. "What if that's all it ever says," he said. "What if it just keeps asking for more and more food and never makes good on the prophecy? Then we become slaves, fucking rat-slaves."

"More," we heard again.

We looked over at the rat. It was sitting on its haunches, wiping grease off its whiskers with its right paw.

"Hot dogs," Messiah said.

"What the fuck's that gonna do," Lonny yelled.

"Technically, that's two words," I said.

I was taking a break—I just had to—and was sitting on the velour sectional, flipping through the American Journal of Opthamology. I could feel the orange fog outside, a kind of damp presence seeping through the walls. I shivered.

"C'mon," said Lonny. "We're in this together." He reached out his hand and pulled me up off the couch.

We fed it hot dogs and nothing changed.

"Messiah," Lonny said, "we keep feeding it the damn hot dogs and it just keeps saying more, more. Bun, no bun, sauerkraut, onions—and it's just more." Lonny was imitating the sound of the rat's voice when he said the word "more." He was doing a pretty good job.

I said maybe we should move the rat's cage from the kitchen island to the dining table, where he'd be able to see out the apartment windows. The rat pressed its face through the bars, took a look at the new view, then waddled back to its usual spot.

"More," he said.

Lonny groaned.

"Him," Messiah said.

Things changed after that.

"I can't just push a button and start thinking of it as some sort of person," Lonny said, so we figured we needed a name. The naming process did not go smoothly. At first Lonny wanted to name the rat after his mother, Lucille. He didn't care that it was a male.

"Names, gender, identity—it's all fluid these days," Lonny said. I crossed my arms.

He came around eventually, but we still couldn't agree on a name. "Why should you get to decide," he said every time I made a suggestion.

Then Lonny woke up in the middle of the night and shook my arm until I was awake too.

"I can't believe I haven't thought of it earlier," he said, and he told me his idea. We named it Ruben after Lonny's best friend who'd been killed in a car crash two years earlier. I was surprised at first; we never talked about Ruben. But as soon as Lonny said it, I knew it was perfect.

Ruben responded very well to his name.

"Clearly the right choice," Lonny said, sounding like a proud father.

"This fog is making everything look orange," I said. "What is that?"

Lonny shrugged. "Emissions?"

Ruben started getting very specific in his demands around that time. There were no more plain mores—now he was naming specific cuisines. He developed exotic tastes, and Lonny didn't mind the extra cost or effort. He wasn't calling Messiah anymore either, and he stopped talking about how his prophecies were bullshit. He was completely invested in Ruben now, entirely convinced that we should allow him the time he needed, be supportive.

Ruben seemed a little less grumpy, too. One day he did headstands and cartwheels for us and then giggled, clapping his paws. Another time he made a kind of self-portrait rat sculpture from the cedar chips that lined the floor of his cage.

Lonny ran through his cookbooks and began to go online to find the most interesting recipes. We went from Turkish to Greek and Armenian, Yemeni and Iranian, then Lebanese.

"He's in his Mediterranean phase," Lonny said in that tone again, as if this were our son who'd just graduated from an Ivy League college.

One day I got out of the shower to find Lonny sitting on the sectional, gazing at Ruben with a look I had never seen on his face before. It hit me then: I was starting to feel left out. Sidelined. Lonny hadn't let me do any actual cooking in weeks. All I was allowed to do was measure out the dry ingredients and scrub pots.

The next morning, around dawn, I couldn't take it anymore.

"Lonny," I said. I shook his shoulder, which was slippery in his satin pajamas.

"Ruben...." Lonny mumbled in his sleep. "Ruben....."

"Lonny, I'm going to make my cherry meringues. Remember the ones I made that New Year's Eve when we had the bottles of water and the generator? Do you think maybe Ruben would like them?"

Lonny reached up and lifted his sleep mask. "What?"

"I'm going to make some meringues for the rat. And also some butterscotch pudding."

"Are you trying to kill him?" Lonny said. He was wide awake now. The orange light of sunrise had begun to filter into the bedroom.

"I just think he might like a little dessert," I said.

"He can't process all that sugar," Lonny said. "Don't you know anything about rats?"

Lonny often didn't remember things he said to me, things that seemed important and earnest at the time, but that in retrospect were just expediencies. Things like: We're in this together. I got out of bed and opened the blinds. I stood there near the window, facing him but looking just past him.

He rubbed his eyes with the palms of his hands. He sighed. Then he patted my cheek.

"Can you make the pudding with Stevia? he asked. Or Xylitol?"

Ruben loved the butterscotch pudding. In fact, after he had his first bowl of it, he said "Thank you" for the first time. Lonny beamed. That night in bed Lonny kissed me on the neck and blew in my ear and wrote his name on my ass with a damp pinky, just like the old days.

Things were good for a while. Ruben was eating well and becoming quite chatty. First he only talked about food. Then he started telling knock-knock jokes. Then he began engaging us in conversations about the weather and politics. We got him his own miniature velour sectional, to match ours, which we all found hilarious and adorable. Ruben added chortling to his repertoire. At night, Ruben lay down on the cushions, and we'd put a tiny fleece blanket over him. Then we'd go to our bedroom. Sex was like when we first got together, with the nipple clamps, anal beads, peppermint oil, and astronaut costumes back in rotation. We were tired from all the menu-planning and cooking, but the orgasmic flush kept us going.

Then, one foggy Sunday morning—Lonny and I were deep in the crosswords and Ruben was doing his jumping jacks, the way he did twice a day now to burn off some of the food—we heard a knock on the door. And I can't explain it but all three of us just knew it was Messiah.

Lonny and I looked at each other. I put down the crossword and nudged Lonny with my toe.

Messiah did not, of course, wait for anyone to open the door. He just sort of appeared in front of us, between the coat closet and the table with the pile of mail.

"My man!" Lonny said in a voice too loud to pass as happy. Lonny never knew how to play it cool; people used to ask me why he was anxious even when he was perfectly calm.

I had never seen Messiah before. It turned out I'd been imagining him all wrong. He was wearing some sort of gold, satin cape, but other than that he looked generic: thick, metal rimmed glasses, skinny denims, vintage sneakers. And he wasn't tall or broad-shouldered or anything. I'd expected him to look like a man who used strength to get his way, but instead he looked like the guy you send to call for backup.

He and Lonny hugged, but Messiah's eyes seemed dead. When he shook my hand, I felt like I was touching ice. Messiah signaled Lonny with his eyes and they started toward the kitchen. I followed, unsure if it was okay, but neither of them stopped me. I looked back at Ruben, thinking he might be tense, but he was midway through his post-workout stretches. At our kitchen door, I let them pass me; I could see and hear from that spot, but felt less intrusive. Messiah and Lonny grew up together; they shared the kind of intimacy men share when they wish they were brothers.

"Coffee?" Lonny asked as Messiah placed himself on the wobbly stool by our kitchen island. That stool always creaked when Lonny sat on it, but now it was quiet. Messiah looked at him funny in response, which is to say his eyes were more alive now and talking, but in a language I didn't speak.

Lonny nodded and poured him a shot of rye, neat. He looked at me, and I shook my head. It was 10 in the morning. He poured another one for himself and sat next to Messiah, on the stool that I always thought of as mine. An awkward silence followed—both men drinking and staring at the floor—and for a moment it seemed that we would all be in that kitchen like that, wordless, until planet earth melted and died. Finally, Messiah looked into Lonny's eyes.

"Enough," he said.

"Don't say that, man, don't tell me that," Lonny said.

Messiah said nothing, which I took to mean he was standing by his word.

"Ruben is my life," Lonny whispered, so low and sweet I could have missed it. Messiah grabbed Lonny's arm then in a way that seemed painful.

"Enough," he said again, and then again, loud. "Enough!"

When Messiah raised his voice, it had a metallic echo. And there was a stillness that surrounded him—I don't know how to describe it—a profound emptiness in the air closest to his body.

"Heaven?" Messiah asked. "Or this….?" He drained the rest of his drink and shrugged a skinny shoulder in my direction. It was the first time he'd acknowledged me since he shook my hand. Then he gestured with his empty tumbler around the kitchen and finally gave the air a jab toward the living room and Ruben's cage.

Lonny asked me to give him and Messiah a moment.

I went and sat on the velour sectional.

Ruben was doing yoga. He finished the warrior pose and wiped his face with his little towel. Then he said he'd been wondering if Scarlett Johansson was actually smart or just good at playing intelligent characters. He also wondered how the Fed made decisions about interest rates, and related to that, where are dimes minted? He added that he would like a sea salt and caramel latte.

"I can't make you one right now," I said. "I wish I could, but you know Lonny's in there with Messiah."

Ruben nodded. We both sat on our sectionals then, waiting.

Messiah glided out of the kitchen after about ten minutes. He flashed me a peace V with his fingers and kept going right out the door. Ruben watched him leaving. I leapt up and went back to the kitchen.

Lonny looked awful.

"What is it?" I asked him.

He got out a new glass, poured some rye in it, and slid it across the counter to me.

"We have to…"

"What? What?" I said.

"We have to let Ruben go," Lonny said. "He's not here to be our pet or our friend. He's here to fulfill the prophecy. Or he was. We've ruined it."

The first sip of my drink burned worse than usual. I took another.

"The line between nourishment and decadence is a crucial one, and we crossed it," Lonny said, sounding a bit like he was reciting a poem.

"So you're blaming me?" I said.

"I didn't say that," he said.

"The cookies, the pies, the frozen yogurt," I said, doing a mental inventory of everything I'd been making for him. "That's the decadence, right?"

He looked at me, and for a moment I could see what he must have looked like as a young boy.

"I really don't know," he said. "I just know we've spoiled him. And now he'll never tell us how to get to heaven."

I tried to think fast. Should I confess to Lonny? I'd only used sugar twice, maybe three times in all those weeks since the first pudding. I knew—just knew, the way you know things about your family without being told—that Ruben could process the real stuff just fine. And when I proved it, I felt closer to Ruben, an invisible cord connecting our bellies. But could that be the problem?

"Lonny," I said, "I have something to tell you." Lonny seemed in his own world.

"A lesbian couple from Toluca," he said. "They're getting him next."

"Mexico," I asked, "or Illinois?" But I regretted my question right away. What difference did it make?

Lonny shrugged. "You can ask them when they get here to-night," he said. He got up and zipped his jacket. "I can't look at him," he said. "I need some air."

I went back into the living room. Ruben was reading *Gone Girl*—the book propped open and leaned against his cage. I stared at him but he ignored me. It was always hard to get his attention when he was reading his thrillers or watching his soaps.

"Ruben, something bad happened," I said.

"Don't ruin it!" he said.

"Not in the book," I said, "right now, with Messiah."

"I know," he said, his eyes still on his book. "Don't ruin it!"

I looked at him, puzzled. He was acting like a teenager, but one who seemed to have information I needed. I knelt in front of the cage and pressed my face against the wire.

"Ruben, can you please look at me?" He finally raised his eyes.

"Are you mad at me?" I asked. He shrugged, and I know that this is a strange thing to say, but I swear—in that moment, he looked just like Lonny.

"I'm sorry I fed you real sugar," I said. "That may have caused some problems." He stared at me, as if trying to hypnotize me.

"Are you trying to tell me something?" I asked.

"I'm trying not to tell you something," he said. I had no idea how to respond, and Ruben was quickly getting impatient. He put down the book. He shook his head with closed eyes, his little claws touching his forehead, pushing into his fur.

"You're supposed to ask me," he whispered.

"Ask you what," I whispered back, because that's what we were doing.

"Ask me for help," he said, much louder now. "The two of you together. You're supposed to accept that you don't know everything, and ask for help."

"Oh, Ruben," I said.

"It's not the sugar," he said, his voice softer now. And his pointy features changed, became more gentle. He smoothed his whiskers with the back of one paw.

We looked into each other's eyes then for what felt like a long time. I had never been so close to his face before. I had never noticed the whorls and cowlicks in his hair, nor his curly lashes.

He repeated: "The two of you together. It's you and Lonny and the prophecy. This is just the beginning."

I thought I might cry.

"Go to him," said Ruben. I opened my mouth to say something—I'm not even sure what—but Ruben heaved *Gone Girl* open and began to read again.

I walked slowly back into the kitchen. The Lucite dreidl that Lonny kept his weed stash in sat on the counter. The window was partway open. Lonny was sitting on the fire escape, with his back to the glass. His shoulders hunched forward; his hair fluttered in the wind. In his hand he held the green glass pipe that I'd given him for our first anniversary.

The fog had begun to clear. Scraps of blue sky peeked from behind the shredding orange mist.

I drank some water straight from the tap, then splashed a bit more rye in my glass from earlier. I knew I was dawdling, that some Mexican or maybe Midwestern ladies were probably landing at the airport, that I should make a move. But I felt a creeping paralysis. I moved my drink to my lips, sniffed its bracing fumes.

And it came to me at that moment, in the kitchen, looking out the window, watching Lonny, watching the pigeons flapping and the steam rising from the roofs of lower buildings and the helicopters buzzing in the distance over the harbor as the fog spindled away: something was going to change, no matter what we did. And not only that: everything is changing all the time.

I knocked on the window. Lonny turned around. He smiled. Yes, he smiled. I could tell he didn't notice himself smiling, which made it even better.

I crooked my finger, beckoning him inside. He pushed the window open and climbed through, dropping to the linoleum floor.

"They're going to be here soon," he said.

"Listen," I said. I reached for his hand and squeezed it. "We still have a chance. It's not too late. We haven't done anything wrong, I think. We just forgot to ask the rat the question."

Lonny shook his head. "It's done," he said. "The lesbians from Toluca…" he sighed and trailed off.

"Listen," I said again. "Lonny. Do you remember how fucked up we were before Ruben?"

Lonny met my eyes. "I guess?" he said.

"We were bickering all the time. You were filling up the dreidl like twice a week." Lonny glanced in the direction of the dreidl.

"You were up every night buying shit on the internet," he said. "It wasn't just me."

"Of course not," I said, "that's my point." I grabbed Lonny's hand, perhaps a little strong.

"Your point is that we were messed up?" he asked. He frowned the way he always did when he felt confused.

"My point is that we were stuck, but we've changed!" I said, and Lonny's hand jerked because I was yelling. I cleared my throat, took Lonny's hand again.

"Everything is always changing," I said, trying to keep my voice steady. "Don't you see, Lonny? We're no different than this tree," I said, pointing at our kitchen window, "or the sky, which was foggy, remember?—but now it's clear and then it will be dark in a few hours, then bright again in the morning!" Lonny seemed concerned, or perhaps disappointed.

"What the hell are you talking about," he asked. I wasn't explaining myself well.

"Look," I said. "If this tree asked you if it could keep its leaves, just for one autumn, what would you say?"

"I would say I must have smoked too much because I'm talking to a tree," Lonny said, and I smiled because I thought he was being funny but his face stayed serious.

"You'd tell the tree it was asking for the impossible," I said, "the unnatural. You'd explain that everything is constantly in flux, that change is beautiful." Lonny looked in the direction of the window as if examining the tree.

"You're saying we should just give up on Ruben," he said, his words sounding more like an accusation than a question.

"No," I said, "I think we still have a shot. I think we need to talk to Ruben together and see. And I think we need to thank him, to tell him we know that he's changed us for the better." Lonny looked straight at me now.

"You got it all wrong," he said. "That's exactly how we fucked up—by being so damn happy. We didn't even ask him how to get to heaven! We totally lost focus." Lonny seemed so sad and I felt an urge to hug him but I knew he'd resist.

"Is that what Messiah said," I asked, though I knew the answer. Lonny nodded. We stood there for a bit; I looked up and tried to choose my words carefully.

"Lonny," I said finally, and he met my eyes, "have you ever considered that Messiah might be jealous of you, of us?" Lonny seemed surprised, then shook his head.

"I don't think so," he said. "Why would he move us to the top of the list if he was a bad friend? We wouldn't have gotten this chance in the first place if it weren't for him."

"Not a bad friend," I said, "just jealous. I saw him today, Lonny. And I'm telling you: he came here to put an end to our happiness."

Something passed through Lonny's eyes then; I knew he heard me and I knew to wait.

"Yeah," he said after a moment, and then again in a softer voice, "yeah. Maybe you're right."

He kissed me then. I tasted the weed and rye in his mouth. I opened my eyes and looked up at his, which were closed. Light flooded the kitchen. It was still morning, but nearing noon. The earth was turning toward the sun, and on the other side of the planet there were people closing their eyes to go to sleep in dark bedrooms.

Lonny opened his eyes. I took his hand and led him into the living room, toward Ruben's cage.

"Okay," I said.

"Okay," Ruben said, putting down *Gone Girl*.

"Do you want to do it?" I asked Lonny.

Lonny knelt before the cage. I could see that he was trembling. Ruben nodded, jutting his tiny chin toward Lonny.

"Rat," said Lonny—and I understood why he used that word instead of the name we had given the rat—"what is the way to heaven?"

Ruben's thin gray lips stretched into a smile. He looked at me, then back at Lonny, then back and forth a couple more times.

"I'm so glad you asked," he said. "I've been waiting for you to ask for such a long time. Don't get me wrong—it's been fun, the waiting. I've so enjoyed the glazed bacon, the hot dogs, the olives and falafel, the meringues and cupcakes. Frankly, this has been one of the top ten stays I've ever had in a human household. Though I never got my caramel latte this morning."

I felt a little jab in my heart then. I'd known we weren't Ruben's first people, of course, but there's always the illusion.

He continued.

"You seem to think that there is only one way to heaven, and that I will give you a simple answer. But there are many ways to heaven, as many ways as there are to get to a lake or a meadow or a volcano."

I felt myself beginning to grow lighter, as if helium was pumping into my veins. Yes, I thought, then, Yes…?

Ruben spoke again.

"Heaven exists in layers, sort of like… like a layer cake." He licked his lips. "The nearest ones resemble the life you know so closely, you might already be in heaven and not even know it. As you ascend from layer to layer, your experience becomes more and more exquisite and joyous, and you find yourself finally in a place with more dimensions and colors than it is possible for you to imagine at this moment."

Ruben looked from me to Lonny once again.

"But some people want to bypass the layers," said Ruben, and his voice sounded a bit stern. "I've never seen it do anyone any good in the end."

I nodded. This made perfect sense to me: shortcuts are rarely good news. You can turn up the heat and cookies will bake more quickly, but they will also be dry and burnt around the edges.

"Other people get stuck in a layer," Ruben went on. "They

get too comfortable there, or they are afraid and don't even know it."

I couldn't see Lonny's face from where I was standing. I wanted to. But I felt frozen, waiting for Ruben to keep speaking.

And he did.

"Now, you two, I—"

Suddenly, Ruben's voice crackled a bit, and he broke off and heaved a great sigh. He pressed his bare little palms together and began to walk in a circle as he picked up again. He took a deep breath.

"You do remember Ruben," he said.

"You're Ruben," said Lonny.

"The other Ruben," said Ruben.

"Yeah…?" Lonny said.

"Where were you the night he died?" asked Ruben.

I remembered the party up in the mountains. We'd all been having so much fun. It was everybody from the cooperative house we'd lived in the year that Lonny and I got together. Caroline made her amazing lasagna, and we danced and skinny dipped and everything felt perfect. I never want to go home, I said to Lonny that night. Can we move to the mountains? I'd asked him. He was the happiest of all—I'd never seen him dance with so much freedom, flinging his gangly legs and arms into the air.

I answered Ruben: "We were at that party."

"And Ruben was, too," said Ruben.

"Yes," I said.

And I remembered Ruben—the human Ruben—drinking and laughing and doing those corny card tricks that everybody indulged over and over because they loved him. Remembering him was painful.

"Who did you leave the party with?" asked Ruben the rat.

Lonny answered, his voice very soft: "Ruben."

"How did you get home?" asked Ruben the rat.

Lonny and I never spoke about that night. It was just too terrible, and it made him too sad. We had just wanted to move on. I remembered putting my sandals and shorts and halter top back on after the skinny dipping. I remembered grabbing my pink canvas tote bag. I remembered walking down the steps from the wooden deck with Lonny and Ruben, heading toward… heading toward Ru-

Shelly Oria and Nelly Reifler

ben's Sentra. Ruben's keys had jingled in his hand.

Lonny must have been replaying the same scene, because he answered.

"In Ruben's car," Lonny said. "We came home in Ruben's car."

I remembered getting in the back seat, with Lonny next to Ruben up front. The worn velour upholstery felt good beneath my thighs.

"In Ruben's car," echoed Ruben the rat.

And then Lonny turned to me and looked up from where he was kneeling. And I looked back at him, right into his eyes.

I remembered seeing the broken guardrail in the moonlight, the Sentra crushed and smoking, the trees broken where the car had bounced into them on its descent. I remembered the sounds of cicadas and peepers. But my body was no longer in the memory: I couldn't situate myself in the picture of the car.

Ruben the rat commanded: "Remember."

I saw a tote bag yards away from the car, its contents scattered across the scrub. Then I saw Ruben's left arm, akimbo against the exterior, snapped at the elbow, dangling. I zoomed in closer to the open window and saw Ruben's torso flattened between the steering wheel and his seat, and I saw what had been his head, now a bloody mass. My heart was racing now; my breath grew short. In the passenger seat next to Ruben was a male form, still except for one twitching finger, three lines of blood—one from each nostril and another from his mouth—congealing on his face. And in the back seat: curled forward and still, with its head between its knees and a bloody halter top, there was a woman.

In our apartment, now, I was still looking into Lonny's eyes. His memory must have zoomed in, too. None of us said anything for a couple of minutes. Then Lonny looked away.

"Oh," said Lonny to the floor.

"Oh," I said.

"Yes," said Ruben.

Then there was a noise, a familiar and jarring noise. I thought it was the sound of metal folding in on itself. But it wasn't. It was the buzzer.

Lonny rose and went to the intercom near the vestibule.

"Hello?" He said.

A crackling female voice responded: "Hi there! It's Mary Ellen and Sakinah!"

"No," said Lonny, "no."

"Buzz them in, Lonny," said Ruben.

"No," repeated Lonny.

I went over to him and I took his hand, and with my other hand, I held down the "door" button.

"It's so much harder for pairs," Ruben said from his cage. "Messiah's a good friend. A bit of an ass, but a good friend."

"But what do we do next?" I asked. I had begun to cry without realizing it. My face was wet and my eyes and cheeks felt hot.

"Well, you're not ignorant anymore," said Ruben. "It's impressive how far ignorance has carried the two of you."

"No," said Lonny. It seemed to be all he could say. He was shaking next to me.

The doorbell rang.

"It's open," called Ruben. The door swung open. Two women, my age—maybe a little older—stood in the carpeted hallway.

"Hello, hello!" they said in unison. Each held a small wheelie carry–on bag. The taller one had long ringlets that curled around her cheekbones. The smaller woman was wearing a felt hat with a brim and carried a canvas bag with knitting needles and yarn sticking out of it. She noticed me looking. With a sweet smile, she said, "Best way to pass the time on a long flight."

"We came from Toluca," said the taller one. "I'm Sakinah. This is Mary Ellen."

I turned from them and stumbled to Ruben's cage.

"Oh, Ruben," I said. "Please don't. We're not ready. I don't understand anything."

He said nothing. He just looked at me with his eyes dark and kind and unreadable.

"Ruben?"

He didn't answer.

"So," said the smaller woman, Mary Ellen. "That's the rat? I guess we take the cage, too?"

"Ruben, do you want some gelato?" I asked.

"Or maybe there's a carrier that fits under the seat?" said Sakinah.

Shelly Oria and Nelly Reifler

I tried to take a deep breath.

"He was delivered to us," I answered. "He came in this cage." Meanwhile, I was thinking, they don't know. These women have no idea yet.

"Okay if we come in?" asked Sakinah.

"Of course," I said. I tried to make a welcoming gesture with my hand.

Lonny had been standing still this whole time, standing like a statue near the acute corner of the vestibule. But now he moved. He was fast. He dashed for Ruben's cage. In a flash, he opened the wire top. He reached in and in one motion he scooped up the rat and stuck him in the pocket of his jacket. Then he zipped the pocket nearly all the way.

"What is he doing?" Mary Ellen pointed at Lonny.

"Hey—" said Sakinah.

But Lonny was already on the move. He pushed past the women and disappeared into the hallway. I followed after him, grabbing my running shoes from the vestibule floor as I went. I ran down the hallway. Lonny was stepping onto the elevator. I made it just in time. I stuck my hand in front of its electric eye, and the door slid open again.

It closed behind me. Lonny's pocket bulged. The rat was not moving, as far as I could tell.

I looked at myself in the convex mirror that spanned an upper corner of the elevator. Then I looked at Lonny.

He looked back at me.

The elevator descended.

Artificial Anatomies

CHRISTINE IMPERIAL

My mother gathers my hair, twists it into a bun. Each strand wound tightly in place. My scalp stretched. I try to look for traces of myself in the mirror. My mother places powder on my swollen eyes. "You look just like me."

It is not uncommon for a cat to eat its kittens, to place its child's head in her mouth, to hear the faint cry of what was once welcomed.

The first response to touch is to flinch.

The *Mimosa Pudica* is commonly known as the "shy plant." It folds inwards when touched. In the backyard, I place my small fingers on delicate petals. I watch them turn away from me.

I sleep with my body curled up against a wall.

Someone grabs my hand in the dark. The first response to touch is to flinch. The second response depends on the situation.

Do not trust me when it comes to facts.

In the Natural History Museum, you can pretend to dust off dinosaur bones. Children use brushes to reveal the horns of a triceratops, while the shadow of the reassembled bones of a Tyrannosaurus Rex hovers over them.

The first response to history is revision.

My younger sister and I cut up old pictures to stick them onto others. We call this "Manual Photoshop." In one photo, I'm cradled by a figure with the head of my little brother. In another, my sister's face is imposed on my mother's wedding dress. We are always covering our mother's face.

In Mary Morstan's "Inversions," pyramids of foil jut out from a black canvas. The reflection cuts my body into a collage.

I see an ad for prosthetic limbs.

When playing Exquisite Corpses, the goal is to mutate the body. A safety pin replaces a head. Two boys conjoined at the skull by a wooden trunk. The machine melds with man.

One form of torture is to pin down prisoners while elephants step on their limbs, to be trapped in the sound of fractures, to scream before the final crunch.

When my grandmother first took out her teeth in front of me, I cried.

The first response to pain is shock.

When I think of potential I think of things already lost.

The only way to get to the origin is to dismantle the whole.

Kintsugi is the Japanese art of reattaching broken pieces with gold. The recreated ceramic glorifies its scars.

My name tattooed on my mother's ankle. The tattoo's script reminds me of romance. The elaborate curling of the letter C. The curve of the letter e elongated into a line. I learn the tattoo used to say "Chris," the name of her ex-boyfriend.

The first response to memory is correction.

Short clips flash on the right wall of the gallery. On one set, Barbara Walters reports the news. Beside it a dog runs across a yard. The channels change simultaneously like the fidgeting of a gambler on a slot machine.

Television preserves what no one can recall. The Internet makes the act of recalling pointless.

A collage creates new memories. Completely separate images arranged to create singularity.

My mother has always lived in a completely separate time zone. She does not believe photographs say otherwise. She splices together images of her in Las Vegas with my siblings in Manila.

The first response to distance is fantasy.

A man was charged for faking his own identity. When the authorities caught the impersonator, he maintained that he wasn't faking anything. To this day, he goes by a stolen name.

I wake up kicking the door of a stranger's hotel room. A woman brings me to the concierge then back to my room. When I tell my father, he tells me to go back to sleep.

If no one else remembers, then how can you?

My cousin told me he dissected a human face. Everyone is proud he'll be a doctor.

The first response to death is resuscitation.

To believe that thoughts can transcend physical boundaries. To believe is to make come true.

We exist alongside everyone else.

The first response to existence is time.

Boy Box

GENEVIEVE HUDSON

I N HER DIARY, FRANCES writes encouragement, suggestions for bettering her life. Tonight she scribbles: Less cautious! More often! Speak up!

Her name: the thing Frances thanks god for above all else. Signing *Frances* to the end of an email does not pin one down: androgynous, gender neutral. Frank, the most popular nickname for Frances, denotes boy. *Frank*. She says it out loud. She tries it on. To the mirror she says, *Frank*. Extends a palm. She gives a turn for her reflection. No boobs need to be taped down, because Frances runs. She runs fast and she runs far and she drinks plenty of water.

Frances likes to walk around topless in just underwear, but she only does it when the Fathers aren't home. Tonight is a night like this: fatherless. Men gone. Shirt off. Frances squeezes her right nipple and studies it. A little fatter than boy. The roots of something lie beneath the skin. The tissue wants to soften and bloom. She squeezes the tit hard enough to hurt her eyes. More here today than yesterday even. This is worrisome. She evaluates the pink wounds on her stomach, her ribs, her armpits. Hidden places almost healed. She resists the urge to rip the scabs away. She dabs salve over the openings: the thick stuff made of comfrey, calendula, witch hazel. It's a concoction from the books of her birth mother: books filled with healing recipes, directions on conjuring spirits, and cautions about dreams.

The cage in her fathers' bedchamber is off limits, but when the dads don't hang around, Frances likes to sit inside of it. She spreads her stash of Riot Grrrl zines and takes out a sharpie to circle the best bits. A blanket is draped over the cage to make it look like furniture, nice décor, just part of the apartment, but Frances wasn't born yesterday. She knows the Fathers' cage is for fucking. For fucking each other, but also for fucking Tim and Marc, men who aren't her fathers, men they met on the internet, at a bar.

Frances sits in the cage and pulls at the strands of her longhaired head. The chick on the Riot Grrrl mag does not have long locks but a half-shaved skull dyed black and a tattoo of a unicorn eating a shark on her neck. The girl is screaming into a microphone. Frances can feel the words drip down her spine. *I just wanna-I just wanna-I just wanna fee-fee-eeee-feeel you!* This covergrrrl is from the band Sunday Sex. Sunday Sex sings about period blood and giving head.

Neither of these are things Frances has experienced, but she gets the idea.

Her zines: the best things she owns. Multi-colored rainbows stitched together with fabric, felt, or cardboard. She'll never know who made them, but she feels bonded for life. The zines came to her by way of Crane's older sister, Kit. They were not a gift. Frances stole them. *Kit.* Just thinking her name makes her thighs scream. Kit is so hot it hurts to look. Her hair is as bright as Lysterine, and her eye makeup smudges just enough to make her seem a little tired all the time. Her bones are big, and her breasts are bigger than any Frances has seen in real life. She imagines standing next to Kit, both of them topless and turned on. Frances puts her hand inside her underwear and starts to touch herself. She thinks of Kit's neck and of fingers that smell like headaches.

A rustle at the door sends Frances to her feet. She clamors from the cage and throws the fancy covering back over it. In the hall mirror she finger-combs her hair to okay. Two at a time steps take her to her room upstairs where she puts on a t-shirt. The footfalls belong to Father First, lighter in his movements than Father Second. Cupboards open. Cupboards close. A glass gets placed on the counter. She traces the motion until she is sure Father First is upstairs and headed for her room. A two-knuckle knock on the door:

Honey? he says. Can I come in?

Yes. Enter, sir, she says.

How do I look? He holds his hands to his side and gives a turn. His voice is warm, his eyes two slices of summer in the middle of a fake-tan face. All right angles. Hard jawline. Strong arms.

Tired, says Frances. You need a shave.

I feel tired, he admits.

Me too.

Lucky girl. You get to stay in.

Get to? says Frances.

Come to the loo and help me shave the back of my neck.

The hand on her shoulder is warm. The lotion she lathers to his skin smells like peppermint. Touching the long tendons on his neck makes her teeth itch. The desire to climb onto his back and sit on his shoulders overwhelms her. She likes the sound of the blade cutting stubble and the pink abrasions lingering on his skin. On the tips of her toes to get it all, the rough patches gone, she pats away the small hairs and leftover cream with a brown towel. Although Frances doesn't share a single gene with either dad, Father First's face is eerily like her own. No one doubts she is his daughter.

One rogue patch of stubble stands near his starched collar. When Frances takes the blade to it, she draws a plump, round speck of blood. The cut is deep, and more red threatens to rise and run. He exhales hard. A muscle twitches under his skin. Frances touches the spot with her thumb and hums one note, familiar, but not rehearsed. She doesn't know where she pulls it from, but it comes from her, like it has before, without warning. When she takes the thumb away, the lesion is gone. Not even a mark.

All done, she says.

Did you get me? he asks, trying to find the cut.

Nope, close, but nope.

He turns. Smiles. You always do the best job. Like a pro.

Whatever. It's easy.

How's that friend of yours, Crane? He says this as he studies his temples in the mirror, pushes at a patch of grey rising up in his black curls. Now he's an odd fellow.

No odder than me.

Than I.

Father First turns the corners of his mouth to a frown. She can see his eyes studying the accumulated age on his body.

Why is everything so much harder for you, honey? You've got to learn to lighten up. Smile more, that sort of thing.

Crane's not my boyfriend by the way. He's my boy comma friend.

Did I say he was your boyfriend?

Father First tucks a hand into his pocket and directs his attention to Frances. He isn't looking at her, but through her, flipping the catalogue of memories: the adoption center, Montessori daycare, Lion King themed pool parties, everything she wanted always.

Youth is wasted on the young and all that.

But nothing is wasted on Frances. She can cry at something as simple as a bug accidently inside the house. Too much everywhere all the time.

I'm going to go read, says Frances. I won't wait up for you.

Hey. Brunch in the AM? Pancakes? Anything you like.

She checks the bus schedule on her phone, but nothing is coming for another two hours. She needs to get there faster, which is where her legs come in. Tonight, Frances heeds her own advice: *less cautious.* The Fathers will not notice she is gone; they will not come and crack the door to check her bed upon their return. They will retire to the upstairs where they will bind themselves in saran wrap and penetrate new crushes and creeps in front of each other. She does not bother making the covers look occupied, as she has observed teens do on T.V. All she needs is to find an outfit that isn't 100% nerd or 99% goody-good. She takes out a grey t-shirt and cuts off the sleeves. She scissors three slashes over the chest and safety pins them back together. She attaches a few more safety pins to the thighs of her black jeans, and pulls on her red running sneakers. Her cell buzzes in her back pocket. It feels itchy-good, like she wants to rub the vibration between her legs. Crane's pic flashes on the screen, so she answers it.

Yo ho, she says into the speaker.

I'm leaving in T minus 10, says Crane.

I don't even know what that means, says Frances as she turns to check how the new safety pins look from all angles.

Time till launch. 10 minutes till launch, says Crane, and she can hear him rolling his eyes.

OK, smarts, sounds good. See you in T.

That's wrong. You're using the phrase wrong on purpose.

Should I wear my purple shirt or? I dunno. I just did this thing were I cut the sleeves off my favorite sweater. What are you wearing?

Just a thing. I'm wearing pants. The usual uniform.

Uh-huh. Is Kit around? What's she wearing? Something black?

Crane empties his lungs into the receiver. Who cares, he asks.

Ok, weirdo, Frances says. I'm letting you go now. Father is on his way out. I can hear him pocketing twelve handfuls of condoms into his pants as we speak. See in you T minus 10. Or whatever.

Whatever, says Crane. See. You. Then.

They disconnect. Frances clips in a nose ring. She stays in her room for a whole 30 minutes after Father First leaves the house, just making sure. Two miles to the venue. She takes off at a slow pace for the show. It's the kind of summer evening with autumn already in it. A couple of blocks away, Frances feels the chug chug chug of Sunday Sex inside her chest. She stops and pulls a sprig of lavender from a bush. She rubs it over her face and arms, shoves it inside her training bra. Kids either too skinny or too fat suck cigs in front of the dumpster.

A lilac-haired boy leans against a bike rack, thank god. His eyes twitch in his face. The fingernails on his hands recede to the cuticles, the collateral of a nervous mind. She walks up to him, and they touch their fists together. She can see Kit's face inside Crane's. The edges of the mouth. The hairline. They share blood. That much is obvious. She must be here. Somewhere. Frances loops her arm through Crane's: the one body she is comfortable touching. Together they are more. The new acne drug Crane is taking makes him more anxious than usual, but the craters on his cheeks are less jagged, his skin less irritated. He spits. No new sores. He swallows. Nothing picked or aflame on his face. Self-confidence can't be far off.

They open the door, break the borders of the venue, and become part of the swarm. Frances fights the urge to itch her eyes or plug her thumbs into her ears. The music is all the way inside of her, thumping and bumping around every inch of muscle, finger, toe, chin. The smell of sharp liquid and unbathed bodies collide and come toward her. People pack tight in front of the stage and lean elbow against elbow at the bar. Frances studies a condom stuck to the floor and imagines the penis it once went on. Crane pulls away, his sticky body no longer part of hers.

Where's your sister anyway. She playing tonight? I have something to give her.

Suspicion falls over Crane's face. Give her? he says.

Like a thing. I have a thing.

She's somewhere. But what do you have to give her?

Let's get a drink! A drink! Frances says. Coca-cola with vodka?

Crane pulls a flask from his back pocket and tips it toward her. You can't order anything. You look prepubescent.

Fuck you, man, Frances says, but takes the flask anyway.

Warmth fills her throat, and when she hums the ringing in her ears gets less loud.

She's there, says Frances, nudging Crane.

So?

Kit sits under an arc of wheat pasted posters. Her fierce blue eyes: so precise and pure and hard-pressed. Someone in a red hat whispers in Kit's ear, but she doesn't change her expression. Her eyes find Frances and settle. Kit's gaze bends Frances's breath. It bends her knees. There is an unearthly quality to Kit's face, in her ability to keep looking at something. Frances wants to touch the warm fabric of her knees. Kit raises her glass at Crane and Frances.

She wants to talk to you, Frances says to Crane. Let's go say hi.

Seriously? What is wrong with you? She's fucked up right now, I doubt she even recognizes me, much less wants to say hi.

I think she does. I think she is trying to get our attention, says Frances.

She doesn't even know your name. She keeps calling you Frank.

She does? Really?

Why are you smiling? That's not your name.

Nothing. You don't get it. The end.

What? said Crane, yelling over the music.

Nevermind!

What?

Frances turns from Crane to the bench where Kit was sitting, but it's empty. She scans the room with no luck. No sign of her curves, no hint of her smell. Bodies twist against them until she finds a flicker in the crowd, green hair going toward the toilets.

I've got to pee, Frances says and points at her crotch.

Frances steps to the end of the line, behind a fat girl with pigtails and a lower back piercing. Someone stuck a rod of nag champa in a vent above the sink and an inch is ready to fall off onto the liquid smeared tile. Kit emerges from her stall, sucking on a lollipop and hysterical at her cellphone. Everyone in the bathroom stops what the're doing to watch. Mascara cuts trails down Kit's cheeks. She doesn't wipe them away, but blows her nose into the sleeve of her jacket. It's loud and the music still swings through Frances' core. She can't hear what Kit is so upset about, even when Kit walks directly in front of her, still trembling at the things being said on the phone.

Cold fingers touch Frances' wrist. Kit's fingers. Kit laughs kind of creepy, then falls silent. She shakes her head at Frances, still holding onto her wrist, as if the two of them are in on something together, as if Frances is on it, too. Kit's eyes glisten like wet pavement. She mouths, *Fuck.This.Guy.* and hangs up her phone. A moment of stillness, maybe a thousand years, hangs between then. Kit does something with her eyes. Something that is almost sexual, almost flirtatious. Then, without warning, Kit begins to choke on her lollipop. Blood rushes to her face. A fear-coated cough lifts from her raspberry lips.

Does anyone know CPR? yells the fat girl next to Frances.

Kit stomps her feet and brings her hands to her neck in panic. Her face is red. Her face is purple. She looks at Frances and mouths the word *Frank,* and something inside of Frances gathers together. She steps forward and touches her mouth to Kit's and hums. She hums three notes. That's all it takes. Kits swallows. There's nothing in her mouth or throat or stomach. Whatever bit of candy that was caught is now gone. She searches Frances' face for a secret, but she doesn't let on anything. She just stares back. *More often!*

Kit grabs Frances' head and kisses her. Soft and violent and there's a little blood on their tongues. Kit pulls her hair and Frances likes the way the sharpness of it travels to her hips. She feels her back hit the wall. Her shoulder blades press into the wood. She wants to bite Kit's lips off. She wants to lick the roof of her mouth until she hits tonsils. The kiss ends as suddenly as it began, and Kit is gone, pushing her way from the bathroom line, through the bodies. She pulls Frances with her by belt loops.

The air outside is thick as tea. They're in an alley, but not the one Frances and Crane came in through, a quieter one. Frances stares into the puddle she is standing in and watches the oil rainbow.

What the fuck, Frank. What the fuck was that?

Frances works hard not to smile. She lifts a shoulder to indicate a feeling she can't name. Kit wraps her sweater tight across her shoulders. She knows something weird just happened. They look like old friends on a warm night, each circling the tops of their drinks with one finger.

What was that? In there? The thing you did?

Frances eats a piece of skin from her thumb and studies the new incision.

You Christian or something? You just talk to God?

My dads are atheist.

Good thing I'm not asking about them.

An idea cold and wet comes to her, and Frances says, Can you keep a secret?

Not really, says Kit.

My mother, I never met her, but I think she gave me something. Some kind of voodoo something. Well, maybe not voodoo, but something that made me different and I think it's her.

Voodoo? You mean like witchery? Like one of those chicks from *The Craft?* That what you're saying?

I'm saying I got something in my throat that makes things better. Like your choking. It makes things better.

Kit sucks on her lips and waits for Frances to go on, but as soon as Frances begins, Kit's interest slides somewhere else—to the gutters, to the blemish on the brick wall, to the past.

What kind of better. What do you mean? asks Kit, still a little glazed over, still only half here.

Not sure where it comes from. I don't make it. This humming thing. It just does it. My body just does it.

Try. Try the humming.

Frances closes her eyes. It doesn't work like that, she says.

Kit takes an earring off and jabs the needled part into a vein in her forearm. A spindle of blood unwinds from the opening.

She shakes her head. I can't, she says. I can't. Just. Do it.

Fucking try it, Frank. Be a little less cautious. Speak up.

A pressure starts in her stomach like trapped gas. Frances coaxes it through her chest, through her throat, until her tongue is on Kit's cut. The taste of coins fills her mouth. The notes flood from her and when she pulls back, nothing red is left. It's just skin. Just some freckles and a few blond hairs.

Kit smiles. Her teeth are not healthy. They are thin and too yellow.

You've got to come with me, kid. The dudes are not going to fucking believe it. We wrung us a witch.

Where are we going? asks Frances on the way to Kit's van, but

Kit is already on her phone, texting someone, laughing.

I have to say goodbye to Crane. He is going to wonder where I went.

Look, Frank. NBD. Crane is a big boy. He's got this handled. Let him get a little wild in there. Shake it up.

But where are you taking me? She buckles her seatbelt, aware of the vodka tinged kiss from earlier and the slur that cuts the end of Kit's words.

Kit holds her finger to the radio volume until the whole place is packed with noise and bass, and Frances can't tell the difference between what's beating inside of her and outside. She pushes her foot into an invisible brake on the van floor, hoping for Kit to slow down on the curves, at red lights, in the woods. They've driven out of the familiar into a park where there's just dark. Kit's eyes press forward and Frances searches for Crane in her features. She needs to see him in there, to make her feel a little less alone, to make her feel like this isn't dangerous, but just another nighttime drive to smoke cigarettes, sip dandelion beer, practice kissing on your best friend.

ELEGY FOR CITY LIFE, PRE-PREGNANCY

ALICIA JO RABINS

vessel yes miraculous yes but sometimes
I miss the office above the city
where we fucked diligently
it was our homework and we
were good little boys and girls
wine and cheese on tuesday nights
instant miso in the break room
it was our spaceship
well as much ours as our bodies
which is to say not for long
will I remember this body
the next time around
as I remember that office
its scars its hidden corners
and the way the lights
undressed themselves each night
before my hungry eyes
rectangular yellow butterfly wings
in the oil slick of summer
wearing the body I used to love
in the city I used to love

THE MONASTERY OF MOTHERHOOD

it's hard to face
my ugly old self again
whether by the pig farm
or metropolitan crossroads
but the hardest is alone
with children
I'd cut my lungs out for her
but then I spray her
in the face with the hose
when she claws for the baby
and so in the monastery
of motherhood I find the devil
in my own heart
and God too in the form
of El Shaddai
nursing as I write
and oh how the helpless babe
grows into an angry being
I pray they'll be better than me
I've done my best so far &
been ashamed of it —
what I thought I'd be like
buried beneath this reality scaffolding
of masks on masks
unholy crown
on my motherhead

Alicia Jo Rabins

Company

JOSEPH SCAPELLATO

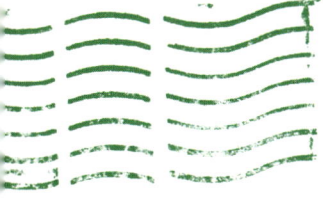

BROTHER, YESTERDAY I SAID to you that there were folks to talk to. That these folks, Mom and me, if talked to, would respond with what we sensed you needed—agreement or advice or humor, say, or silence—and in doing so, offer you what no one can deny needing, the water we pour on our grown-lonely insides: company.

"Company!" our Uncle Nunzo used to shout, the goofball, when we were kids and Mom would take us nearly to the end of the Red Line to see him, when we raced to be the first to punch his buzzer. He'd skip around in cartoony circles, screaming "Help help help, company!" like he'd opened the front door to flames.

"You know that," I said to you, tapping the table, not knowing if you knew it. "You can. You can talk to us."

You said you knew it. I watched you watch your hands scratch the label off your pop bottle. It fluttered in shreds to the floor. I'd guilted you, as you let me do just once a month, to a lonely Mexican joint in the Loop. Mariachi music plugged on around us, going places proudly. If I scooted my chair I smelled bleach and black mold.

You knew it, you said, but you couldn't.

I said, "It's that you *won't*."

You made the face you make when you're trying not to feel what's obvious to everyone.

I made the face I make when I'm trying to stop myself from yelling, You don't understand what's obvious to everyone.

Understand isn't the same as *agree with*, said your face.

My face had nothing to say to that.

When the bill came it came with two candies. I cracked mine in the back of my mouth. You knew I was thinking, If I let you pay, will you feel like you've participated?

You picked up your napkin. I picked up the bill, half of which was my three beers. I hoped for the hundredth time that you'd some-day have a drink with us.

"For the holidays," I said, tilting my head this way, that way, "if you come for the holidays, I hope you do, you don't have to talk. Even though you know it's hurt Mom. That you haven't. Talked."

You tore the tiny corners off your napkin.

I gave up: I said, "Thanks for answering my call."

You put down your napkin and said you're welcome but come the new year you'd stop paying for the phone plan you never used.

I didn't know what to make of that—everything inside me sunk. You folded the napkin and put it in your pocket.

That you intended to no longer have a phone through which we could continue to try to reach you felt even further out than all the other acts of isolation—your acts, my acts, Mom's acts—and made me remember, not for the first time, that for longer than we liked to admit we'd been misunderstanding who we were on purpose.

On the street we shook hands limply, like kids, you wearing your gigantic gloves. Our eyes flicked away just before they met. The meanest wind we'd had all month ripped in from the lake, herding trash, bending everyone who hustled down the block. You walked off wearing the coat I gave you last Christmas—the last Christmas you said you'd ever go to, which was the last thing you said to Mom in person.

"Waitaminute," Mom had said that day, stepping away from the sink, making your exit certain, "scusi, stronzo—per favore, wait wait *wait!*" but you were in that coat and out the door, shutting it so hard the silver bells suicided off. At the window Mom slashed the air with her hands and scourged herself with curses—the first steps of the smashy-dance—as if doing so would get you to look back, to look up as you crossed the courtyard. I crushed her with a hug in case she moved to bust the glass, which she hasn't done since Dad. Together we watched you stiff-walk through old hard snow.

Yesterday I watched you stiff-walk through the Loop's lunch hour foot traffic, between the businessmen and -women, the work-jacketed blue collars, the street-cool students, the poky tourists—tourists even in December, even under all their layers.

"You're a tourist," you said to me years ago, on the first of the lousy Christmases. I'd come home from half a year of living in a different neighborhood, eager to club you with my hipness. That you churned with a bitterness more awful than what I'd expected was in every sentence you didn't say: you were even more alone, and it was and wasn't on me. We moped in the kitchen, not doing dishes, as Mom readied presents in the parlor. I'd been drinking a can of beer because I was old enough. I took manly swigs. I wanted you to want some, to ask for it. You wouldn't. You turned to the sink. I waggled the can in your face, I pressed it to the back of your neck, and that's when you called me a tourist.

Do I need to say what I did next, or why I'm sorry?

I hit you in the head with the can until the can was crushed and foaming.

I'm sorry—I can't stop plunging my head into the past, even though it's hard to breathe in. You know I plunge the most when I've seen you. You know I know you're not actually okay with leaving everything where it is, Mom alone, old wine in old bottles.

"How do you like that," Uncle Nunzo used to say, mock-serious as he sniffed a popped cork. "New wine in a new bottle."

What I'm telling you, brother, is yesterday you walked and I followed, I followed because what you said about your phone plan made it hard for me to get out of my chair. You walked your stiff-walk, which was cocky if not nerdy, your arms looking like they were strapped to your sides, and you whacked shoulders with anyone who didn't give—a many-scarfed grandmother, a jock of a businessman whose bulk nearly knocked you over, who stopped to turn and glare. I waited until you neared the corner, then I hoofed it to catch up, to keep a bead on you. My lungs crackled with lake air. I leaned on a parking meter and burped pukey backwash into my hand.

You puked into Uncle Nunzo's rubber workboots. When we were kids, playing in the mudroom on the plastic rug. Me and Mom thought you'd been faking, acting sick at every Red Line stop to dodge the visit, even though we knew you loved Uncle Nunzo. I didn't want you to turn us around. Watching your miserable face on the train, I'd thought: I can let myself be angry, or not. This knowledge made me feel enormous. After you'd lurched over the toys to yak into both workboots, you wiped your mouth and looked at me that same way—I saw you deciding to be or not be angry. I could have laughed. If I had, you'd have joined me, and before long we'd have slapped the floor and flopped for breath, in cozy hysterics together. Instead I saw my look in your look. I stood up, above you. I grabbed and raised the dripping boots.

The backwash I wiped on my jeans. I managed to keep half a block between us. Your pace was steady except for when you slowed in front of an alley, as if window-shopping. When I got there I slowed too: a grinning two-coated bum sat in a shopping cart, tossing seed to a family of pigeons that muscled dumbly through themselves. "This one, that one, this one," the bum sing-said.

For half an hour you walked an expanding square-like path, a maze you were making from the inside out. That's how I knew you'd lost your job. What I didn't say at the Mexican joint was that I could take the long and beery lunch break because I'd lost my job too.

"A promotion," said Uncle Nunzo, when he got too sick to work, when he was hospitalized. "Pay's different. Different benefits!"

You agreed without saying anything, and he was grateful for it, and I disagreed but said he'd be better soon, and he forgave me for it, and Mom wept in Italian. She always wept in Italian in hospitals.

"Mi rompe i coglioni," she said, and from his bed our laughing Uncle Nunzo took a bow.

When you weren't there he'd say to me, "Always kiss your brother on the head." In his last months he'd demonstrate. "It's easy!"

I want to know: what did he say to you when I wasn't there?

It had to be something, something just as easy.

It had to happen—your squares within squares broke on car-choked Lake Shore Drive, which you crossed. Then you crossed the Lakefront Trail, where bundled cyclists and joggers with sweatered dogs exercised insanely along the lake: a wind-whipped plain of caulk spilled from the sky's bucket. You trudged onto the nearest public pier and all the way to the rail closest to the water, furthest from the city. When you passed an old man he turned and left, as if piers were for one.

I stopped just short of the pier's concrete lip and stomped feeling into my feet on the frozen sand. Behind us, if you'd turned to look, skyscrapers stood, broad and black.

You didn't turn to look. What you did was take out your phone. You held it over the rail and dropped it into the lake.

You took off your glasses, folded them, and dropped them into the lake.

Then your gloves. Your keys. IDs and credit cards and business cards. Your wallet. The napkin.

You unzipped your coat and wriggled out of it and in it went. Your fleece, your button-down, your undershirt—I hadn't seen your torso in ten years—you shook as you undid your belt.

A bearded man in a peacoat jogged past me, to you.

I came up from whatever I was in and into something else, something even worse, and shouted, "It's okay!" to no one.

As you stepped out of your jeans, the bearded man slowed, like you slowed at the alley. He set a hand on your arm. The whole time he was talking.

At first you didn't do anything—you looked like you looked when I slammed the can of beer into the back of your head or dumped the two boots of vomit in your lap or lied and told you, to get you to speak to her, that after the wake Mom had broken both hands while breaking a table, that Mom was out of desperation going to marry Drunken Stanley, that Mom, wanting to make sure she died before you did, had resolved to kill herself with cleaning products.

You sat on the concrete. The bearded man sat next to you, like a dad.

He scooted a bit to unbutton his coat, which he offered you. You shook your head. He put the coat on you anyway. You took it off and gave it back, and said something—a long something, with gestures that went from small to big, from hands to arms—and he listened, his coat on his knees, and when you were done he stood up and pointed back to the city. You said something else, to which he listened, and then you turned to face the lake. He left.

He came towards me, putting on his coat and looking grave.

A young woman had appeared at my side. Pins and buttons peppered her jacket and a sprout of green hair ran from her knit hat. That she was interested enraged me.

"Think he's okay?" she said.

I looked at her and laughed. I laughed! You're no addict, brother, you're not insane, you haven't been beaten or abused or abandoned. You're okay! You're okay, so what is it, what is it always, and why have we only ever talked around it?

The bearded man came up to her and me with a face that said, I tried, and the young woman hugged him. A kid with a beard, not a bearded man. They were students. Kids.

"I'm going to wait," he said. "Dude might jump."

I said, "Wait for what?"

"The cops," said the girl, "I called them."

"The cops! The cops will tell him to go the fuck away. He'll go the fuck away, they'll go the fuck away, he'll come back and they won't, and if he's going to jump he'll fucking jump. He won't jump."

My voice was high and tight. When I spoke I spat.

The bearded kid came out of hugging his girl in such a way that he stood between her and me. "How do you know?"

Muscles flexed around my heart. I said, "You're crying?"

"I'm—what?"

I peered into his face.

"It's the wind," he said, not backing away. "It's windy."

I grabbed his arm. I was crying.

"Okay," he said. He put an arm around me.

His girl tugged at him but he didn't budge.

A pair of cops passed us, the casual walk they reserve for the homeless.

"He won't jump," I said into the kid's arm.

"Jump," I said when they helped you up, when their hands kept the blanket on your back.

Your Name in Veins

DANIEL GRAMMER

You wear this ridiculous ten-gallon hat now
In the saloon with a match in its brim. At the bar
You load a cigarette. You're pissed that the juke-box
Ran dry. You drink your wine like it's water and your voice
Keeps on trickling because By God you'll finish what you've started.
You're mixing blood with thinner blood, going broke as the
Ten Commandments because for you, it's never been about the body.
On Sunday you said that since blood is no more than sacrificial
Wine then you've always had an altar for that preachy son of a
God—dammit, you're a desperado whose fingers raise hell from a matchstick.
You turn the air to smoke performing the Devil's work, a prophet
Burned too many times by past certainty,
Cowboy Killers, Sweet Jesus!

Bonus Round

KARA VERNOR

AND THEN ONE DAY your molester turns up as a contestant on *Wheel of Fortune*. He's standing at his station clapping as the wheel he just tugged spins. He's gray now and liver-spotted, but it's the same man who lived four houses down from your parents until sometime, while you were away at college, he moved.

When you regularly watched *Wheel of Fortune* you were not the age you are now—the age of meeting friends for walks in the hills, which is what you'll do after you eat your chana masala and feed your cat. You were not the age when you met friends for cheap beers and angry bands, nor the age when you gathered by the loading dock behind the mall to share cigarettes. You were the age when being with friends required adult supervision, except on your street where you could play in driveways but not inside, though you sometimes went inside when you thought nobody was home. You lived with your parents then, four split-levels and an empty lot down from Mr. Gorman. You remember now. The lot, too. It's where you fell on a steel can and sliced your knee. Four stitches was all it took, but the pain, how you howled.

He solves a Before & After: 'There will Be Blood Pressure'. He points as he says it, stresses each syllable. Then Pat Sajak is next to him, shaking his hand. Pat looks like he did on your parents' TV, chipper and bronzed, but Gorman, he's a shrinking man. A deflated balloon. You see his hand shake the next time he reaches for the wheel, the same hand he pretended wasn't touching between your legs as he talked of his new sailboat, the maiden voyage he would take to Sausalito. He looks like someone you might extend an elbow to if you saw him at an intersection, if he hadn't caught you in his house with his hands, if he hadn't pulled you onto his lap in his Barcalounger, promising not to tell your parents about your sneaking... *if*. His spin clicks to a stop a notch away from Bankrupt, and he lets out a sigh.

You shut off the TV and sit there remembering old thoughts of nailing his hands to the hull of his boat, of loosing it into a storm. Then you get up and bring your plate to the kitchen because you have that walking date with a friend, and you are the age when that's the perfect way to spend the evening. You don't smoke anymore, you don't drink until you throw up, you don't wake from dreams of suffocating under sails, you don't even avoid the ocean. You pay your rent on time, you have a boyfriend who tells math jokes, you have a job that builds you more than it breaks you, and at some point along the way, you did loose that boat. You don't need the TV to show you Rob Gorman is as good as dead.

There Are No Children Here

JASMINE AN

The Karen community of Huai Tong Ko is one of the least accessible villages in the mountains of Thailand's Mae Hong Son province. Even so, the community offers homestays to students and tour groups several times a year.

Muga means something approximating "aunt." But when *Muga* opens her small photo album and lays it on the floor between us, she is nothing but *mother*. She points to the faces of her children and tells me names in a language I still strain to understand. I ask ages, and she tells me those too. I was born the same year as her first daughter. I don't ask where, but learn anyway: the oldest son a soldier, the daughters *bai tam ngan* in the city, the youngest at boarding school five hours away down the mountain. Later, I find a spare blanket snuck underneath my mosquito netting, an extra scoop of rice in my bowl, a bite of chicken deposited onto my spoon. All week, the *mugas* tug their host daughters from house to house, handing us snacks of boiled corn and coconut milk, sitting us in front of their looms and laughing as we fumble like children half our age.

Jasmine An

Ancestry of Objects
excerpt

TATIANA RYCKMAN

W HEN HE PUSHES US over the kitchen sink and lifts our dress, our eyes hold the glint off the faucet like a dead bird. Something we wonder if we could have loved or saved or should be relieved to have done neither. On the first strike waves move through our skin and he pulls his hand back, we hear the hollow crack before we feel the sting. We anticipate the second slap. We brace ourselves with whitening knuckles against the edge of the sink. We grab for the narrow ledge that separates the two deep basins, but quickly draw our arm back. A ceramic finch watches detached. The edge of the sink is smooth but unforgiving where it digs into our ribs just below our breasts. We think "tits." We command back at him in our mind to "feel my tits." We grasp finally at anything.

The first waterfall of moisture runs down our thigh with the sweat. It splits into two streams at the knee. His fingers wear the memory of her hair and the sweat of our low back mixes with the salt of her tears and the salt of his come landing/a flock of birds on our back. He smoothes the cream over our spine like icing. He licks and puts his hand in our mouth to taste.

We watch the dead bird faucet in the distant sunlight while the glaze of his fingers fill the air in front of our face with the scent of warm dough.

We bite a finger. Her tears and hair and our sweat and his come scrape onto our teeth and we taste the hollow sound of each slap echoing through the porn of our memory. He relaxes his hand in our mouth until we let go. His own teeth sink gently into our shoulder. His lips touch down on our back in the erratic pattern of ejaculate. He rubs the come in like lotion and it dries into a tight flakey skin peeling like a sunburn.

He sits and the chair rolls a few inches as if a grandmother, our own grandmother crippled by polio, slides across the kitchen tile before bumping into the table, shuffling papers and silverware into stacks exhausted.

We don't think about what we've done, we think instead

about this man: the clean crease pressed into his pants, the good shape he's in, considering, about how easily he manufactures a smile, a history, money. Our thoughts are made from all our memories of him, we are watching the cavern his shirt makes where it is missing a button—the fabric opens into a womb of a few straight chest hairs and when we enter that tangle with our eyes, they are all the women that have gone before us to wander that forest. We think about the wife's starved fingers wandering that sparse wood. Think the phrase "snake in the grass." Think "Babes in the Woods." Think Hansel and Gretel and their trail of bread. Think of the trail of tears, think of the tears the wife/woman with boney fingers leaves when the man says first I love you, and then But:

When we think of her, her eyes are the clearest blue in watery sockets, a womb warm and wet and tight. Nothing like the man's bird nest chest. Nothing like the marsupial pouch of his unbuttoned shirt. Nothing like the cups of our emptied hands.

     We will not be distracted by the long straight slope of her nose or the labial pink of her lips. Her existence is the distraction, her absence palpable between us.

When the man wipes the tears away his fingers claim he is sensitive. And she whispers But:
     and then,
     I love you.
     and even they do not hear the things they are not saying.
     He wipes the tears on her hair and his long fingers remember the weight of her head: a mother holding a stranger's child. She thinks this means he is changing his mind, he'll take care of her. He wants to feel the weight of her head in his hands until they fall off in their rotten grave, to press his mouth to her mouth and to keep it there.
     But he is saying goodbye.
     We leak onto the linoleum floor at his feet while he pets the come left on his hand into our hair. We think of the stain he's made in the house, in us, and wait for the moment when he will leave and we can toy with the lonely wetness of our cunt and the house, the whole house cupping us in its warm echo. We will come fondling the bruises he's left.

W E LEARN THE MAN:
When he comes in with a bag, he wants to stay the night. When he cooks at our stove, we pour another glass of wine. We rub the dry fabric of his shirtback lightly until the prints burn off our fingertips. We grip loosely the knob of his elbow and he tells us the history of the day. A good day. Money in an old coat pocket, a client pleased with his work, he's made them a sum of money that we don't understand to the extent that we understand more clearly how little we know—about his day, about his fingers when they are not wrapping themselves around our throat.

When he finishes his story with a smile and "It was good— Now it's good," and moves his mouth to ours and sets down the old spatula, plastic handle disfigured with heat, we take his hand and examine the roadmap of his palm. We joke "This long one must be money, maybe the shorter one is life."

He slides his hand from our hip to soft flesh and pulls us to him. He says he can be very generous and we resent instantly being bought. Indentured. Our sex stolen when it is owed to the man for his generosity. He radiates a salesman's thin integrity. We enjoy the tottering infant of hate we've conceived and cultivate it, so we laugh, we pretend that he's said nothing. We are thankful for the distraction of water boiling over, spilling white foam on the oven top.

The first time:
We meet him at the expensive bar. With a book in bad lighting we privately celebrate the end of our life.
The toaster we might throw in the bath.
The car that might run too long in the garage.
After "we" and "regret" and "to inform you" the words mean nothing: Streamline, technological advancement, efficiency. So we manifest fantasies of the end of our job and house/home and life as the end of times our grandparents warned of in lectures we did not listen to. But here it is, to be followed by The Beast and flight to the

Caves, and finally the third or fourth or millionth advent of nothing.

And the end of the delicate balance of days spent recording death onto a cassette. The equilibrium of waking up, of sitting at the long table each morning, the plastic stickiness of a cheap American flag tablecloth under the computer surrounded by the relics left over, we are the relic left over; to protect these things around us, to protect the things we are, we listen.

The necessary and comforting weight of everyone's fragile lives is dictated through headphones, the lives taken first from them and then us in the familiar cadence of a woman's voice reading without emotion the tumors and fractures lit up from behind *comma* from within—the voice of quick and unremarkably slow deaths of strangers so ingrained in our mind that it is our own slow death *period* Our own calm voice the voice of all/no life, the voice of our thoughts on the traffic in the street outside the window or the narrators of great literature. Our voice, the woman's voice, the invisible doctor recites the pain of strangers over breakfast. It is the only voice we have when we cannot think in the thick drawl of well-meaning admonishments, our grandparents' image of us in negative like x-ray film; the emotionless voice of dictation is ours when we are notscolding ourself in the mirror with voices past the suffering recorded by the woman, it is too late for them. They are already dead. We remind ourselves, again and again.

At the bar the woman dictates the book through our eyes: *I told him,* period, *And as I walked on I was lonely no longer,* period. When he sits at the bar waiting for his table and woman we can see, from the corner of our eye, that he will speak to us, and when he asks what we are reading we know we will hate him, our desperate and bottomless loneliness taken like the ready hum of the recording.

He takes her out for dinner, and while she is in the bathroom he takes our time because he does not know it is ours. But he is generous and asks about the book, as if we brought it for him, brought ourself for him. We cover our face with the book so he can read the title without giving him our attention. We imagine him mouthing out the words, reading them like an analogue clock. Letters and meanings and anything we might know foreign to him, we think angrily without evidence watering the seed of our malice.

"First time?" he asks and we shake our head no, rereading *Now* comma *don't think my opinion on these matters is final* comma *he seemed to say* comma *just because I'm stronger and more of a man than you are* period As she returns to the bar from the restroom he adds with confusing compassion: "Somehow I never expect him to die."

We look over the yellowed pages and see the delicate lines by his eyes make an estuary of sadness. We believe his smile, fresh and controlled, could have cracked easily like the thin bones in her wrists.

"Me too" we think/say without thinking to the nothing that is listening. His face is a painted mask of politeness. We nod to her, but she doesn't see us, doesn't need to see us because she is wearing a new dress, and he is generous. They are shown to a table and float on the privilege of life empty of complication. When we try to pay for our drinks the tab has been taken care of, and we are ashamed. We think only of his confusing sadness.

Of the celebratory red of blood merging with water.

At night the house holds us like the thin shell around a yolk. We slide out of our shoes at the door a small dark enclosure with sweaters and rain boots smelling of roses and mothballs leading to the kitchen and we stop to notsee, notlisten, notthink about what is or is not in the house with us. The persistent nothing, and we walk through the long open rooms, past kitchen and dining room and finally in the soft cushion of afghans and eyeless stuffed animals no longer seen, we bend to run fingers through the thick weave of carpet. Plastic fibers catch our nails and we lower ourself onto its bed. We think "fur" and "counting sheep" and of his woman's forearm in an x-ray, tied at the wrist to the table so when they order her favorite meal she can never quite reach. Can never taste it. Our grandfather would say *patience is a virtue.* He would say, *good things come to those who wait.*

And we fall asleep, our hair weaving itself into the fibers below us.

When he sees us filling bags with rice and beans and grains we will forget in cupboards, dried and organized in bins, he approaches, switching a gallon of milk to his left hand. He extends his right and says Hello, with an easy smile, his name is David.

We do not reach out, and he wipes sweat from the jug on the

lap of his dress pants. We wonder what day it is, if he's coming from work. The sun is up. But we don't pretend to know how people pass the time.

"I'm sorry I didn't introduce myself the other night," he reaches out again.

We take the hand, it is cool and moist and soft. We let go. "You seemed busy," we say in the way of an excuse. We cannot muster even a polite smile but remember the paid tab and add "Thank you. For the drinks, I mean." A concession we have been trained to make but do not wonder what training we've received, what the lesson is in giving up before:

"Oh," David says, waving as if he'd made himself forget. As if he is as embarrassed of our impotence as we are.

It is quiet and we undulate our fingers on the bottom of the thin plastic bag so the desiccated bodies of seeds surround our hand in a loose dance held back by the frailest barrier of plastic. We forget to try, that it is uncomfortable to stand with a stranger. With us.

We drop the bag into the red basket on our arm. "It was nice to meet you, David," we've learned to say and "Be well."

He mumbles something but we are already walking away. His milk sweats onto his grey pants and we turn to the next aisle full of cardboard boxes with cellophane windows, food looking out hungrily.

We stand in front of a cooler, the low refresh rate of the electric bulb blinding. A child is singing ninety-nine bottles of beer, and when we reach for one he sings ninety-eight. The mother smiles apologetically without knowing who her embarrassment is for.

Behind us David says, "That's a good one." We turn. "Sorry," he smiles and we think being charismatic is something he practices in front of a mirror, something he does for money. "That," he starts again "didn't go as I'd hoped. I don't mean to be forward, but I'd like," he grows shy and maybe in a hiccup of professionalism extends his card "I was wondering if you'd like to get a drink some time." The mouth of his flowing unhappiness opens and there is the same unidentifiable current of sympathy, a nothing that pulls between us like a rope, David's: *I never expect him to die.* And we, too, never expect the man to die. Still can't quite believe that he could.

And we capitulate, moving from one nothing to another is

made easy by the appearance of this man.

We consider his persistence and our day and more: the last six months alone in the house and maybe in a dare with some part of ourself we thought dead or simply without thinking or from too much day/night alone in the yellowed house we move out of the way of the cooler and gesture to the many bottles with our own. The light makes him look pale and glistens off the short greying hairs on his square jaw. The hand, the card, hovers between us like a lost animal and his look is first one of notunderstanding then "Oh, I meant any time. I didn't mean tonight, I mean—" he calculates and grasps to recover any ground he's lost "unless you're not busy?" He watches the thick paper of the card as he flips it between his fingers and into the dark of his pocket.

We know we are inviting a man into the tight hallway of our home. We know the dry air and slick sweat of crossed thighs in the tunnel of hot rooms. We know the overhead kitchen light on the formica counter and our grandmother's recipes and measuring spoons and juice glasses and cookie jars and doilies and—all piled across the plasticy white as if anyone might use them.

As if in the other room our grandfather is quiet, reading seed catalogues and she is sponging herself in the bath, and from our back on the thick rug we listen to the whispered tick of the clock above our grandfather's fake leather chair, greenish and hard and would it mean everything if he saw us, just over the fine print of catalogue pages just once.

Even in this place we expect David to expect sex. In the white light of the cooler there is a golden glint on his finger and we expect him to absorb the mess he makes into the lap of his own life without yet knowing if we want him to.

"If you want," we say.

The child is bored and kicking at his mother's cart and she begins to roll away, through an unidentifiable shiny spill, the wheel of the cart making an erratic pink trail across the tiles flecked to disguise filth and the woman is distracted by the long list of her family's needs. David smiles in a way that looks like laughing and opens the cooler door. "Ninety-seven bottles of beer" the child yells when David selects the same bottle we are holding, and the mother drags the child away by the hand.

The first thing we regret about bringing him in to the washed-out yellow of the kitchen is the casual way he moves things—picks up blue tin cups duck-shaped salt & pepper shakers napkin holder still holding three folded napkins and puts them down somewhere else. We resent the rings his drink leaves on the wood of the kitchen table before he takes it up for security or courage, while a cardboard square printed with poppies sits embarrassed by its uselessness beside the wet circles. "This feels so impulsive," he says suddenly with a note of boyish adventure that surprises us for its openness, its familiarity.

"Sure," we agree, turning to hide our irritation among the groceries as we put them away—why have we invited this man here to look at the things, to touch to pick up to move to look, always touching, looking like a child?—why is he here and we notice only then that David does not come up behind us to authoritatively take our hips in his hands. David does not make the same assumptions about our body as he does about our things as if we are not one of these objects we are not an abandoned thing baking in the hot hallway of the house. He steps a few feet to the counter and when we face him again he smiles, happy just to be seen. Simple.

The warm yellow glow of the hanging light paints him as a piece of furniture. Like the only thing that's been dusted. For a moment he takes on the golden sandy color of the brocade couch and we stop resenting the time he is taking from us/we allow him to belong. We do not think about the other things we would not be doing if he were not protecting that small piece of counter, bit of floor. We feel nothing in the air. We are home, and David is with us.

David senses this softening, he grows uneasy in the silence and immediately fills it. "I don't normally do things like this," he says to the gold flecks in the linoleum at his feet. He wants us to say Me too. He wants us to say You are special. He wants to say We are special. He wants an occasion to say the idiotic thing: anything being any different than it has ever been before.

"What do you do?" we ask, forcing himself to make himself a real thing among the other real things littering the room. Separate himself from the dream of us in our house with the yellow light.

"What do you mean?" he asks, punctuating his question with

a drink "For work?"

"For work," we say, to make it easy.

"Finance," he replies as if unsure of the answer; not saying so proudly the thing we imagine he is trained to say proudly.

Our response is a thought made from a feeling. Something as satisfying as: *Oh*. David's life becomes the puzzle of assumptions we've pinched together by frail nubs to explain the bright ironed blue of his shirt and careful haircut. In one seamless reversal of thought we see ourselves in his eyes. We see young flesh made of body smell covered in a loose lid of cotton, easy to open. We believe in that image instantly. When we are the man with money in our thirsty kitchen we know we are clearing an inevitable path through the clutter of our life, and only a part of us grows sad, because now we are the that man too, and we can see David, the salt and pepper and the softness where his beer is going in that very moment. We feel the coarse hair growing on his shoulders moving all day against fabric, we make the muscles in his arms slack from disuse. When we are him, he is just David, and this makes him tangible, possible, bearable.

"Personal finance," he adds, "Retirement, things like that." And maybe it is our lack of understanding that tricks us into thinking this means anything at all. That he is accustomed to long days of wading through thick curtains of paperwork, of numbers, of solitary work, something familiar. A rare wisp of wind blows through gauzy curtains. We step closer and lean against the counter, facing him.

"What else?" we ask in the way people say For pleasure? We want him to wrap his cold damp fingers around the hot chords of our throat, to pull us toward him.

He performs, says casually: "I keep busy." His smile is knowing or suggestive and our rumpled dress heats to translucent.

He looks at us from one eye to the next, we are unflinching and meet each gaze. His jaw softens out of his winsome smile and he reaches out a hand, cool and moist with condensation, to run fingertips down the hot, dry skin of our arm.

"And your wife?" we ask without emotion. We are not satisfied to be the dust that covers everything but must also be the death and termites and endless exhausting summer days that make the dust. His hand falls to his side. The corners of his mouth move up, but he is not smiling. Only sad.

"I told you, I don't do this often."

"Ever?"

"No."

"What is This that you never do?"

"Going home with a woman—" we study the clouds of emotion as they move across his face and are edited. "I didn't mean to imply—" He watches the empty bottle as he taps it on the counter. "She's very nice."

"What does she do?"

"Lara?" And as if he doesn't remember saying it, or maybe for an effect he repeats: "She keeps busy." When there is no reply he says "She used to be a therapist but she hasn't practiced in years."

We reach out imitating certainty. We rest a hand on his shoulder.

He draws us to him like a man grieving, and lowers his head like praying.

For the time we stand this way, we think, we could have fallen on the dull sward of a butter knife, or died slowly in countless other ways: organized the bookshelf by color, rearranged magnets painted to look like ladybugs on the freezer—could have moved the to-do list of pills our grandmother tucked under the magnets' red wooden bodies two years ago to a less prominent place, could have watched our face grow sleepy in the matte reflection of the rusting bathroom mirror, sat alone with the hollow tap-tap of the keyboard under our fingers and the arid empty words of disease blowing through our ears.

He lifts his head to look around, as if for the first time, because he needs something to fill the space between where he is and where he should be. "This is an interesting place," he says. We nod against him. "A lot of unusual stuff," he adds, looking for the answer to a question he doesn't know how to ask.

"My grandparents built it," we say to the floor, our eyes open and comparing the slick black of his shoes to the pale toes of our feet, and below us the dark wet of basement empty and blue-black, faraway in our mind from the pale gold of the house. And in that dark, a smaller house. The rooms built from scraps of the house that is its home.

"Looks like you haven't changed a thing" *comma* "Looks like my parents' house" *period*

We are notlistening distracted by the smell of his laundry detergent and press ourselves against him. We wonder if he can feel the prick of our nipples through his shirt. When he straightens, our hands drop as if they expected to be left empty.

His hands are warm and dry and hold each side of our face while his lips linger lightly at our hairline. His fingers slide back, behind our neck and into our hair, the hands hold the whole weight of our head and he kisses our cheek. We want to be near to the man we saw when we were the man with money, something easy and confident and uncomplicated, because suddenly we are that man. We rest against his chest and he strokes our hair as it falls down our back. A finger is caught in a tangle for a moment and instantly we are angry with ourself for bringing him here, bored with this man who should be home, fucking the woman he loves. Or doesn't.

We pull away, say "Do you need to go?" For a moment we believe the concern in our voice.

He looks at the oven clock unoffended and says Yes/He hadn't meant to stay so long/He should get going/Here is his number/call any time. And we stop listening. We make it easy for him to leave us—easy for him/us. We walk with him to the front door and he brushes our cheek with his thumb, kisses the top of our head.

"Goodnight David," we say. And he is gone. His body has vanished and the house sighs with relief and the air hangs itself in the still kitchen.

We sweep everything from the evening, bottles and David's number, into the trash. We move to the living room to be held up by the thin floor, suspended in the room as if on adrift on a flimsy raft. We think only of David's bottomless sadness, of his eyes when he remembers the man will die.

Woodbine, By the 401

ROBIN RICHARDSON

PRIORITY

JOENSUU
23.12.05

Her intuition means he calls her *Lucky Charm* —
     arm-in-arm outside the stable, claiming
she can dowse a winner. All the jockeys
     wear the sun like suits of armour, stern

as new spells cast to change this child's fortune.
     45 to 1 they'll notice the disgruntled groundskeeper
slip cyanide into the fountain pop. She is as sure
     she'll die here as her father is he'll win enough

to pay his way to Vegas. *Simple mathematics,*
     he says, and the whole track opens like a dirt-
lipped mouth, makes stew of all the horses.
     Can't stop calculating firearm per losing streak,

sees Derringers in pockets, box cutters, mid-
     life men with hearts like S.O.S pads wearing
through their white. What a mess. She changes
     in the bathroom, custard on her hard-earned

Terry Fox tee, learning not to look long
     in the mirror above the brass horse statuettes.
There is her face. There is the less-than graceful
     way she bats her lashes at a stallion.

Her love is unconditional and lingers long
     as mustard gas. At twelve-years-old she knows
she'll pass from charm to trinket: picture
     in a wallet, whipped out at casinos for good luck.

Delicate, Colors, White

YEJI HAM

EVERY MONTH, THE MAN brought the sky and three dollars.

"Usual?" the boy asked.

The man put the sky on the counter.

"Double wash?" the boy asked.

The man laid down three dollars.

"Double wash?" the boy asked.

"Double wash and iron," the man answered.

The boy took the three dollars and pointed the man to the corner. In the corner were a bookshelf, a heater, a table, a chair and no one. The man tapped his fingers on the counter staring at the creased sky. The sky was black, the blackest out of all the clothes that were brought to the Laundromat. The man looked at the boy, nodded, pushed himself from the counter and walked to the corner. The man slumped down into the chair. The boy put the money in the cash register.

People always spill on others' shirts. That was what the boy's mother said. That was why the boy's grandparents had started the Laundromat. Grandmother told Grandfather that the Laundromat was always. Always, people clean their clothes. Always, even when raining, snowing and thundering, people come and will come out to clean their clothes. Washed, pressed, dried and ironed, the clothes become dirty again, because as Grandmother said, people always spill on others' shirts. Twenty-six years ago the boy's grandparents opened the Laundromat, and a few years later his mother bought it from them. She paid half less for the place and never saw them again. People will always ruin your clothes, the boy's mother said. Always, sometimes, often but it will never be never, she said.

The man rose from the chair and stared out into the street.

The sky was black, the blackest out of all shades of black.

The boy put the sky into a basket.

The man was looking at something.

The boy took off his shirt and put it inside a washing machine. Every day, early in the morning, the boy washed his shirt. The whole day the boy was half-naked. Shirtless, the boy said almost nothing, wrote down whoever's name and contact information and took their clothes and money. Late at night, before his mother came back from her full-time shift at the restaurant a block away from the Laundromat, the boy put on a clean shirt. The next morning when she put him on the stool behind the counter and left, he took his dirtied shirts off and put it in the washing machine. If he could wash the purple and black on his body, he would. The boy shut the lid and pressed delicate.

The man was staring at an old lady.

The boy took one of the baskets and dumped the clothes into a washing machine and pressed white.

The man dropped his head.

An old lady was wearing a dark green coat. She was trying to grab. Something and somebody. She reached out her tiny trembling hands for sleeves or tails of coats. She opened her mouth but only her breath came out. She caressed her neck perhaps trying to save the warmth and breaths left inside her. The old lady looked around, left, right, behind and down but never up. Her feet were bare. For a long time, her feet had felt the cold concrete of the city and had forgotten the warm texture of a carpeted floor. For a long time, her feet had walked the streets of the city and had forgotten a way out of it. The old lady bent over, picked up a penny and put it in her hat. Leaning against the wall, she held out her dark green hat.

"The last time I saw her, the coat and the hat were emerald," the man said.

The boy dumped another into a washing machine and pressed color.

"They are dark green now," the man said.

"She should wash them," the boy said.

The man turned to face the boy.

"Yes," the man said, "she should."

"What color was the sky?" the boy asked.

"Everything and anything but black," the man said.

The boy dumped another into a washing machine and pressed color.

The man sat down back in the chair.

The boy grabbed the basket with the sky.

The man's fingers were black as burnt match heads.

The boy's fingers slipped and the basket fell on the floor.

The man got up.

The boy grabbed the sky and stuffed it back into the basket. Long and large. The sky could be a cape or an overcoat or a poncho. The boy could imagine himself wrapping his body with such long and large clothes, clothes that had the color of everything and anything. On Monday, it'd be sky blue. On Tuesday, it'd be yellow. On Wednesday, it'd be cotton candy pink. On Thursday, it'd be green. On Friday, it'd be red. On Saturday, it'd be ivory or pearl. On Sunday, it'd be purple. Grandmother was right, though. The boy's dry cracked hands became slippery. His dark skin became darker. The boy coughed. People always spilled on others' clothes, even on the sky. People ruined it. People must have spat, trampled and threw things on the sky. The sky was greasy, stained and no color of everything and anything could be seen but black. The boy put the basket on the washing machine.

The man was looking out into the street again. He tapped his fingers on the glass. He was looking at a young girl staring at her cell phone. She seemed to dial a number but then put the phone back into her pocket. The girl bit her lips, took the phone out, dialed again but shoved it back into her pocket. Trembling, she tried to get up but her legs were shaking badly. She could not stand. The girl fell back onto the bench and she clasped her purse and stomach. The man muttered:

"A dead baby in her purse," he said, "there's a dead baby in her purse."

The boy looked at the large sweater that she was wearing.

"That isn't her sweater," the boy said.

"No," the man said.

The boy dumped the sky in the washing machine and pressed delicate.

"Those are not her clothes," the man said.

The boy's mother always gave him a shirt that was too large. That was because she said wearing clothes that were a size larger was better than wearing smaller ones. The boy's mother said that her parents had always bought her clothes that were too small. Even now, her parents mailed her clothes that were too small to wear. Grandparents wanted her to come back home. The boy's mother

Yeji Ham

never did.

The washing machine tumbled and rumbled.

"Did someone spill on the sky?" the boy asked.

The man looked at the boy.

"Did someone step on it?" the boy asked. "Did someone spit at it?"

"Does someone spill, step and spit at your clothes?" the man asked.

"People always spill on others' shirts," the boy said, "they always ruin it."

The man pointed out to the street.

A tall man was screaming at a man in a suit. The man in a suit lowered his head and bowed. The tall man seemed to grin but also frown. The man in a suit kept his head down. The tall man's mouth was wide open. Whatever came out of his mouth weighed down on the man in a suit. His back bent over lower and lower. The tall man threw some papers at the man in a suit, turned his heels and went into a building. The man in a suit knelt down on the pavement and collected the papers. The building, like the tall man, was high and lofty and loomed over the man in a suit.

"His pants are dirty now," the boy said.

"Once more," the man said, "once again."

"He should wash them," the boy said.

"Clean," the man said.

At night, the man with large hands came back to the boy's and the mother's apartment. Only by early in the morning, the man with large hands and wearing workers' boots left the house. From night to morning, the man was awake. The boy's mother was quiet. The boy was kept awake. The man spilled alcohol on the boy's shirt. The boy's mother spilled smears of blood on the boy's shirt. Worthless, the man said of the boy's mother. New beginning, the boy's mother said of the man. Watching the sky dark and darkening, the boy waited for the morning when the man was gone, and his mother was moaning, and there, lying somewhere floor of the house, the boy imagined himself at the Laundromat.

On Strike

REBECCA LEVI

In the dark, something's burning. The bus
has stopped at 13,000 feet. My neighbor
turns to me, I wrap my face in my scarf.

At dawn, the mountains are pink and gauzy. Voices
seep in, I hear hot breath in the altiplano's
cold air. Still, the burning. Pulling wool
from neck, I find the place where you last kissed me.

Their faces wake me, too close to mine through dirty
glass, too young to fear. Until their rocks
explode the windows. I cram my body beneath
my seat. The leather sole of my neighbor's boot.

In bed, your fingers drew the Andes on
my back, the mountains bleeding scarlet quinoa,
sold to distant gringo yogis. Will killing
me bring down the price of grains? Potatoes?

Faces disappear, we stumble out
from shattered glass. My breath mists. The roadside
fires warm our hands, the mountains harden.

My neighbor, Vincent, answers to several different
names and makes mistakes in his mother tongue.
He's fluent in no language. We walk past truck-tire
walls, around a pile of flaming shit.

The town appears like a dust-swept set, silent
before the show. We find warm beer, which turns
the mountains back to gauze. If you came looking,
you'd never find me. At dusk, the driver calls.

Through the holes where the windows were, we toss
five soles to the mamachas, bundled at
the barricades. They drag away the tires.

Moonlight turns the giant lake to silk.
Vincent breathes on my neck, avoids my eyes.
I look out the hostel window, search for mountains,
see only floating islands made of straw.

Far across the altiplano, chapped young
hands pull down the walls, put out the fires.

Drift Sessions

TONY Y. FU

February 2013
Matthews, North Carolina

In the records of the earliest dynasties, events were (in absence of a portable standard) measured in the time it took two people to have dinner. When will the emperor's forces surround the rebel encampment? The time it takes to eat a meal. What length was the traitorous general's serenade to his favorite concubine before he headed off to battle? The time it takes to eat a meal. For how long did the horses drag the general's decapitated corpse through the muddy roads of his hometown? The time it took to eat a meal.

When the only Chinese restaurant in town folded, we didn't find out until we arrived for dinner on New Year's day and the dragon was gone. For years it had nested above the entrance, its body coiled and electric like some kind of mythical beast. But in its absence, only discolored concrete remained, weakly illuminated by the neon signage of the Fuddruckers on the other side of the parking lot. We peered inside and the banquet tables were all pushed to a corner; the red cushions had been ripped out of their booths and piled up in the center, slack as body bags. My father joked that we should leave before the People's Liberation Army finishes its executions and starts cleaning up witnesses. My mother gave him a look and changed the subject, asking me what a Fuddruckers was. I replied, "A terrible thing," and we drove away.

January 2012
Marvin, North Carolina

I let my mother dredge the deep fryer. It's a fry bucket to be precise, no lid, all electric, just a rubber pail with enough space to make three chicken legs or a sandcastle's primary turret. Last month it appeared on our doorstep inside a giant box also filled with pots, a rice maker, pans, two kettles, coffee tins, an electric iron, and a pressure cooker so outdated even our relatives in China would dismiss it as provincial. My father, it seemed, had not asked my mother what she wanted to spend their MasterCard reward points on. All his choices were terrible, except for the deep fryer. We forgave him.

The things we deep fried were largely determined by novelty. My sister resisted at first, suspicious of the things bathed in half a gallon of oil. Then the afternoon my mother and I discovered anything dipped in pancake batter would turn golden and crisp—strawberries, sliced bananas, sweet potatoes, yuan xiao, dessert never ending. Then shrimp, salmon cuts, whatever meat my mother defrosted the night before. One night my father asked if we wanted hot pot, he had bought special thinly sliced lamb from the Chinese grocers. We deep fried the lamb. We're all watching our weight now; we don't want to end up like Americans.

If I worry at night, it's about the deep fryer after it's unplugged. For thirty minutes it stays scalding hot while left unattended in the middle of the kitchen counter. My sister says she's old enough to pour a glass of tea without knocking over a bucket of boiling oil. "Duh." Still, I'm uneasy. I don't want her to look like a burn victim. When I was in high school, there was a transfer student whose face was disfigured because her stepfather threw acid at her—so the story went—and we were all nice to her. I mean, we would hold fingers to our noses and oink when pushing past fat girls in the hallway. We would hand out party invitations to the whole class and skip the girls whom even makeup couldn't turn pretty. We would throw our leftover carrot sticks at the girls who couldn't afford the right clothes. But we were, all of us, nice to the transfer student. We always smiled, we always waved, we always said hello. We must have felt terribly sorry, looking at her. She wasn't like the other girls. She was so ugly it was tragic.

January 2014
Marvin, North Carolina

By evening the squall line weakens. Our mother leaves once the rain starts to taper. Clouds roil across the sky, as if a lake frozen at high tide. She pulls the garbage can out to the curb. Twilight seeps past the cracks of a horizon that will take months to thaw. Alone at the bottom of the driveway, she looks underwater, her way lit by the pairs of lamps hanging above garage doors, each installed at the same height, an unbroken string that, as far as we see, encircles the earth. If she could keep traveling west (or is it east?) she might reach the places where her sisters have scattered. The sun wanes an ashen blue, a wound we left after falling through the ice.

Trash strewn across the street: earlier the wind toppled recycling bins while rifling through the neighborhood. A slurry of grease and alcohol flows toward the gutters; the rivers glisten with bluegill bass, channel catfish, and ten thousand tons of coal sludge that local officials deny responsibility for. We head downstairs and help her wrap dumplings, our six hands gathering with flour until we become indistinguishable. She doesn't say it, but we can tell, once we leave for our own families, we'll never know this home again. Our grandparents' fields are decades gone; the farmland paved into suburbs, strip malls, highway bypasses. Pinned to the refrigerator, there's a sheet of paper brittle with age, a trail of phone numbers belonging to our aunts and uncles, written and unwritten like the rough draft of a poem on drifting apart. We too will chase shadows, believing they're our dreams, and lose touch like geese caught on opposite seasons, or pollen that the wind flings in all directions.

Rain returns, dangling off empty tree branches with a teardrop's sag. Our mother finishes loading dishes into the washer. The full moon is piercing, but not bright enough to be seen across four continents. Whatever sky hangs over her kin tonight, home is as distant a wish as the cities their lives have portioned out.

Tony Y. Fu

December 2009
Beijing

Sister, I've forgotten the rules to our childhood games, and the snow keeps falling as if no matter how many decades later, the city that should have raised us will never forgive our leaving. We land in Beijing, no better than tourists.

I hail a taxicab and we try to pass for locals around the old imperial palace. On the way out, you point at an intersection and say maybe that's where grandfather and his wooden cart were detained by the Red Guard for selling kettle corn. I laugh and wonder if mom will ever stop telling that story every time she sees a popcorn machine at the movie theater.

Our mother, still jet-lagged, meets us for lunch at Pizza Hut. We plan the evening over garlic knots, bubble tea, and the hulking din of construction machines. The blizzard worsens and tower cranes go dark. Work falters. Those nascent skyscrapers through the haze are too much like Goya's half-devoured colossus. Kitchen doors open and the tang of liquor and roast pork wafts out.

The next morning, a petitioner's carcass thaws out kitty-corner from the railway station. Trains to the seaside will be delayed. Those drawings our small hands carved into the dogged red walls of the hutongs have long eroded.

November 1997
Holland, Michigan

My cousin and I were the biggest fobs in the Midwest, but we still had to go to school every Saturday morning. In winter, snow sagged off the sharp angles of the church roof, smearing the brick walls and stained glass panels with ice hued darker than soot. We trudged into the charmless single-story building without wiping our boots.

When class started, the five of us boys still in middle school would sit as far back in the bible study room as we could, almost crashing into a bookshelf full of New Testaments and Jesus themed boardgames. We whispered about new releases for the N64, our beloved Lions' playoff chances, and let the girls and the two highschoolers occupy the instructor's attempts to teach us how to write and speak Chinese.

Everyone's parents waited out the time in the cafeteria—which wasn't more than a couple of folding tables and a soda vending machine—and played majiang or eights while talking about whatever there was to say to the only other Chinese adults in town (and, as far as we knew) the only ones in Allegan county, in the lower peninsula, the rest of Michigan, the GMT -5 time zone, the western hemisphere.

Our eyes often wandered toward the slit of a window that lead out to a field of grass long enough to play two first downs on. But nobody ever brought a football, and we weren't permitted to sift through the equipment closet during our lunch break. It wasn't our church; we only belonged on Saturdays between 9am and 2pm.

Eventually, we came up with the rules of a game that would let us tackle one another and declare losers. We called it Hiroshima. Whoever scored highest on that week's vocab quiz would become it. He had to run as fast as he could. The rest of us would be Americans.

Brothers

JAC MARTINEZ

A.

B.

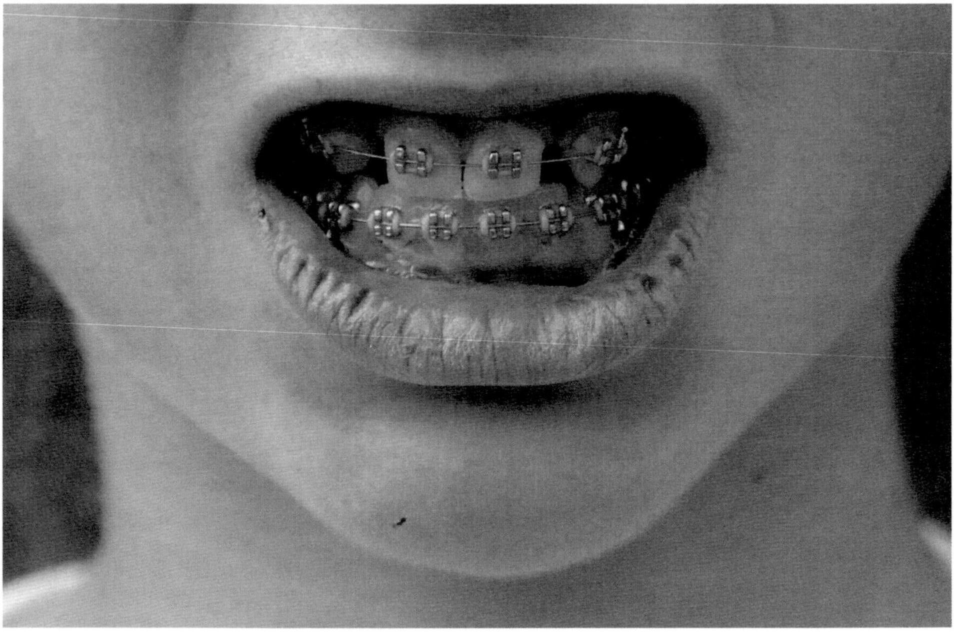

E.

F.

Shroud of Darwin

NICK CRISCUOLO

Catharsis

MOHD AZLAN MOHD LATIB

MEDIUM: Caffeinated art paper, digital print, collage and hand tinting

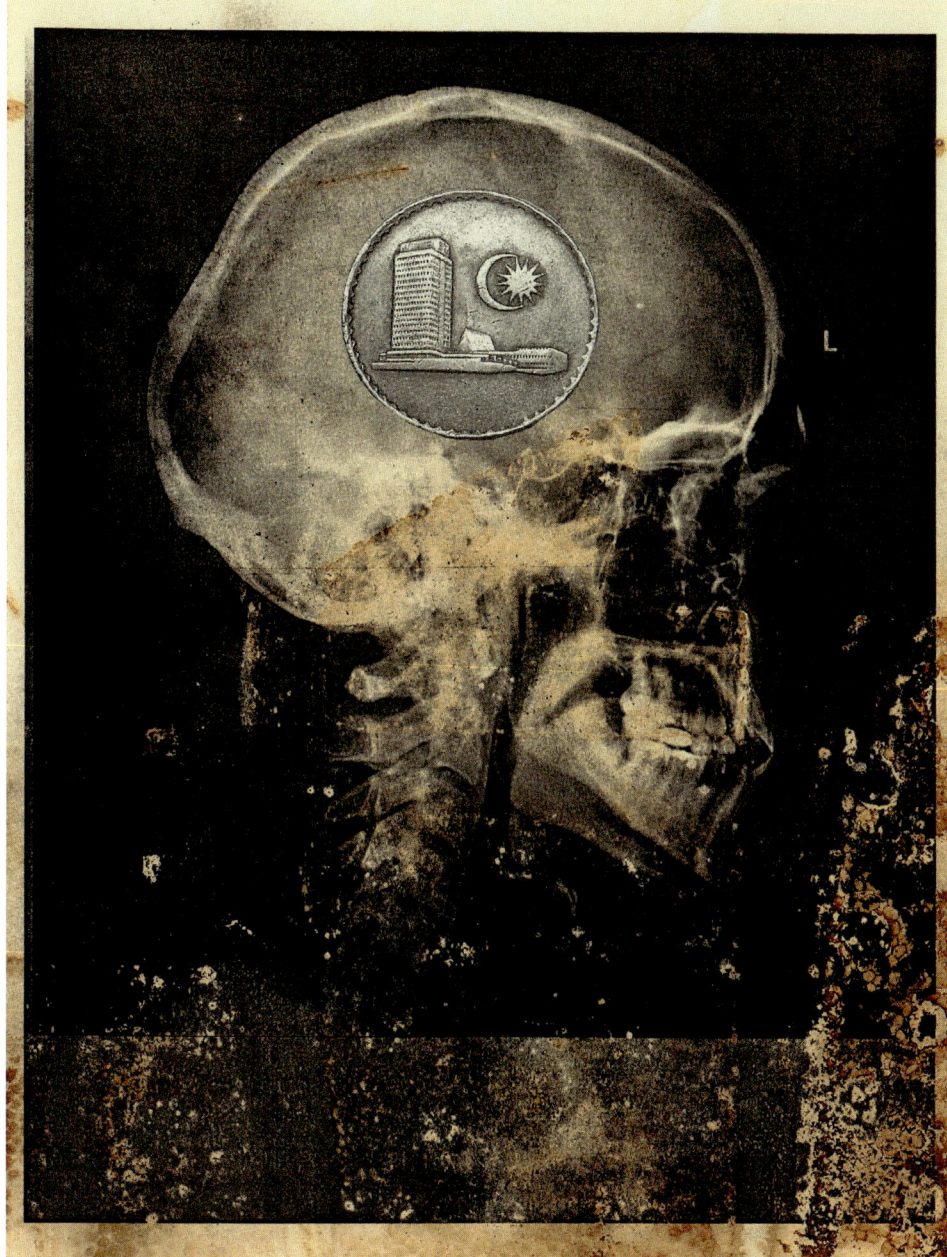

L

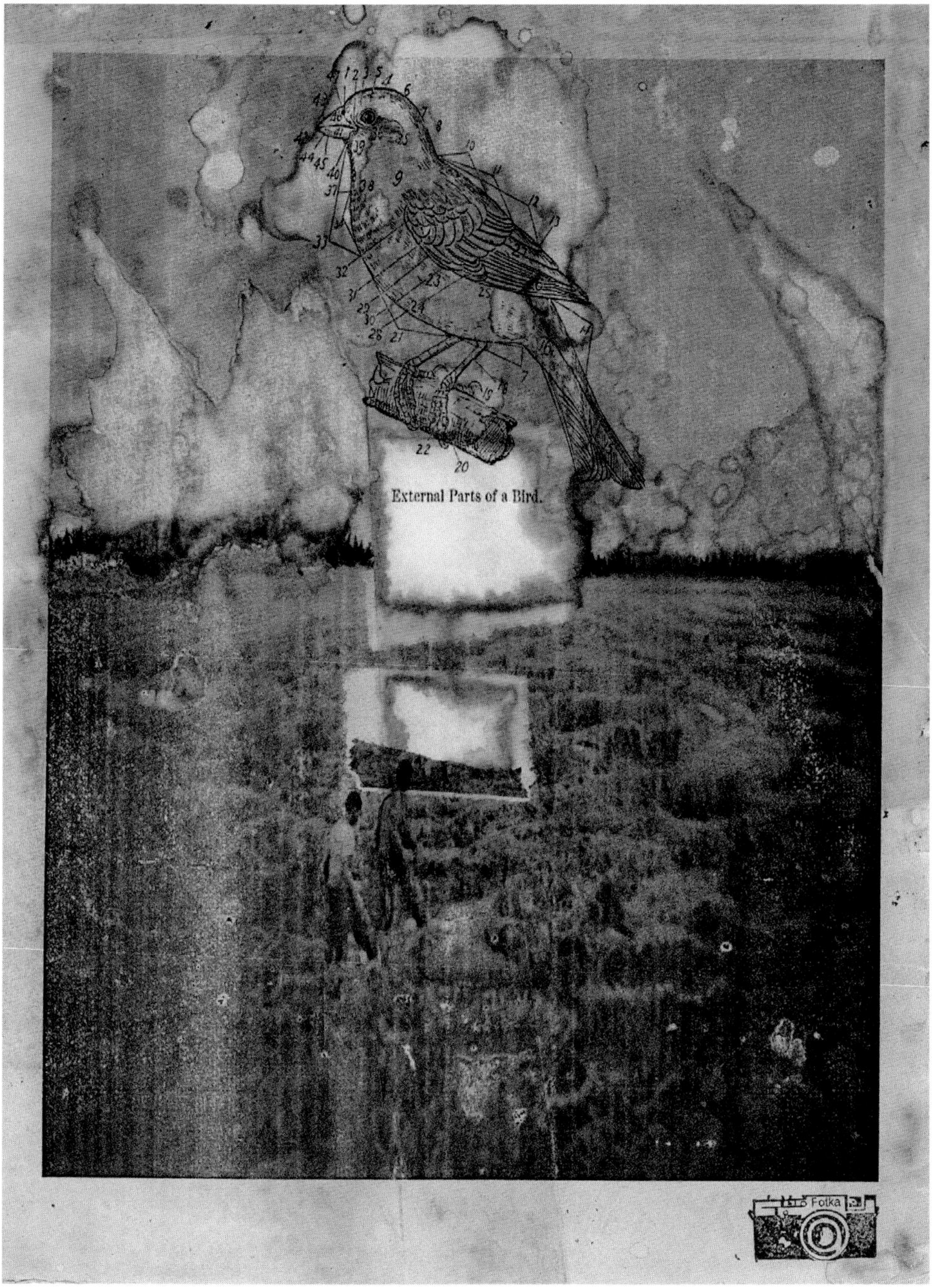

External Parts of a Bird.

2016 Letter Contest

Congratulations to our winners and finalists! We are pleased to honor the following writers and artists for their extraordinary letters:

1ST PLACE
Chad Simpson, "No More Ghost"
2ND PLACE
Sofia Stambolieva, "Confetti"
3RD PLACE
Awuor Onyango, "Zuhura: Bridges to a Post-gender World"

FINALISTS:

Katherine Bowling, "Richmond, VA 1978—Typewritten letter"
Bridget Brewer, "Star Dog"
Laura Lark, "Cellophane Sky" & "Dear Johnny Depp, It's Not About You"
Matt Nelson, "Please Don't Make Me A Character (excerpt)"
Okwiri Odour, "Untitled Letter"
Clio Velentza, "Postscript To A Thank You Note" & "Dear Sister"

AN INTRODUCTION BY CONTEST JUDGE

Mary Gaitskill

DEAR READERS,
I almost never write letters any more even though I love them. I used to write them regularly to friends and family, pages-long letters that sometimes had illustrations even though I can't really draw. I have a whole chest of old letters, the love letters tied together with ribbon or something.

For a while I wrote email in the same spirit—but it wasn't the same. The difference is hard to describe, because really, it's very small; the content of what you say is likely the same. But email is not as tangible or physical, and so not as intimate. You don't see the way the person appears in their handwriting, which lights up their words like the tone of their voice (in a letter to his wife Vera, Nabokov writes, "I love your handwriting, that running shadow of your voice"). There's no stamp for subtext (beautiful Grace Kelly, angry Bette Davis, playful Krazy Kat bouncing a brick off the head of some stuck-up guy in a suit; the mute, gleaming first telephone ever). You can't keep it in a chest, tied together with ribbon, or if you did it would look funny. You have to wait for letters, even if you choose, as I and my boyfriend of years ago chose, to Express Mail every letter you send. You also have to wait to react because it takes longer to manually write, and then, if you're like me, you have to re-copy it so it isn't a mess and so it says exactly what you want it to say. Then there's the patient ritual of envelope and stamp, the mailbox or the post office.

This ritual is not only delicious, it also has a practical effect, at least for me. Email is so immediate that you don't think it out, or feel it out, even if you save the first draft and look at it again. You don't use your whole arm to do it, your arm connected to your shoulder and chest, where your heart is. You don't have to put anything in an envelope or walk anywhere. You just hit "send." I have had ridiculous misunderstandings and even fights with people because of email, mostly because I completely misunderstood the tone of something that was meant to be funny, or just not as serious as I thought—people have made the same mistake with me too. This happens with letters, but with letters you can't just write some sarcastic rejoinder and hit "send." It takes a lot longer and even if you do send your pissed-off or completely off-the-mark reply, there's a really good chance that one of you will call the other and...the misunderstanding will evaporate instead of solidifying. For some reason that doesn't happen with email, people don't call to talk it out, they just react and hit "send." With text, forget it, why talk when you can furiously work your thumbs and send? Perfectly nice people text like insane, murderously angry stalkers when, if they had to write a letter, half-naked and angrily weeping, they could just vent their deranged feelings without the recipient ever knowing because...they'd have to get up, get dressed, address the envelope etc.

For all these reasons, if you love someone or even just care about them, or even just used to care about them, write them a letter. Even if you barely know them but you want to comfort them about a death or illness, write them a letter. Give them something to hold in their hand, it just feels better. It's closer to touch. I admit I hardly ever do it now, and when I do it's usually pretty short. But if it's important, and I want the other person to know, I write a letter. If it's too awkward to say in words, or say it's an uncle with whom you have nothing in common, write to him. Email can work fine. At least it's not a text. But really, a letter is nicer.

AN INTRODUCTION BY

No Tokens

D EAR READERS,
I've spent many evenings taking walks with Mary Gaitskill through the New York freeze. Walks during which we've discussed the letters we've written, the best letters we've received, love letters, break-up letters, too-late letters, more-soon letters, Nabokov's letters to Vera, all the letters we wrote but never sent. Some letters, we can't even remember. We sent them off and now they live somewhere in the world—a shoebox, a drawer—with former versions of ourselves pressed inside of them.

We did not know what to expect when we made the decision to run this contest. But the submissions—full of fire, bravery, earnestness, wit—exceeded our expectations. Each letter, each ode to a letter, meditation on a letter, essay about a letter, contained its own world and powers, and we feel rather voyeuristic in our love for every one of them.

The week Mary wrote her introduction, I received a voicemail. "I thought I'd take my own advice and call you," she said. Mary is not one for lengthy email exchanges, which is one of the many things I admire about her. "The thing is," she continued, "letter contest entries aren't *really* letters, and the reason they're not letters is exactly what we're getting at here. If you submit a real letter, it's going to be too intimate. You don't want everyone in the world to see it, or even, *some* people. You just don't want it. But that's exactly what letters are—that's what's so special about them."

The three winning entries by Chad Simpson, Sofia Stambolieva, and Awuor Onyango offer tremendous range. These entries travel from Indiana to Bulgaria to Nairobi; they examine themes of fatherhood, mortality, politics, sexuality. But here's the thing—these letters also have something in common, the only element we found that matters in the end: an urgency and need to communicate, to break through, to connect with another person as if it's life or death.

Mary was right in her voicemail. Some things are better kept. All letters are secrets, in a way. But better, at times, to have somebody hold your secret in their hands.

Yours truly,
T Kira Madden and the staff of No Tokens.

No More Ghost

1ST PLACE: CHAD SIMPSON

DEAR DAD,
You are asleep in your recliner, and I am in the next chair over, typing this letter into my phone.

I have driven you to your surgery and returned you home. I have stood over your chair and directed medicine from a dropper into your naked eyes. The TV is on, and you are sleeping fitfully. It's as if you want to stay awake, though I've told you not to worry about it, to get some rest. I'll stay until the next round of drops needs to be administered, and then I will go home, to Jane and the cats and the last few weeks of summer before school starts up again.

I just realized that behind where you're reclining, in the space between you and the laundry room, a ghost may be hovering. That's usually where you sense his presence, right?

Hello, ghost.

There is a realtor's sign in the yard.

Soon, you are going to sell this place and move into some condo or another.

You will have new eyes, a new place. No more ghost.

You and I laughed on the way to the hospital about how many people, after you told them you were having cataracts removed, replied that their grandmother had endured the same operation. You were sick of hearing it, sick of being compared to somebody's grandma, but still you were capable of laughing about it. At the hospital, when you looked at me for the first time with your new eyes, you let me know that I had red spots on my face—there, and there, and there. You literally pointed them out.

I've had those spots for a while, Dad.

Under my right eye is some sort of burst blood vessel.

The rest are acne scars.

I'm wondering now what I'd looked like to you with your old eyes. I'm wondering what it would be like if that's how all of the world saw me.

I've been meaning to tell you: I've known since I was twelve years old.

I'm pretty certain that if you were my child, and not my father, it would be against etiquette to say such a thing.

If you'd actually come out to me, that is.

Chad Simpson

Since you were/are unaware of it: this discovery of mine happened back in September, a little over two months after Mom died. You and Brent and I were in the living room where Mom spent the last couple days of her life with a fan blowing on her face, sweating, suffering fever dreams.

Already, July felt like a long time ago. For each of us, though you were the one still waking up alone in bed a few times each week and wondering where Mom might have fallen asleep. You were the one still putting on your glasses and going looking for her, then chiding your sleepy brain for not remembering, for being so stupid.

You sat in your recliner, and Brent sat in the chair opposite mine. We made a kind of acute triangle. There was something on the TV, but mostly the three of us were experiencing the soundscape and texture of Mom's absence. It was the first time the three of us had been together in the house since the days following the funeral.

The tablet was new. It had been charging next to my chair, and I picked it up as a distraction, began reading the latest article about the Sheley trial. That guy had shaken certain convictions of mine, and I was a little obsessed. To be more precise: I'd recently begun to believe there were people in the world who might truly be evil; I'd begun to think maybe the death penalty wasn't such an untenable option.

When the email notification appeared, I tapped the envelope at the bottom of the screen on instinct. Mostly, I was confused. About five minutes earlier, before I'd begun scrolling through articles in the local newspaper, I'd asked you if you wanted me to set up your email on this new device. You'd shrugged, said you'd worry about it later.

Before I read the message, I realized that if the notification wasn't some glitch, what I was about to do was a kind of invasion. I glanced first at Brent, whose leg was now slung over the arm of his chair. He seemed about to doze off, probably wanted a cigarette.

Then I looked your way. None of us had said anything to one another for several minutes.

I registered immediately that the messages were being conveyed through a certain website devoted to classifieds and personal ads. The latest note in the chain said only, ok. I could have stopped reading and closed the app right then. I probably should have. But

I'm human, Dad. Just like you. I checked the room one more time. It was filled up with television noise and fatigue and sadness. I think we'd had lunch at the lake that day. Rachel was in Rockford, working. Jane was in Carthage at a bachelorette party. There were probably other places the three of us would rather have been right then, too.

Beneath that first message was a solid block of text filled with letters, numbers, acronyms. I skimmed everything once, afraid of what I'd find, trying to take in the words imperfectly, and then I decided to go through it all more slowly.

You wrote in complete sentences, detailed your height and weight, the dimensions of your penis. You capitalized certain letters—HWP—and words—THICK. Your grammar was decent, your tone formal. You seemed to want to impress him, convince him you were worthy of giving whatever it was he happened to be seeking.

Beneath that message was the guy's original post, only eight words long, all lowercase: will suck or fuck for ride to airport.

I read the messages again, in reverse order, and then one more time, as they'd originally unfolded for me, word by word, as if to punish myself for all of the suspicions I'd held over the years, or maybe to revel in the confirmation of them, I really can't say.

The thing about the exchange that made my heart ache the most was not the fact you'd lied about your age—you've always been vain, hated aging—but your eagerness. That block of text, how thorough it was, indicated to me naïveté, desperation.

Later that night, after I bought a big bottle of cheap wine on my way home, I sat on our front porch alone in the dark, drinking and looking out at the night sky, imagining the worst. I imagined that guy who wanted the ride to the airport was some homophobe with cannon fists, sharp knives, a gun. I imagined you showing up to some collapsing apartment building in your pristine car. The guy had thick wrists, long and tangled hair. Tight jeans. The knives and gun I'd imagined dissolved, and a small aluminum baseball bat took their place, tucked snug against the guy's thigh as he walked to your car. I imagined shattered glass and you wounded, bleeding from the head, having to call me to come and pick you up from one of the hospitals in the Cities.

I imagined the drive home. The story you might concoct,

Chad Simpson

the fabrication.

The sutures beneath the gauze secured to your head.

The shame.

I called Jane late that night to tell her about the messages I'd read, but she'd been at the bachelorette party for hours and was drunk, ready for bed. We agreed to talk about everything the next day, when I met her in Carthage for the wedding. By the time I arrived there, after imagining for most of the night several violent scenarios by which Brent and I might be rendered thirty-something-year-old orphans, I realized that you would probably be just fine. The truth was, I knew, you weren't naïve. You weren't in over your head. You'd been doing this for years.

I never told you how I knew, what happened when I was twelve.

I could claim omniscience, or a son's intuition, though I'm not sure what the point of doing so would be.

I should preface this with some etymology. I'm thinking of ancient Greek, the word epistomai, which means "to understand, to know for certain, to believe."

The first and third aspects of the definition are most applicable here. When I was twelve, I began to understand that you might be gay. I began to believe that you probably were. I cannot say I knew this for certain.

Before I was twelve, though, I was ten, the year we all moved from Illinois to Indiana, to Logansport, for your work. Before Mom and Brent and I joined you there, you lived alone at the Holiday Inn for three months. At the age of 32, this was the first time in your life you'd ever lived alone. What a part of me is trying to say, Dad, I think, is that I can understand the sense of freedom you must have experienced when you moved without your wife and boys to Logansport that summer. How liberating it must have felt to be alone for once, to just be you.

We'd only been in town for a few weeks and already you were going for nightly walks at Spencer Park. Then one night when you were out I broke my hand in the backyard playing football with the Pyle boys. My pinky finger was bent at a terrible angle, and I showed it to Mom, who was sipping vodka, watching TV. The first words out of her mouth were, I could just kill your father. I swear to God I could fucking kill him.

The problem was that she was a little drunk—and she wasn't quite sure where the hospital was in this new town where we were living. By the time she got Brent and me loaded into the car, it had gotten dark. We were two headlights in the quiet Indiana darkness, driving from street to street, looking for you. The whole time, Mom kept muttering, her face tight to the steering wheel, I swear to God I could fucking kill him.

I didn't know about Spencer Park when I was ten. I didn't know that it was a cruisy spot, that guys came there from all over that part of Indiana, seeking what they knew could be found. I couldn't understand why Mom was so mad at you when I was the one with the disfigured hand, the reason we were out there in the dark, scanning the sides of the road, hoping to find you.

By the time I was twelve, though, I knew the kids in town called that particular park the Butt Hut. And I knew it was where you still went on walks most nights. I never fully connected the dots until I was sitting in the Lincoln Middle School gymnasium one morning before classes started. In middle school, all of the kids— whether they were dropped off by their parents or herded off of some bus—were forced to congregate in the gym before classes started. This strikes me know as a horrible idea, bringing together six hundred sleepy-eyed eleven- to fourteen-year-olds and asking them to sit relatively quietly on wooden gym bleachers for twenty or thirty minutes every school day, but that's how things went down.

This being middle school, there were cliques. There were spots on those bleachers where you did or didn't belong. By the time I was twelve and in seventh grade, even though we'd only been in town for a little over two years, I was popular enough. Brent and I would split up as soon as we walked in the gym doors. He would head toward his group of quiet and frail-boned friends with their uncombed hair and weak eyes. I would find some of the guys I played baseball or football or basketball with. Sometimes, I'd sit with a couple of guys from my accelerated classes and talk about the previous night's homework. I was flexible: I don't remember the social politics of those mornings being particularly stressful, though they must have been for a lot of kids. Maybe I was just oblivious, not fully present.

Boys sat on one side of the gym, girls on the other. If I was oblivious, it might have had to do with the fact I spent much of middle school in love with a particular girl, Lauren Richards. When I was sitting on the bleachers, I was often staring across the basketball court trying to find her, to see what she was wearing that day. Even now, I can recall the section of bleachers where she always sat. Which seems strange, since in my memory of it, I am always looking at her from a different vantage point, from a different part of my side of the gym.

There must have been fights some mornings, but I don't remember any. The teacher in charge of maintaining order in the gymnasium was one of the shop teachers, who also happened to coach the middle school's football team. He had thick fingers and a broad forehead that looked like it could withstand a lot of punches. Everyone was afraid of him. If he whistled to get our attention and told us all to quiet down, most of the time, we quieted down.

The most disobedient thing I remember kids pulling off on those mornings involved bouncy balls. This being middle school, we were too old for them, really, but some young genius must have had one on his person some morning. He threw it from the boys' side of the bleachers off the wall above the girls' side, and we all watched the ball arc from one side of the gym to the other until it finally rolled to a stop somewhere near the center of the court.

Our supervisor, the shop teacher, Mr. David, walked slowly toward the ball and then dropped to one knee to retrieve it, began scanning the boys' bleachers for a face in the process of betraying its owner in some way. He stared in our direction for a long time.

After that first person, that genius, got away with it, bouncy balls became a thing for a while. Even the girls started throwing them. Sometimes, there would be six or seven balls bouncing simultaneously from wall to wall. Mr. David remained vigilant, whistled loudly, made announcements about how the business with the bouncy balls needed to stop, but he couldn't watch both sets of bleachers at once. When he focused on the girls' side, some guy would launch a ball and then hunch back down. When Mr. David then turned to the boys' side, his eyes slits beneath that wide forehead, his hands clenched into fists, some girl would send one sailing. I don't remember him ever busting anyone—until I was the one who'd just let a ball fly from my hand.

That morning was like most other mornings: a slow waking, a shower, an early bus pickup, the gymnasium. I'm remembering now another detail about those mornings: the kids who were bussed arrived to school earlier than the kids whose parents drove them. And my bus, it was one of the first to arrive. Maybe that's why I was always sitting somewhere different on the bleachers. Maybe I would just choose a spot to sit and then watch everyone else filter in, wait to see who joined me.

Already, a few bouncy balls were flying around the gym that morning. The place was filling up with kids. I'm sure I'd already spotted Lauren Richards. She was probably wearing a turtleneck. She wore a lot of turtlenecks back then. I was probably sitting with Andrew.

Not far from us were Zach Hall and Casey Bryant. They were the un-bussed, the late arrivers. There were certain popular/rich kids in Logansport who still seemed to resent me a little—for arriving out of nowhere and getting better grades than they did, for being a little better at sports, and decent-enough looking—and Zach and Casey were two such people. Zach and I actually got along OK most of the time, but Casey was just a remarkably average asshole, a loudmouth and a bully.

I'm remembering now the din of the gymnasium, the sound of six hundred chattering middle schoolers, echoing.

I'm remembering how it seemed to quiet that morning, to go still. Zach Hall was saying my name.

There were people on the bleachers between Zach and me. When the noise seemed to quiet and Zach's voice made its way to me, it also seemed as though the people sitting between us weren't paying attention. It seemed for a moment it was just the two of us—and Casey Bryant, whom I blurrily sensed was snickering at Zach's side. I dislike the word snickering, but that's the only word for what he was doing. When he wasn't being a loudmouth, Casey Bryant was snickering.

Then the stillness diminished, dissipated. I was having a hard time hearing what Zach was trying to say.

So he shouted, his hands cupped around the sides of his

Chad Simpson

mouth. I said, I saw your dad last night at the Butt Hut.

The quiet returned. All of the guys sitting between us on the bleachers turned to look at me. Casey Bryant's snicker became much less blurry.

This was a kind of challenge, and I recognized it as such, in my twelve-year-old gut. I don't think Zach Hall was wanting to fight me, but I do think he wanted to see how I'd react to this. As did the small horde of guys whose heads had now turned my way.

I could have stood up out of the bleachers, said, What the fuck did you say?

I could have made a joke. Something dismissive. Something derogatory about you.

I could have pretended not to hear him at all.

I said, Yeah, he goes for walks there sometimes. It's not far from our house.

Zach's face turned serious. He seemed to be attempting to solve a math problem that was beyond his capabilities. Casey Bryant stopped snickering.

Zach said, OK. Just thought I'd mention it.

People stopped paying attention. The place grew loud again. I was staring at one of the basketball hoops, at the two-foot wide rectangle on the backboard behind the ring. I was imagining the rectangle filled with Casey Bryant's suntanned and snickering face.

Then it was just about time to go, and a bouncy ball had materialized in the palm of someone's hand near me. The person— maybe it was Andrew, but I doubt it—was offering it to me.

As you know, I was not the kind of kid who broke many rules. I probably learned this from you. When you move around in the world in small towns in states like Illinois and Indiana, in the Midwest, I'd learned, there are things that do and do not look good. There are ways you should and shouldn't behave. Breaking rules only ever drew the wrong kind of attention.

I had stopped imagining Casey Bryant's face trapped in the rectangle of the backboard's glass and was thinking now of that night two years earlier when I had broken my hand. I was thinking of Mom's anger, of her saying over and over again, I could just kill your father. I swear to God I could fucking kill him.

I was twelve. I connected the dots loosely, abstractly. All gut, no brain. I remembered how angry you'd been when we finally found you, how defensive you became. Sitting on those bleachers in the middle school gymnasium, I might not have known with certainty that you were gay, but I began to understand that you probably were. I began to believe it.

I reached for the ball, took hold of it, and stood, threw the thing with all of my body.

Most kids, they sat back down as soon as they threw a ball, but I'd forgotten this part of the act. I stood there watching the ball sail through the high-ceilinged gymnasium until it reached the wall above the girls' bleachers, and then I watched it begin bouncing, weirdly proud of this thing I'd set in action.

Then the sound of Mr. David whistling loudly through his teeth returned me to the moment, to the school, to seventh grade. His thick index finger pointed my way and curled into a fat sickle, calling me to him.

You say you sometimes hear the ghost walking on the hardwood floors. You say he has stopped the dryer mid-cycle, left your clothes damp.

You've worn hearing aids and glasses since you were in grade school. You're still going to need glasses, but the lenses will be much thinner now. When the doctor removed your cataracts, he inserted intraocular lenses into your eyes.

I like that word, intraocular.

One day, back in October, I texted you to ask if you were home so that I could bring by some food Jane had made for you—and show you the galley of my book, which I'd just gotten in the mail.

When I arrived, you were out in the driveway, half inside your car by way of the driver side door. I could see your shoes and legs and butt, but the rest of you was hidden. Near your feet: a bucket of soapy water.

You extracted yourself from the car when you saw me. You were cheery, maybe even a little manic. You told me to go on inside, you'd be there in a minute.

The floor mats were on the driveway. There were several rags strewn about. You'd only had this car for a month. I could smell its newness from where I stood. You saw me looking at the bucket of water, the floor mats, the rags.

There was a little accident, you said. I'm just about finished cleaning it up.

I let myself in the back porch, then the back door. In the kitchen, I set down whatever it was Jane had made for you on the counter near the stove. When I turned around, I saw your tablet in its stand near the breakfast nook. Because you had been outside cleaning for however many minutes, it would have made more sense for the display to have gone into sleep mode, faded to black, but there was an email message still loaded on it.

I looked at it only long enough to note that it was another Craigslist exchange. Then I grabbed something to drink from the fridge and began to head for the TV room, to the place where I am right now sitting, the galley of my book still in my hand.

You entered the house just after I turned from the fridge and were suddenly standing in front of me, the tablet on my left, its display still bright. I was trying not to think about the accident that had occurred that had you scrubbing out the inside of your new car. Your hands were soapy.

Good! you said. You got something to drink! Sit down!

I've been thinking lately about these little manic episodes of yours.

Maybe manic isn't the right word. It's more like ecstatic, derived from the ancient Greek ekstasis: "entrancement, astonishment, insanity; any displacement or removal from the proper place."

I haven't mentioned this yet, something I realized only months later. That first message I read, way back in September, it popped up as a new message, but it wasn't actually new. It was two days old.

I don't know why it would do such a thing, what kind of loop it was stuck in. You've told me before that you delete everything, that you don't even store anyone's number in your phone, not even mine.

You believe there is a ghost in your home. You talk to it. Every now and then, you say things about Mom looking down on you from the afterlife and noticing when you do something stupid, like leaving the oven on for a couple hours after you've removed your dinner from it. You imagine Mom laughing. I'm wondering if Mom or some ghost was inside that message, making it new again when it should have been long gone.

The meeting you were trying to arrange, it had actually taken place the day before, on Friday. That morning, after you worked from five until ten, a half day, you stopped by my house for something before you left for the Cities.

We talked for a few minutes on the front porch. I don't remember why you'd come by, what we said, but I remember your behavior. You were ecstatic—entranced, insane. Everything you said came out too fast and through an enormous smile that barely moved when you spoke. Anything I might have said back to you, it wasn't registering, I could tell.

At the time, I think I wrote it off as grief. I think I blamed your recent lack of social interaction, your solitude. At home back then, it was just you and that ghost.

After I figured out the message I'd read was somehow old but had reappeared new, I realized your behavior was more likely due to nerves, among other things. In the seventeenth century, mystical writers used the word ecstasy to describe "a state of rapture that stupefied the body while the soul contemplated divine things." I believe the stupefied body is an appropriate way of addressing what was going on with you at that moment, though I have no access to what your soul might have been contemplating. Whatever it was, it had nothing to do with our interaction. With the conversation we were having, face-to-face, on the front porch of my house.

There in your living room, a month later, you were in that same ecstatic state. Whatever had mucked up your car, it had been cleansed, made pure. I'd set down my can of soda and was holding the galley of my book in both hands, wanting to show it to you.

You began to talk. You were thinking about selling the house, moving somewhere new. There was something going on at work. Your buddy Troy had taken up running again. You went on and on, as you do.

At some point, I stood to leave and reminded you about the book, part of the reason I'd come over in the first place.

It's true: Mom was the reader. She was the one person in the world I most wanted to see me succeed at this writing thing. You like to brag that you haven't read a book since the late 1970's, and I'm mostly OK with the fact you don't really understand or care about this particular aspect of my life. Still, I handed the book to you. I said, This is just a galley. The real version will look like this, but it will be nicer. Better paper, better cover stock.

You held the book out in front of you, looked at it through the lower half of your glasses. There was still a little sweat on your face. You turned the book over in your hands, looked at the author photo. Neat, you said. That's really neat. Then you handed it back to me. It won't be long, you said, until I can have my own signed copy.

I don't know what I was expecting. Not much, I suppose, but still: you maybe could have said something about Mom, about how you wished she'd been around to see it. You maybe could have shown on your face a little bit of pride.

Maybe you were thinking such things, or feeling them in your ecstatic heart. Maybe inside you were full of astonishment, overcome with it. Maybe everything you were wanting to say, everything you were feeling in that moment—the joy and sorrow, the wonder and shame—kept any tender word you might have spoken from coming out of your mouth.

You don't really believe that Mom is somewhere out there watching over you, do you? I mean, maybe the idea brings you some kind of comfort, but you do realize all that she'd be privy to, right?

Or does her presence come and go, make only selective appearances?

If this is the case, I can see the appeal. But still I can't help but wonder: what if she shows up at the wrong time? What if you'd thought you were alone—or that it was just you and some other person—and then there she was?

What would you say to her then?

What do you imagine she might say in response?

I have no real attachment to this particular house. I've never lived here.

Several years ago, I helped remove some wallpaper in the dining room.

Three years ago, Jane and I stayed here, in the basement. We'd moved out of our rental and were supposed to have moved into the house we'd bought, but the FBI raided the place issuing our federal loan on the day of our closing, and things became delayed for a bit.

The first night we stayed here, we went out for a nice dinner, because it had all been such a pain in the ass—moving our stuff into your garage and onto the back porch, knowing we would have to load and unload it all again in a couple of days, playing phone tag with our bank, waiting to hear what the next steps would be. We'd wanted to treat ourselves.

Later that night, Jane awoke with food poisoning.

It was so dark in the basement I couldn't find the lamp next to the fold-out couch we were sleeping on. She couldn't find the toilet.

She put her face close to the cement floor when she vomited so that it would splatter less.

I listened, tried to find my way to her in the dark.

I said, I'm sorry, baby. I said, I'm coming.

More recently, of course, Jane and I slept in the basement one last time the night before Mom's fifty-seventh birthday. I'd told Aunt Glo I didn't want to be in the room when Mom died, but she woke Jane and me up anyway the next morning around 6:30. You were at work. Jane went upstairs, and I stayed on the fold-out with my eyes shut tight, trying not to even listen.

I can't remember whether Mom ever sensed the ghost in this house. I feel like maybe she did, but you've been talking about it more lately than you used to. You're pretty certain that it's a friendly ghost, that it means no harm.

I hope this is the case. Truly I do.

It's almost time for your next round of drops.

Soon, I am going to retrieve the medicine from the kitchen counter. I am going to stand next to your chair as you tilt your head back and look up at me, capable of seeing now even without your glasses. I am going to hold the pipet steadily over your face, let one drop fall and then another.

Soon, you will no longer need me to do this for you. It will have become a forgotten thing. You will be healed.

Love,
C

Chad Simpson

Confetti

2ND PLACE: SOFIA STAMBOLIEVA

WE WROTE LETTERS TO our pen pals in USSR, who we called "unknown comrades." The teacher would come in with a bunch of letters from Soviet kids, or the "little Russians," and randomly give an envelope to each of us, careful to match boys with boys and girls with girls. This is how we started our relationships with the only country abroad who would care for us. It also helped us to practice our Russian.

We told all the Oksanas and the Seriojas what we were up to, how great things were, and asked them for their diary entries. We exchanged wrappers from chewing gum, chocolate and candy, the smell still lingering on them, and we inhaled, like junkies, the sweet scent of "abroad." We had two kinds of chocolate wrappers, one was blue with a cow's face, and the other was yellow with a cup of milk. When guests would come over, they'd bring over a chocolate bar for the kids and a bottle of wine for the grown-ups. The "little Russians" had a hundred different kinds of candy which they called *konfeti*. In Bulgarian, *konfeti* was the small colorful paper dots left over in hole punches. Stores would sell it around New Years. We would throw it in the air and it would stay in our hair as a sign of festivity. Here in America, confetti is anticlimactically emptied from the office hole punches into the trash, without a party or hair to adorn. So, to thank Oksana for her gifts, I would send back foil chocolate wrappers, carefully ironed with my index finger.

Shortly after all those transactions, communism fell and I immigrated to New York.

Once I had the stupidity of sending my tips back home to Bulgaria—20 dollars in an envelope. I wrapped them in wax paper, on which I reported how good everything was and how great America felt in person. The tip was a sort of proof that yes, she's correct. My family in Bulgaria never received that, or any other letter that came from me since. Mailboxes in the building had these holes at the bottom, big enough to push in two index fingers and push other people's mail up out of the slot. People used to pilfer like that whenever someone received *Parallels*, a black and white magazine with highly censored reports and photos from around the world. We didn't think it was the neighbors, though. After all these years, everyone in the building knew everyone else and *Parallels* was no longer in circulation. There were tons more colorful and interesting magazines that no one could afford, so nothing worth stealing was delivered.

We knew that some aunty in the post office was meticulously combing the international mail for money, finders keepers. She was probably still eating the little Russians' candy that she withheld once upon a time, leaving only the wrappers, since you were supposed to give something to the kids after all. I imagine the naked candy aligned in rows in front of her, like a communist parade.

More than a million Bulgarians had immigrated in the 90s, so it was a good business venture she had going on in there. Once I wrote on the envelope: "Dear aunty in the post office, there are no money here, please deliver to family so-and-so." No, she would not. Naturally I stopped writing, and would rather call once or twice a month, if I made enough in tips, since phone cards cost a fortune then.

My family would be very careful about what they said, because they were convinced the phone lines were still being tapped 9 years after communism fell. They wouldn't tell me if someone divorced or drank too much or lost their job or got sick. Negative information somehow exposed us and we didn't want to be exposed. When I told them how much I earned, they started singing to cover up the number so someone wouldn't come running and kidnap the entire family for ransom. I made like a hundred dollars a week, but it was a fortune in their eyes.

There is this expression in Bulgarian slang, where someone asks you, "How are you?" and you answer, "I'm a bomb!" So my father would say, "Everything is a bomb!" which meant things were great, even though they never were. It is an ironic way of saying things are as good as they can possibly get under the circumstances. Once he said "We are a bomb!" and we got disconnected. From then on, he's been convinced the word "bomb" sets off the big brother listening on the other side. They interrupt our conversations, for the sake of the world peace.

So now dad is saying, "Things are as good as 'that word.'"

"Which word, the one that starts with f?" I would torment him, because sex is another thing we don't talk about.

"No, the one that starts with B and makes a lot of noise."

"Baking soda?"

"No, the one that rhymes with 'mom' and starts with the first letter of the word 'baking.' It behaves like baking soda in a cup of coke."

"No, dad, we shouldn't say the word coke either." So he would hum loudly to somehow erase the word after I said it, like squeezing the toothpaste back into the tube. "Ode to Joy" was my father's default melody. It somehow worked every time, and made big brother more understanding, so they didn't cut us off or send the police.

In a yard sale in Brooklyn Heights, I found this postcard reproduction of a painting by the Spanish artist Joaquin Sorolla—two girls holding hands, the taller getting into the ocean, the shorter one following. The taller girl is wearing this oversized tank top and her shoulder strap has fallen down. The shirt, the sea and the task somehow are bigger than her, but she is trying. I felt this image described my relationship with my little sister and how I wanted her to come here, America being the big dangerous but also enticing ocean. I mailed the postcard, thinking it's not in an envelope, clearly no money are hidden. It never arrived. The aunty in the post office probably has it pinned up on her wall, being either a younger or an older sister, since most women statistically are. Speaking about statistics, there is a thirty percent chance her sister or another family member ended up in the States, so that adds even more sentimental value to my postcard on her wall. What can I say, we are a bomb and I am happy to help.

Zuhura: Bridges to a Post-gender World

3RD PLACE: AWUOR ONYANGO

ITT WAS AS DELICIOUSLY frivolous and delightful as any Saturday could be in Nairobi. The sun and the clouds were playing their endless game of peek-a-boo and the tourists' vans made a beehive for the Maasai market where they would be swindled out of white guilt by smiling hawkers with the gorgeous ability to apply accents on their tongues to aid their cause. Your aunt Hellen, her friend and I had ventured past the realm of our safe, secure and even reputable neighbourhoods, to the wrong side of Moi avenue, not for some adventure where we pretended to be less wealth privileged than we were, or watched what the other-tiered Nairobians were up to, but because my sister's friend had won tickets to see a movie and the particular cinema happened to be all the way on Mombasa road. Just when we had selected the best seats in an empty Nairobi premiere of a movie so insignificant even your elephant-memoried Aunty Hellen can't recall, your mother called me. Her voice snaked out of her mouth hitting everything on its way out and hissing as it went; she was at the hospital, the doctors thought she was having a miscarriage and she needed me to tell everyone. Aunt Hellen's phone was off because we were in a movie place, and your grandmother had not yet mastered the art of moving a mobile phone so though it rang, it probably lay by her bedside where it always was and she could have been anywhere between church choir practise and Lolldaiga.

Aunt Hellen decided to rush to the hospital, and my task was to retrieve your grandmother and find our way to the hospital from there. We ran across Mombasa road like lunatics auditioning for the part of the black woman who always dies in Hollywood films and somewhere in the traffic between Mombasa road, Waiyaki way and Limuru road I realised, with my heart thrashing against my ribs, that I was actually going to be an aunt…that I wanted to be an aunt! I reached into myself, into that deep eternal recess where I belonged before I manifested into a physical entity. I swam there in search of you. I promised that I would wage wars and fight battles to offer you a life you could call your own, a life in which you weren't tricked into mediocrity, a life where you could know peace regardless of who you were or how you chose to be. You were already black…the odds were against you; but I vowed to fight the odds for you, if you would only just live! If I do not succeed, I leave you this, a labyrinth of sorts that should lead to a bridge to a post-gender world, a world slightly more suitable and worthier of you.

Being born is like being tossed from the clouds right into a viscous sea of humanity. You have to decide whether you will sink to the bottom forgotten, unimportant and wiped from existence…or if you are going to swim in whichever incomprehensible direction your mind, soul, heart (or whichever metaphysically transgressive pseudo-organ you adhere to) tells you to. It behoves me to say that even if you swim, you may tire and lose energy and drown in mundane mediocrity. But you might find an island where you make a home and slowly watch the sky turn against you once with the insidious realization that you were never meant to win and the light of your existence will be washed away at high tide, leaving no mark behind. And still I will urge you to swim. Swim! Do not drown in mediocrity of your own volition! Do not let the currents of the world carry you to the bottom of the viscous sea! Wade, crawl and thrash through the thick waters with your all; if only to feel futility with your own body rather than hear it in the whispers of frightened fools.

When I realized you were a black girl, I could easily have wept for you; I understood immediately why women prayed to long-gone gods for the lumps in their wombs to be boys. I would not have wished the burdens of elegant and demure female suffering on my worst enemy. Men have a way of reducing a somewhat functioning individual into something inflexibly sensual and far removed from reality. You will hear claims that they are visual creatures, somehow more entitled to what they see than you are, that they have a right to demand something due to this purportedly unique nature of theirs, that you weren't saying no, and if you were it was not clear enough to their all seeing eyes, that you are so beautiful they couldn't control themselves yet, they are the best to control a country, a government, a business and a household. It is your fault you are so easily degradable into a thing! Your body is less linked to a personality, individual, name or history. You are but a lust invoking thing.

 I had dreams of cutting my breasts off and throwing them at ogling beastly men, running freely into a desert where I could die in the sand never to be found or bothered again. I was going to escape the fate of this dismembered body part that aroused men felt entitled to carry off into their sick fantasies, but what good would that have done my cause to save you?

You were not to be saved from misogyny; you were to be saved from mysogynoir. You were not just doomed to the fate of a thing, but that of a black thing and there was no room for black things, not even among other black things. Black things, you will be told, have no history except that of running around in bushes like a tribe of forlorn monkeys calling to spirits as they waited upon people for salvation. Men might run around recklessly in this world, but you must understand that women brought men into this world. Women raised them to think they own it, and women sit back in this universal silent elegant demure suffering. I have always held it as the most unfortunate tripartite truth; the risky thing about child bearing was in these three things: that men could impregnate women, that women could love unconditionally the children they bear, and that born children could quite easily be, for lack of better words, the flawless anti-christ. The entire world is fed on hate, and the thing most hated is the black woman. She is hated by the black man, the white man, the man of colour, the woman of colour, the white woman and her fellow black women who measure the lightness of their skin, grandiose achievements and thinness of their waists against hers. You will not hear them say outright that the darker a woman the more worthless she is, but you will see it with eyes just as all-seeing as those men possess. You will pass it in billboards glorifying the white "bitch" as the only acceptably sexual female. You will hear it in inexplicable secret laughs between friends trading light-hued dolls at the playground. You will bear witness to statements masked as compliments about how light you have become or what a black beauty you are. You might even hear it in songs about delicious skin the colour of alabaster or novels about beautiful throbbing blue veins itching with infernos of desire. It will be there in silences too, in missed opportunities where one word would have made a great difference, in preferences that have unfair origin and no explanation. Some people with ladders that reach the heavens will tell you that there is a man up there who created two humans, and that the female one brought us to this hell we call earth and therefore all males bear the resentment of females from this! Do not swallow these things, no matter what candy is wrapped around them.

The world will be filled with hate for your kind, insidious hate that will leak into everything you touch. Hate begets hate. It is natural for a wounded animal to see only the depraved poacher in everyone. You may find yourself tempted to return this hate tenfold. I myself was in this position before I saw you. I realized what I am about to tell you now; hate is a legitimate reaction to hate, indifference never won a war, love dies in a flash at the battlefield but compassion always wins. It is ok to hate those who hate you, those who can be affected by your hate, those who are touched by it… it is not just ok, it is important that you do so. Hate is bound to explode and destroy everything in its path if left inside you too long. So hate as openly as you can while you find your way to compassion, do not hate silently and in clandestine ways, do not whisper hate to someone else so that they may join you, do not seethe in it and let it stain the people that you touch. I have found that it is easy to hate something, slightly harder to speak against it but even harder to do something to change the situation that breeds this hate; however all three are very necessary.

Stronger than hate, there is silence. A few years before you were born, Kenya fell into a state of civil unrest. The air was thick with revolt; at first it had been foggy with riot. A choice had been made by those who hadn't felt the loving kiss of the economic number growth, those who had tried it on and felt that its touch pinched rather than soothed thin pockets. Those declared a minority for preferring social change to economic growth were filled with a rage, bitterness. The air was fogged in riot because those who were down had been dealt another blow. The veil of paranoia had bridged conspiracy with tribe and class and what had been a riot to hurt an unforgiving economy, thickened and solidified into an animus that had only been whispered from wrinkled lips to milk-whetted ones. The currency to pay for life was your name.

I often noted that in Kenya there were four tiers of citizenship: first class citizenship reserved for men, second class citizenship reserved for men of Somali origin, third class citizenship reserved for women and fourth class citizenship reserved for women of Somali origin. In my time of conscious awakening it was people of Somali origin, before that it was those with dreadlocks in their hair, before that it was people whose names required a heavying of the tongue; your grandfather, my father among them. We may be many things but discriminatory is not one of them. We intend to isolate and torture everyone. When we have banned women from wearing short skirts because the attorney general thinks the legs are the ugliest part of the female anatomy, and we have carried young men off into torture chambers because we didn't like how soft on the upper palette their last name was, and when we have forced a people into trucks and dumped them in a defunct state of which they know nothing because their names made our tongues belly dance and our throats expunge sounds we attribute to snakes, and when we have cast aside all the women without families to tend to for attempting to tend to the nation, and when we have turned against everyone for every possible reason we could conjure up for the gain of some retribution for something our forefathers suffered while they watched. I am confident we will chance upon a new criterion for hate. A Swahili saying asks that if you see that your neighbour is being shaved forcefully using razorblades then you would be wise to prepare your head (for you are surely next).

I fight for a world in which you will be free to choose how to be who you are, a world in which you can taste both freedom and security and choose for yourself what is most important. I have failed at times. At a film genre lecture I watched the dean bemoan the fate of Kenya; apparently we were heading towards South Africa 'where the gays run free'. In another film class another lecturer expressed distaste about our priorities as a nation; he went on to call a country in which you can only be yourself if you do it in silence and darkness 'too liberal'. In his view, Kenya could never stand up for its customs and tenets the way Uganda did with its "Kill the Gays" bill because Kenya was too busy kissing the feet of foreign investors; I said nothing. You will be told that this is homophobia, that the history we have been taught nothing about does not allow it on our continent, that the queer person is being forced down your throat by puppet masters with evil intentions, that loving outside the realms of heterosexist viewpoints is sexual deviance. I do not know who you will love just as I cannot say who I will love but I should never wish you to fear who you are; for that is the only reasonable use of the word homophobia. A phobia is marked by fear, and you will want to run away from what you are scared of, just as you now run away from birds and insects...but what the world offers is not fear but disgust for people outside shambolic heteronormativity. It is not homophobia, it is heterosexism.

Part of swimming is finding your own path, in hearing what you are told and questioning what it means to you. There is no such thing as a shared reality; we see only what we want to see and what we are taught to see. I ask only that you want what's best and teach yourself, though it seems easier to fall back on the opinion of crazed demagogues who claim to have the answers. See humanity where others see boys, girls, demon-possessed sexual deviants, hues and hierarchies; this is the first step to escape. Girls are oppressed in ways that you cannot possibly imagine; we would be none the wiser if we weren't aware of our capabilities and how they match and at times even surpass those of men. We are oppressed in ways that even the strongest of us fail to withstand. We are expected to bare these humiliations suffering in graceful silence. Let not the glue that holds the world together fall apart, you will be told. Suffer, but suffer in silence so that the men can enjoy as loudly as they wish. You are the glue. I humbly submit that this is not a world worth holding together...that if the glue fell apart perhaps we could start again, this time learning from our mistakes. Men are oppressed too, they suffer from too many responsibilities peppered with few freedoms they must first qualify for in a world they are led to believe they own and have all rights to.

Girls, all the people in the world who see themselves as girls, are going to grow up to be oppressed in ways that are incredible and even the strongest of us will find it hard to fight it. Boys and all those in the world who see themselves as boys will be oppressed too but they will be of the idea that they are not oppressed but are in fact the oppressors, those who are neither girls nor boys will know oppression too. To this end, the sexes will battle at best and switch roles between victim and victor at worst without stepping back from the war-zone to realize that we do not need a patriarchy nor a matriarchy but a humanarchy alone. This is the world I wish for you, this is Zuhura; a place in which you are a human among animals and plants; in which you live deliberately and without fear of yourself and others, a world in which your history is restored to you and violence is never a worry; neither invisible violence nor the visible kind. I wish a world in which you do not have to hear about corrective rape, or little girls like yourself being slit open from their reproductive parts, where you don't have to work but want to because you're passionate about it. I wish for you a world where the souls of children dying of preventable diseases do not visit you on your birthday wondering why you survived or how they would have made better of a life if they had one. I wish for you a world in which you do not have to be a professional mask-switcher, adept at playing the social mine-sweeper game that guarantees your survival. I wish for you a world in which you don't have to wait for someone else to realize your self-worth and potential for you; just for you to half-heartedly scream 'appropriation' and take it as a back-handed compliment. I wish for you an Africa and a blackness that does not instigate pity, ignorant assumptions, othering or puzzled looks when presented to someone. Perhaps you can take all the skeletons of our colonial, neo-colonial and post-colonial history and build with them a bridge to a post-gender world. If I cannot bring you to Zuhura, I hope you can find it for yourself.

Awuor Onyango

Star Dog

BRIDGET BREWER

NEW ZEALAND-U.S.A
AIR MAIL SERVICE
VIA NEW CALEDONIA, CANTON IS.
AND HAWAII

OUR MASTER POINTS.

Star Dog, he says.

We tilt our faces, search the night, and find you there: a spangled star pattern of a star beast we've never in our lives met before. Snaggle toothed summer dog. Baring your teeth, wagging your tail, howling and spitting comets from behind your tongue. How could we have missed you for so long? Come play with us, we want to say—but the man who owns you stands at your side, swinging his three-star belt. We keep our invitations to ourselves.

Our Master kneels, frost crunching under his flat knee, and points his telescope in your direction. We take turns to gaze at you with our seven eyes, and you are closer to us now in the glass than in the air. Your fire burning in each of your joints and in each of your eyes and in your snaggledy tooth, your mouth, your loins; and our fire quiet under our skin. You surge, you froth, you are hot in the star hunt, star blood spilling on star tongue, your three-starred Master urging you on. We stand with our feet firm on earth, our dresses swirling, our Master's eye pressed into his eyepiece and his mouth humming words: Isn't this beautiful, my girls, my doves? And we say, Yes, Master, yes, it is yes.

Now we dance around the telescope, we dance like this, one two three one two three, we spin on the cool grassy ground behind our house, late autumn hours licking at our chilled skin. We roll and we roil and we're all made of fire, you and us, we're all burning up with love for these Masters and love for these stars.

Dear Star Dog. We are seven, eight if you add our Master. The oldest of us has black eyes and a mean tongue. The next oldest of us can be found hiding behind the woodpile. The third of us knows how to set rabbit bones to heal. The fourth of us is the smartest of us. The fifth of us has only nine toes, doesn't like to be touched. The sixth of us is afraid of snakes. The youngest of us has never spoken. Sometimes we find our Master by the woodpile, weeping. The youngest of us goes to him and holds his hand, and he lets her. He says she has mothereyes. We try to have mothereyes too, but we are not successful.

Now you know us, it is so good to meet you, we love you, goodbye.

Dear Star Dog. Please don't write us back. Our Master doesn't like us to receive letters. He says: What can you get in a letter that you don't have right here? He may not be able to read very well, but he knows what a letter looks like, which is to say a letter looks to him like leaving. Our Master says we must never leave. He says: The world is cruel and creative, and if the world ever caught you, it would gobble you up. He says: I know this for a fact. His head hangs down on his chest, heavy as the belly of the crooked moon.

Please let us sit on this stone and speak our letters to you, without reply. We know you can hear us. It is enough.

Dear Star Dog. Our Master says: Tell me the sum.

Summer is done and now is the time to set to work; we must be bridled all over again. We sit before him in chairs in the house. Inside our mouths are numbers. Between our legs, we are told, are virtue and a good pair of bloomers. In our ears is Master:

Tell me the sum, girls, tell me now.

But our minds move like sap slow to ooze from the bark of a tree. Twenty-one? Fifty-seven? One-hundred-and-thirty-five? Any of them could be the sum, the sum, the sum of this equation he has set before us. Our Master's nails dig into the soft wood belly of the table.

Not one of you motherless idiots studied a lick of this, did you? he says.

We are bad little girls. We did not study a lick of this. We studied the grass and we studied the hair in our armpits and we studied the sky for your wagging tail, but we did not study a lick of this.

Teach us to be good, we beg him: Teach us to be good; show us the telescope again.

Our Master looks at the ceiling and sighs. You must earn it, my girls, my doves, he says: You must earn your keep, or your brains will never grow, and seven idiots are good to no one.

We long to earn it, Star Dog. We long to wash the dishes before he even says it. We long for him to put his belt away. To put his hand on our foreheads and say, Good.

Dear Star Dog. Tonight we do all the laundry before our Master comes home: We bring water from the river to the basin by the stove, we scrub each and every rag of clothing, we hang them on the line until it snows, and then we move it all back inside to dangle, down, in the cellar below. Our Master is pleased—though he grumbles—and yes, oh yes, now he brings out the telescope as a treat.

Our Master shows us your enemy. That's Taurus, he says: See his red eye glaring at the three-starred man? Your Star Dog hates Star Bull, girls, remember that. And our Master pets us, because tonight we have earned it.

Ugly bull. Ugly bad bull. We hate Star Bull, too. We don't know why you hate him but the why is not important. One day you will give to Master Star Bull's head. The rest of his body you will chew and swallow, and you will shit him out and smear him on himself. And your Master will be proud. And down on our planet, we will cheer for you and pet you between the ears until you sleep.

Dear Star Dog. We can be his best little girls, we can, nobody will see us but him, we swear, we will never be noisy when he wants us to be still, can't he see us burning up with love for him? Even with the belt and even when he talks with the liquored grumble. We can sit on this stone, we can look at you, and we can forgive our Master anything. You understand. You good, good dog.

Dear Star Dog. We have made a game so we can play with you, even when the telescope is sleeping in Master's room. Our game is called Snaggledy Tooth and this is how we play:

We pretend we are bad little girls and that Ghost Master is on the hunt for us.

We sneak and we hide and we tiptoe about, and when one of us makes a sound that is too loud, Ghost Master sees us and we must run and dodge his whip.

And when he catches us and he has us against the wall of the house and he is ready to thrash our legs, we pretend you leap in front of him, your snaggledy tooth gleaming and your star paws hissing on the old crusty snow, and you give a great roar and your star teeth find his leg and Ghost Master screams before disappearing, goodbye Ghost Master, and then we get on your back and we ride with you out into the sky, and now it's our turn to find your Ghost Master and return your snaggledy toothed favor.

It is our favorite game. We do not play it when Real Master is here.

Dear Star Dog. It is a bad day. Here is the snow and here is our Master's truck and here is the hutch of dead rabbits we did not bring into the house before the storm, like he told us to. So many ice-stiff rabbits in the corner of the hutch. All these ice rabbits, no good to us. Our Master brings his belt to our backs forever. When he is done, the snow is red and the rabbits are still dead and we are crying and press into a circle of bleeding braided girl spines.

Goddamn birdbrains, goddamn daughters of a whore! our Master screams. You sleep in the woodshed tonight!

Does everyone have a Master? Is everyone like us? Bad and stupid and always wrong? And never stepping a foot outside? You're like us, too, Star Dog. You are stuck points in the big black sky. You can never run away. Can't even try.

Dear Star Dog. At night we whisper in our ears about birth. Some of us remember a woman: a soft warmth who held us and fed us buttered milk from her body. Some of us remember blankets. Some of us remember bits of songs. Some of us sing them: *To sail, to sail, my Pleiades, upon the warmest ocean breeze.*

Some of us remember only Master.

Where are you from, Star Dog? Who made you?

Dear Star Dog. Our Master is away. We are gathering more ice rabbits and shoveling a crusty snow path, and suddenly there is a man, a man, a man. He carries the pelt of a great bear on his shoulder. He could be your Master.

Are you Star Dog's Master? we call to the man, ice rabbits in our small girl hands.

The man does not answer. He swings his pelt higher onto his shoulders and stares at the oldest of us. We turn and stare at her, too. Is she different from us? She sticks out more in places, she is worse at braiding hair, she gets Master's belt longer than we do and she does this on purpose. Is this what the man likes? His eyes travel her body like a road and he smiles, and we try to make our eyes travel that road too but we can only see all of us inside her. The oldest of us is silent. She drops her ice rabbit in the snow and she walks to where he waits by the white birch trees.

Don't go, we tell her, we stomp our feet: Don't go, don't go, if you do this to you it's done to us all.

But the oldest of us reaches for the hand of the man, her black eyes hard, and she takes him into the forest, where we cannot see her. We stay with her in our minds until the man's mouth is upon her, and then we come back to where our bodies are, and now we are minus one, our arms full of ice rabbits and fear inside our heads.

Dear Star Dog. We sit on our stone but we cannot find you with our eyes. Are you hiding? Are you locked in a star house? Are you like the woman who birthed us? Have you left us and run away? Don't you love us anymore?

Dear Star Dog. Why can't we see you? The snow is melting. We are minus one. Master locks us in the woodshed. We eat potatoes raw. We shit in the corner and we cannot get clean. Our new name is sluts. Star Dog, come back.

Dear Star Dog. We can see your Master but he is low in the sky. Where did he send you? We rub the ears of the ice rabbits until they thaw and are soft again, but the wet fur does not comfort.

Dear Star Dog. You are gone, we are minus one.

Dear Star Dog. We dream of the wind in our hair, of falling down through broken glass into the hot spring mud. When we wake, the next oldest of us is gone and the window is broken. Now we are five.

Dear Star Dog. Master does not like to look at the next oldest of us. He will not go near her. She is so broken and still. Master says: Leave that thing be. At night, we dream we can feel flies laying eggs in her eyes, foxes nibbling at the flesh of her feet.

Dear Star Dog. Master drags us outside by our hair. Even if our scalps hurt, it is nice to be outside at night again. The next oldest of us lies in the snow like a broken dove. Our Master yanks harder, our hair like so many leashes. He points his finger at the churning stars, where you are not anymore. Master looks at us with wild eyes, the trees screaming above his head.

You would like to know real things about your Star Dog? he says slow. Your goddamn Star Dog?

He tells us the story of Bad Star Dog. And we weep. And we know you now. We cannot un-know you.

Before the three-starred man, your first Master was Europa. She was a tiny good girl. She liked yellow flowers. She liked petting the hairs on your dog head. She liked when you kept her back warm at night on the floor in her house. We know how that feels. We keep each other warm on the floor at night, because we have no dog.

You were bad, Star Dog, lost in your star head. You played in the field too far away one day. And Europa put her hand on white bull flesh. And the white bull was pretty, so Europa got on its pretty, wide back. And the bull liked the soft froth between her legs. And the bull was a trickster: He ran into an ocean, and took Europa away, and made her cry again and again, his loins on fire, his loins made of fire, like the oldest of us and the man in the woods, and you, bad Star Dog, running in and out of the waves again and again, howling on the island, howling for Europa, couldn't swim, bad Star Dog, can fly and can run and can hunt but did not, could not, swim that day for her.

We dream of how she felt.

Dear Star Dog. How can we forgive you for that? How can we forgive you for leaving us while down below we cry at the hands of our hard, hard Master? How could you? How could you? How?

Dear Star Dog. Here goes spring. Here goes summer. We lie on the floor and pretend you are licking our faces. In our dreams you love us.

Dear Star Dog. The youngest of us can talk now.

Dear Star Dog. You runaway. You are good to no one.

Dear Star Dog. We might see your paw, but we don't believe you.

Dear Star Dog. We see you, through a loose shingle in the woodshed we see you. You're there. You've come back. What can you promise? We have new hearts, thinner bodies.

Dear Star Dog. We could be your best little girls, if you would like. We could be your good, good girls. We will never be noisy when you want us to be still, if you would like.

Dear Star Dog. How would you like us? Tell us how to be.

Dear Star Dog. We met your brother. We did not cry all day, and our Master was pleased, and out came the telescope, and he showed us: Little Brother for Star Dog. No snaggle tooth for Little Brother. Twin dogs in the sticky black sky. Little Brother looks afraid. He tucks his tail between his legs and hides behind other stars.

Little coward, crows our Master: That small dog is just a little coward.

Make Little Brother brave, Star Dog. Tell him what we tell ourselves. Tell Little Brother to face the sky like a hunting beast, face it like Star Dog has faced it for years, before Master was even alive. Crawl closer to thundering enemy hooves and dream of when coiled star intestines will rip and spill onto the dark star floor. Tell him to be brave. That's what we want, Star Dog. So we can see your Master's face glow. So we can see his face and we can hear his glittering laugh and know that someone, somewhere, is good. Is burning up with love for you.

Cellophane Sky

LAURA LARK

BY AIR MAIL—PAR AVION

Dear Johnny Depp,

One time, when I was in my twenties and I kept having psychotic breakdowns because I either couldn't get my lithium — or I just didn't want to take it (when I first started on that shit, I gained so much weight, all I could fit into was this mammoth pair of overalls and this elastic-banded skirt in a really bright shade of aqua and a tee shirt I found at a thrift shop that said, ironically enough, "no fat chicks", and then it makes your mind into a bowl of fucking oatmeal, like every thought is something you're slogging through)

Laura Lark

I was running around all manic in the street one day and I realized that I hadn't eaten anything for a long time.

Like a couple of days.

Maybe more.

So I decided to just march right on over to Kroger. It was a hot day in Houston. Most of them are, especially in summer, and I think this had to have been in summer, but anyway, I was walking along on the sidewalk on Montrose Boulevard, a couple of blocks south of Westheimer, and you know how sometimes you look up in the sky and you see those floaty things that look like they're right in front of you in the air but are really in your eyes?

Well, I had a bunch of those.

②

So there I was, standing on the sidewalk in the heat and looking at those things that are just like the magnified germs you see in those toilet bowl commercials?

I was just there.
Nobody's ever standing around on a sidewalk in Houston, Texas,
by the way.
Nobody walks anywhere.
So standing there in the blazing heat, this skinny, hungry, tall chick with hair that hadn't been washed in whenever — that was me.
And I was really hungry.
It occurred to me, all of a sudden, that I hadn't slept for

③

Laura Lark

a while (two? three days? I'm not really
good with facts. Kind of a liar.
Whatever. I totally remember this),
and then it was like this film –
you know, the kind that comes on top of
plexiglas? Clear, but colored? But this
wasn't any color. Just a grayish film.
It was like this invisible hand was
slowly peeling away the dirty grayish film,
and there was the sky: blue like in
movies where they want you to think life
is perfect and that people will be in
love forever. With a trail or two of wispy
white cloud.
And I stood there.
Staring straight up, like I was
expecting a piano to fall right on me or
whatever, and everything that was
exposed from under that mucky film

④

was like a gift being unwrapped that no one else could get their hands on.

I don't remember if I cried.

But I do remember that I just then realized I would pass out if I didn't get something to eat.

So I quit looking at the sky and ran to the Kroger and I went straight to the dairy part and I got one of those half-wheels of Colby cheese, you know, like an inch thick and really an orangey-yellow which looks like a color straight out of a tube of oil paint, and I opened the plastic-y wrap from that, which was cleaner than the filmy looking stuff in the sky, and I stood there and ate it in the dairy product aisle of the grocery store.

I was chewing on a big chunk of it when I showed the empty wrapper to the cashier, who looked at me weird.

⑤

And the kind of slow girl with thick rimmed glasses kind of like Tootsie or Kathy Whitmire told me my bra strap was showing (I said "Thank you.") And after I paid I ran home to my apartment and slept on the floor and dreamed of a big rolling gray ball that I sort of rode on, like a roller coaster in slow motion.

And when I woke up, I felt like I was God.

But Really I didn't feel like anything — I knew I was God.

⑥

Richmond, VA 1978— Typewritten Letter

KATHERINE BOWLING

Hey like Im back in the 60s tricia is playing this really queer
      MUsic and there is lots of wailing going on Oh yeah let me hear me say
   ILOVE YO_u or something like that   It is 100 in the morning and only thursday

    and hell these machines ere fun to monkey around with if you know what I MEAN
      Like i really feel like im doing something when i type   Oh god so
t did i write you im the last letter   Gee melissa When i came home today after a hard d
 ay at the studio (amartistswork is never done) I opened the mail box and d said "oh
shit" more love letters and RELIGIOS mail and WOW pie im the sky and RAINbow
  trout and all that "news from the coast" You sure are a FUN girl ti get mail
  from" I am doing a series of Drawings about neurotic DREEAMS and Fears of a single
  girl   Nancy Hart gave me the idea but dont tell her   I mean i guess i have
     exagerated a little   Im just really tired of running into wallflower girls
who say they cant do anything   Idont knoe wow   Icant Icant Girls cam do anything
I mean WOMEN I AM WOMAN   -------------------------
      Last nite i went to am opening at the anderson Gallery   14 Women artists
 I talked to joan Watson and she was so elegant and slim and didnt know what to do with
her legs . she folded them up like a flamingo   and swims 9o laps
   a day in a pool in nyc   Judy Pffaf Ha d this real wacko room
   where the offices used to be   Lots of little tin foil things flung on the walls
      and stuck in cactus plants   and line drawings on the floor and ceiling and

   places you couldnt see.   the anderson gallery is being remodeled and boy
   does it look tacky   the front room downstairs is covered with some kind of
       neutral colored burlap   and the upper walls are painted BLACK
       they are also trying to eliminate individual departmental shows
   and ---just have one big show at the end   33333333333333333######
       SURE can you believe that?

       It is the next day FRIDAY and i guess ill make this a continuing saga
       like maybe a week or two

    writing like this is just like having a conversation on the phone
       you know?   i can just say when i feel like It or when something happens
              SOMET HING

    Well friday nite is almost over   and im sitting here sort of dazed
     this afternoon i had a critique with Jewett campbell   there was all this crap abou
 minimulist art   Some skinny guy with a gauntlooking beard   kept emotionalizing
 about the reverence of his drawings   and there was just this piece of white paper
     with a black ink mark on it   I mean i cant believe we sat there for an hour
     and talked about nothing.

   also there was all this funny talk about the night before and Jewtt and this
 guy kept exchanging looKS   Like oh YEAH we really understand each other
   and frankly i thought the whole thing was just a bunch of you know what

        after that was over (paul Greenburg had some beautiful Drawings)
     I went to Hair Nouvou to meet tricia   she was gettting her hair
   cut by Tonyella   there was nobody else there so we could play disco music
     real loud and gossip   but there was nothing really good to goossip about
        tony gave tricia a really great pair of sunglasses   and we were goin
 to get photo booth pictures taken   but GOD it was only 500 and woolwoths was clos
 ed   so then we went to see Maggie

maggie and renee and tricia and i are going to the beach tomorrow
to nags head we are staying at the welcome mat cottage or something like that
and im sure it will be alot of fun   because maggie and renee are pretty FUN girls

            thenafter a few beers and much loud talk we went to see john and nancy
    because we are borowing there cooler.   you had just called nancy
        i havent seen her for awhile   and she sure is a pretty girl   but semmed rather in a q
        quiet mood and didnt speak much.

        i dont know sometimes you cant tell with her but i
        (thinking about it) you can

    Monday and hot outside I have been riding around there is a half moon and the stree lights
    are shining   1 !!   you should see my legs! there are 20 zillion mosquito bites or at least
a few   the mosquitos at nags head were scary and big and mucho numerous   the water was DEE-
lightfull the sun was hot and i hate to get tan marks. maggie and i made faces ooh! ahh! eek!
    renee was moody and tricia slept and ate cookies. we played pool and played blackjack and swam and
    ate. on the way home some young girl ran into the back of renees van with her pinto and renee
    started to cry. i really had a good time but i also caught a cold.

    I am listening to records on the stereo and watching this movie about carol lombard
    without the sound and ....
....i keep spacing out
        I am really list interested in carole lombard because in High school i had this
friend carol and she was carole lombard and this friend Brian and his psuedo name was Miles
            and me and i was Gidget and we all three hung out together. they were my only real friends
    in that school(except my last year i did have a boyfriend that was a drummer whom i met at
    a Rolling Stones concert but he lived 30 miles away)   and we used to excel at doing fun thing
    what we really liked to do the best was to dress up in funny costomes and go to midnight
    movies. the highlight was when we saw Miss DIVINE in person at the Biograph theatre in washdc
 . i really wore red in those days. like the time all three dressed up in dresses evev Brian
and went to see Bette Midler (This was before she was popular) and everybody but everybody was
dressed in drag. yeah. We would skip school00000 whenever caroll got her fathers Mercededs
Mercedes that is, and drive into dc . sometimes we would go to the Hare Krishna temple and chant
(those times are the only experiences ive had with temples in reality)   or to dulles airport
to watch the planes and on that road you can drive swiftly quickly fastly   i guess youd call it
speeding.   then we had to split up and go to colledge our last outing we all did a hit
of acid and went to a carnival and i think it was kind of depressing.
    now caroll is planning to go to Russia (thats what she studied) because she is in love with some
    russian chap. we still see each other. and brian who was from canada is now back north
and is teaching art at some school(minor) and we dont see each other too much because of distance
    but he still sends me funny things like small rubber babies.   and well...
nats the end of that story.

    Umm now lets see...   Have you run into any vicious chinese punks
    I hear they are rampant.   I am really glad you have a place to work that is so close
what kind of work are you doing are you doing much work
    I hope you dont get too lonely   and is billy happy?

Having this typewriter is like having a friend to come home to
and it doesnt talk back today which is No wednesday i recieved a   NICE
compliment this young fellow who delivers the mail at vcu and no he is nottDOuglas
said "Katherine with your HAIR UP you look just like Lucille ball   Ilove LUCY ILoveLUCY
and this guy was wearing a rather snappy panama hat   i mean   i could tell he had taste

          Every day from 1100 to 400 i go to the studoi today brett wilson and i
    were going to meet with Heather and we waited and waited   but she never came
    I was pissed because she did say she was going to come but she didnt
   and it really makes me nervous to wait for people   and i hate to wait .
them from 400 till whenever i go to the public library and read art magazines
because i feel really dumb about what is happening.   I mean there are just so many things
     that i am not in touch with.   like i didnt know thatt Ree Morton got killed in an automobile
accident in April am d it made me feel bad   that i hadnt called before
    that i hadnt found out before i dont know what im thinking about
ting about   maybe its this beer.   yaeh blame it on alcohol. i swaer
last weeki bought a whole bottle of southern comfort and drank the whole thing
   . that was the night we went to disco night at the rollar   rink
   and i only fell down once   but tricia fell down on her elbow and reaally
     hurt it   and we had to go to the emergency room its all right just a bad bruise sprain
   something,   o my GOD and you would not believe the traumatic
experience we had the other nite late at nite . I was lieing in bed   when i hear a blood curdli
   SCREAM!   Tricia tricia are you all right?   !!!!!!!!!!   I really thought the mad r
apist had climbed in the window and gotten her   but you would not believe the size of this
roach I mean you would really not believe the size.   !!!!!!!!!!!!!!!!

!!!!!!!!!!!!!!!!!!!!!!!!!

IT was so big and it was flying around

_____66666_____

the room.   .   melissa i am not squeamish about mant things but this was a monster
and i was really terrified!   tricia killed it with a big pan.
and today they exterminated the place, for which i will go down on my knees and thank god for
because the kitchen and bathroom were off limits at nite   the suckers   fuckers
          God i really hate roaches   .

what did the other pictures look like? i just love to look at pictures.
     last night i made calling cards be cause whenever i go visit people they are never
     home   sometimes i feel like i have no friends at all.
          but i guess i do   they are just never at home.

     well melissa i think i will be winding this letter up soon.

     as i think i am rambling.

The Wedding Present

DAVID RYAN

RECEIVED
DIRECTORY
SEP 24 1944
SEO.

THEY STOPPED FOR HER eyes. Hanna had trouble with them, how they looked in the morning, so Curtis had pulled into this strip lot and parked, watched her disappear into the drugstore's automatic doors, the sign above, *2 for 1 Easter Eggs*—Easter having passed, what, a couple of months ago. He could use the chocolate right now, the sugar for his blood. He imagined Hanna grabbing some of the chocolates on a whim. She was good that way. Glancing down the aisle, tucking a few into her purse. Paying for something else, something small—a pack of gum, a tabloid, a wedding anniversary card—when she reached the counter.

He waited outside in the car. In the lot. She would take her time. It didn't seem to matter what all she actually needed. Time slowed, sped up, passed. Himself, he hadn't stolen yet. But he'd borrowed a lot, he'd never gotten back to people, sure. He watched a car with a *Student Driver* sign on its tail roam gracelessly about the lot. As if the transmission had been accidentally left in neutral and the car were moving of its own agency, rudderless, threatening in relentless slow motion anything in its path.

After the carnival they might drive back to the city, or they might stop by the motel. The motel was free if you didn't mind the dank, the outside chill breathing through broken windows. The electricity gone, its circuit breaker broken and glazed with years of rust. He'd checked the box. He'd broken into the utility room. She'd be out any minute now. Only a couple of shops left here in this strip—a Chinese take-out, a Salvation Army drop off, this drug store. White paper, red lettering *FOR LEASE* repeating along all the windows, as if saying it once along the low block of yellow brick and tinted glass wasn't sufficient. As if one banner didn't express enough how blown open this town was.

What did you make, teaching people how to drive? Could you live on it? What if someone you were teaching how to drive recognized you? What if a student driver said, Don't I know you? Weren't you famous once? In that band?

He and Hanna were on their own short tour. The go-lower tour. He wanted to leave this one. Wanted out. He had no idea how. You got the cheaper drugs out of town. Then you drove the hour back. You might stop at the abandoned motel along the way, but it didn't have a television. She called it *The Bates. Let's just go to The Bates.* Tall grass coming up through the cracks in the asphalt, orange spray painted *DEMO 9* where there used to be a front office. The rooms had water stains on the walls and a smell. But the price was right: any room had vacancy where the door could be kicked in—should the traveler need a place to stop and hit, to nod off a bit before returning to the city. The pool's tarp sagged, sunken beneath eons of green rain. Someone had driven a gleaming shopping cart into the water, a television's shell around a shattered cathode tube. One night they walked past the pool and found a family of possums bathing.

But no electricity. She liked the television on. Increasingly, she needed the sounds. Well, always now. Often they hit up a little in the car, just to get them through the hour or so back to their apartment in the city, for the voices on the television. It made him crazy sometimes. The louder the television, the more frantic the voices sounded, the more empty the apartment felt.

He had left the engine off here in the lot. But the car was getting hot now and his breath felt thick. He made out two silhouettes inside the Driver's Ed car. The car kept stopping, then lurching forward, wandering around the lot like a stunned insect. She'd be out in a minute now. He glanced into the rearview. There was some saliva running down his chin.

No, he hadn't stolen yet. Yes, he owed a few people. Mostly in LA, but there everyone owed a few people. You either owned or owed. His owning anything belonged to the past, just like LA did, just like New York. The shows and the audiences had long ago fallen off. He'd missed a couple of shows, well, several, many. He'd gotten flak. Promoters were less inclined to take a chance on him. He and Hanna had burned through the publishing advances he'd gotten for his songs. It wasn't her fault; they'd both been foolish. There was the greeting card jingle—that money too was gone. Still, occasionally, you saw a comeback. He'd been teaching Hanna guitar until he had to sell off all of his gear.

It parallel parked again, the Driver's Ed car. You'd have to just let go. Just let yourself go if you were sitting there in the passenger seat, teaching this sort of thing to some frightened kid. The car drove over to the parking spots reserved for the defunct muffler shop that faced the main road. Another *FOR LEASE* sign. On the way into town they'd passed a *McDonald's* that had gone out of business. When did you ever see that? Curtis felt the drug hangover pull just then: as if the sound of the word McDonald's had sent a windup inside his head, the small seizing, the snap-back in his brain from the heroin the night before. The flash of sickness like a gnat or a mosquito knitting the space closer and closer to his ear. His head flinched and he heard a little gasp and it was his own gasp. Then silence. The sun etched light into the dash. The student driver blew another parallel parking job. Tried again, screwed too far to the right, tried again. Better, now. That sort of a job you'd really have to let yourself go.

The Driver's Education drama made Hanna's exodus from the automatic doors of the drug store seem epic, an angel entering the morning light. She had her purse and her shearling puff, no shopping bag. It was too warm for the coat but she was always cold now. He turned on the ignition and let the warm breath of the air conditioning start to cool. She was fine, doing fine. Walking more or less steady, not too fast. That slight lurch, as if stepping in heels even when she wasn't. They both had that now. He saw it in the windows they passed.

Behind Hanna, the automatic doors opened again. An employee, some kid in a blue shop smock, the little white lettering of the logo, was following her. A rushed skip to his step. Curtis tapped the horn toot toot, might want to pick it up a little, Hanna. Hanna reached the car door and opened it just as the stock boy, this kid, reached out and grabbed at her shoulder. Curtis said, *just get in, will you?* but this stock kid had tugged off a bit of Hanna's once-expensive shearling puff and there was her stained silk blouse now where her thin and still-beautiful shoulder arched forward, blouse tugged, the smooth skin over her collarbone, cream camisole strap. She called the stock kid something cruel and her hand reached back, swatted, whip-scratched his youthful minimum-wage mill town face and she tumbled into the passenger seat and slammed the door on the kid's hand, his fingerbones jacking audibly in the cleft. The stock kid screamed like a cowboy, a scrappy howling falsetto. Hanna opened the door again, just briefly enough to slam it this time up at his wrist. Slammed and opened the door and freed this tenacious hand reaching in.

—Employee of the Fucking Month, she said.

But the stock kid's other hand slapped down on the front windshield, palmed the glass, as if trying to reach around the girth of the car and give them a big hug.

—What the fuck did you get in there?

—Just shut up, she said: Drive? And Curtis pulled the car away slowly, this kid still there holding on, chasing alongside. Curtis continued easy, letting this kid canter beside them. Slapping the windshield with his good hand, holding fast above Hanna's door with his other. On the hand pressed against the glass, something written in a pen, a note to himself, a to-do list. Curtis gunned a little and the kid started running, the one good hand with the palm scrawled in pen remaining there on the front, as if still gently guiding the car to a place where he could read Hanna her rights. Curtis let him hold, kept creeping along through the lot. He braked then turned a bit, the speedometer at a rolling 0. The kid tripped a little, regained his hold. A lamprey. The kid was panting.

—Jesus, You grab the fucking till? Curtis asked. Hanna, cackling; it was all her voice could do anymore, these mornings, when she expressed something other than the verbs of basic need. The cackle troubled Curtis and the longer the kid ran beside the car, the more he hated this kid for the sound coming from beside him. And the more he hated this kid the slower he drove so as not to lose him, so as not to let his little flimsy tentacle detach its suckers from the front windshield, so as not to lose the savor of this feeling. Of any feeling.

And just then, Curtis recognized the kid. As if staring back at himself as he was many years ago—the chin the same, the hair the same color, though a different cut, a different style. The eyes, the shape of them: They were Curtis's eyes, the whites still white, the retinas as yet unfaded. This kid could be a little brother, a nephew.

—What did you take?—and she, Shut up, he's a boy scout: some fucking mascara, fingernail clippers. Hanna's long legs and bulimic fucking waist, she looked like hell on a stick right now. But Curtis could remember a time seeing her sleeping beside him when she was beautiful, waking up to her when they were both beautiful and possibly kind. When they had every reason to believe they were good. Curtis suddenly wanted to hit the kid, the kid's mouth now open in another howl of rage.

Suddenly the kid's hand peeled from the windshield and his body dropped back and away from the car. He stopped in his tracks. He was looking forward. Curtis turned to look ahead too and slammed into the Driver's Ed car, T-Boned the passenger side. He paused, registered the silhouettes, the grand-matron instructor in the passenger side, thrown back, barely tall enough to peer over the window, slammed back by the car's air bags, burst open. He jammed the transmission, backed away. Then, another slap on glass there by Hanna, and Curtis thought, *are you kidding?* Kid hugging the car, pounding his fist, teeth bared in silent outrage beyond the window. He shifted into Drive. Hanna turned on the radio, some *Classic Hits* station out in the middle of the dial. The kid infuriated by the sound of music. There, Curtis felt the world pull away from the window, draw back from this kid, from himself. A stock boy who looked like an old high school photograph of Curtis back when, this spitting image cut out of some lost yearbook and stuck to the window. Curtis gunned the car, peeling the fucking kid off, pulling away down the lot toward the exit now. The car bottomed out sharp and hard on the turn down onto the cross-street, left. The car sounded okay. He hoped the people in the Drivers Ed car were okay. Some mascara, fingernail clippers. From a cost-benefit angle the morning was off to a bad start. The car filled with the banjo outro of the Eagles on the radio. Hanna, sitting there, as if nothing had just happened. How? From there to here—to now? She was once gracious, soft spoken. She did things for people. *We used to be attractive.* Her eyes, those eyes. Now depthless, blank. The makeup from last night, stale, flaking on the bruise-like circles beneath. All of this morning devoted to a little glass tube of black smudge she trusted might, this time, give her eyes back to her, make her beautiful again. To draw a last light from them. Eyes that once stunned—a hazel like some exotic polished stone that gave off light. The art directors knew this, the photographers did, the magazines. But look at her.

They caught the yellow, then red stoplight with a corner

church and another giant crucifix, another Christ stretched out in agony, the cross seemingly larger than the church itself. You could tell how destitute a town was by the number of churches. Everyone praying for something to change. Here there were many churches. Most, small and plain, shacks with a little marquis sign out front with pressed lettering announcing an upcoming social, or with a funny quote, or something batshit crazy, or perhaps just *Welcome!* But this one, another they'd passed this morning already with so large a cross, so large an effigy hanging from it. The third. Curtis had a numerologist's interest in three—everything good and bad happened in threes. Past the third of anything you entered the unknown: of curses and wishes, of fable. If it took three match-strokes to light a spoon of heroin, Curtis would toss the match, strike a new one, even if they were low on matches. He'd had three songs that charted—three hits on the radio, the royalty checks long ago having dwindled to pennies a month. The payments, he assumed, continued to gather at the lower Manhattan PO Box thousands of miles away. He'd long ago lost the key. And he'd had three publishing deals, his advances shot to fuck all, burned up, pissed away, each deal for less money and worse terms than the one before. The last advance had the finality of a mob loan. But you need to eat, and sometimes you need a little more.

The traffic light seemed frozen on red.

—Oh god look, Hanna said. The church doors opened and now a wedding spilled onto the sidewalk like a rush of water from a gate.

And three managers, each of which, when he was high, he blamed for destroying his career. When he was high, the burden, the fault was all theirs.

—Oh, she's beautiful! she said. Overdosed, he had, three times, though he'd probably come close a few others. Was it really Saturday? Sunday? The charm of three, he'd used it up. Sober, he saw this. But when he was high, the moment he peaked, he could believe that anywhere past the three of anything you were just a fucking pioneer. The light changed and again Hanna coached:—Green—but his foot was already on the gas. She said:

—I'm not hungry.

—Let's just get a little something. I don't want that carnival food.

—Did you hear the sound?

—What sound?

—His hand—the door.

It was the space behind her eyes that had changed. Her soul. She couldn't get to that space anymore. It was dream memory. Her soul had been replaced just as her laughter had changed to a cackle. But the memory of that laughter kept coming around, flitting off before you could grab hold of it. They passed a vast concrete lot surrounded by high chain link fence.

—Are we lost?

—No, we're just going. They sounded married, he thought: *He* sounded married. Some rusted truck trailers scattered about the lot, dead shells, in the distance a large brick conglomeration of buildings, long abandoned, sprawling outward. She could get it back. The soft laugh, her looks, the good space behind her eyes. The decency. He knew they both could. Part of it all, at least. Already now she'd peeled away at the package, torn it open. The sun visor down, another little dirty mirror. Already she had that little wand on her eyes.

—I was just trying to get away.

—I know.

—From that kid.

—I'm not hungry.

—I know. You said. Neither am I. Is that all you got in the store?

—Oh, also. She stopped dabbing, fished around in her bag: —And this. She took out two boxes of Robitussin Daytime.

—I hope they're okay.

—It's cough medicine. What's not to—

—No, the student driver. Them. The other stuff had to match the skin tone of the rest of her face. She put it on a little thick, mornings. Under her eyes, the circles. She did a better job when she was straight or at least not waking, shaking off something. She had always known her makeup. He turned up the radio. Remember them? Jesus. Used to love this song. What it was like to be a teenager. Butterflies before the parties. Thirteen, fourteen years old. You didn't need anything, just your young, beating heart. At the light he cracked open a Robitussin. Drank it down in a pull. Thirteen, fourteen years old. That feeling in the gut, the butterflies. Just showing up at someone's house and calling it a party. Bunch of other little kids like him, no alcohol or drugs. Not yet. Just the anticipation of something. Maybe you'd kiss a girl by the end of the night. Maybe you'd just live the next few hours like a thirteen-year-old—to whatever conclusion the youngness of your hours chose for you. God, the bounce in his heart, the light in his gut. The light was green.

—The light, she said. Where are you, my space man? He pressed the gas. She'd been thirteen once. He hadn't known her then. It felt so romantic to wonder about. Her, then.

—Thirteen, he said.

—What? They'd gotten the last of the morphine the night before. Enough for the night, just a little in the morning. Old Mike had said he was tapped out. It would be a couple of days before any more came in. Curtis and Hanna had come back to their apartment, this worn studio flat out by the docks. The television was on. Some show about Ireland as a vacation destination. Some travelogue. The television was emitting a lot of green into the dark room. The green came off the screen iridescent. It seemed impossible to believe a place could be so beautiful. Sometimes she asked him to take the belt and slap it over her ass. He didn't care for the treatment, but he never said anything. He remembered the Irish travelogue, because, last night this is what he did once they were high. He slapped her with the belt while on the television a fucking pan flute danced along with the sound of the belt on her ass, this announcer talking about Egyptians migrating to Ireland some ancient time ago: He slapped her with the belt until she nodded off. And then he just sat there in the flickering light, the colors of the television playing off the room's windows. An outdoor festival, now, a beer garden party on the screen, an Irish fiddle and a squeezebox knitting the space behind his eyes. Green, a ghastly television blue scoring the walls, his face, her nudity turned on its side. Old Mike said he'd call ahead, the carnival, the forty-five minute drive out of town. Her ribs in the television light. Light flickering over the thin bones of her arms, the rise of her shoulder blades as she stirred, then turned onto her stomach. The ribs, the curve of her body now. Like a bat, sleeping—and he winced. She used to put on a wedding ring. It was meant to turn men away. She was good in her heart, he knew this. Her heart could still turn you on. He couldn't remember if she had sold it. The ring. It would have been worth something.

The next light changed to green. Another church, another bright red door. *Will you marry me?* He'd asked her a couple of times. Maybe three times. They were high, but he meant it. Being high just loosened his tongue enough to say it. He thought about it a lot. Sometimes the thought of asking her to marry him was like the impulse he had once or twice to buy a handgun. It gave him the same butterflies. Three times, yes, *will you marry me*. He didn't remember her answer. Had she asked other men to use the belt, to slap her ass? Oh Jesus. You did whatever you needed to do. She was thirteen once. Drove, spanked her, proposed, shot up. The carnival dope, his expectations weren't much—low-grade tar. But it would do.

Over there, the place they'd seen on the way out. A former Big Boy's. The new owners had left the sign there like the old days: the giant cartoon boy holding a tray, racing forward with an eager smile, eager eyes. The sign looked like it might topple on you as you passed beneath it. Beneath that sign another placard that said *AZARS New Mgmnt*. Curtis squared into a space and recalled the air bags bursting open a few minutes ago. Flinched reflexively, as if it had just now happened.

They got out, both with a hitch in their step, like they were about to come apart. They passed the glass wall outside. It reflected back two shapes, a glass Curtis and Hanna, looking like people you recall but whose names always escape you. Their reflection, they looked like that. Each, a mental block, blue-ish in the morning shade of the overhung sign above them. The glass man staring back at Curtis had straw colored hair, combed back, lightly oiled, thinning. An older faded version of himself, the image he held in his mind. Here, his lined skin flushed red, maybe tanned, it was hard to tell in the glance of shadow. The reflection cinematic, de-saturated—bleached in shadow. This faded couple walking into the AZARS under new management in a town with many churches.

Inside, a long row of vacant booths. It was early, too early for a lunch crowd, too early for anyone. They ordered at the counter, sat themselves at a booth, and waited. You always waited. Wherever, they made you wait. Even back in New York, six AM, all the junkies lined up along 3rd Street. Between C and D. *I walk down the aisle, like some foolish bride.* Like a song he remembered. You stood outside, waiting like all the others. At six the line started inching forward, like an egg passing down the throat of a snake. A peristalsis of addicts processing along the sidewalk.

He and Hanna had left New York to get away from all of that. They'd kicked for a time, a spell at the rehab in Minneapolis, then come out west. 6 AM you got up to the heavy red door and the eye-slot slid open, then the transaction, cash first, the little jewelry baggie passing through the opening. They made you wait. Six AM. You could trust the dope, though. For as long as he could remember they made you wait and you could trust the dope.

You thought you lived in the present, but the present never was. The present was memory before it had a chance to be, when you were straight. Being high was the only way to feel timeless, to feel like a hit song you heard on the radio and loved, suspended in your unconsciousness, in that privileged, impossible space.

Then the kid behind the far counter called a number as if a number were needed. Hanna lifted her head. Is that us? Laughter in her nose. And Curtis glanced at the slip, as if this too were needed, and said, Us. The kid called the number again. Curtis got up. He tried to steady his gait as he walked. But still, he noted how the kid regarded him. Wary. Curtis, just a minute ago had been reflected back a ghoul in the glass outside. *Fuck you,* he thought, directed at the kid and his reflection as if they were the same. Curtis came to the counter, took the paper bag without looking at the kid, returned to Hanna at the table. She'd never had a problem with food. She could eat anything. Nothing could touch her figure. Today, two french fries—he counted—a bite from her cheeseburger. That was all. Curtis finished his, then ate the rest of hers. He saw a ceiling fan reflected in the surface of the unused spoon by his plate, the ceiling fan above, spinning in the reflection. But when he glanced up to the actual ceiling all he found were the speckled white tiles of the restaurant's lowered ceiling, a bulge of rust stained like a cloud hovering over them. He slipped the spoon into his pocket.

They were driving back now, back along the four-lane cut into the drag, followed through a string of broken intersections, the hanging traffic lights just blinking yellow, as if having given up the pretense of green, yellow, red. Then they were on the highway, driving until he saw the fairgrounds ahead, the Ferris wheel, a speck of colored trash it looked like, coming closer. Like a horizon of little cups and wrappers, a coiled wire, a stray wheel, scattered under the big sky.

—Wait. She reached over and turned the radio up, the *Classic Hits* station. Caught it just past the intro, Curtis' voice, singing. The second hit that broke, and his least favorite—it had always felt a little facile, a little too much of a sing-song to him—but it was okay. Right now it was okay to hear. If people liked it, that was fine by him. It had gotten a lot of play. It had paid the rent for a long while. *Classic hits?* Had that much time passed? Hanna turned it up louder, as if his thoughts were getting in the way. His younger voice filled the car. They both just sat riding along, listening, drifting. It was okay, it wasn't his worst. He pulled into the fairgrounds. Then a string of commercials that felt endless. Now a hair metal band whose name he could never remember. Shiny hair, Max Factor in satin tights. The song finished. He and Hanna were still sitting there, staring straight ahead.

The carnival girl's legs were braced. Aluminum crutches extended, strapped to her arms. She looked like a broken doe, lovely and bent. Mike, their dealer back home—and Curtis's tour manager in their prior life—had described her, the crutches, long ago—can't miss her, she's pretty, makes you feel vulnerable, but she has the heart of a spider.

Mike said he'd call ahead this time, let her know they were coming. He took care of Curtis and Hanna, like old times, like back on the road... The doe said:

—Walk this way. She had taken their money and now she moved fluidly, her steps dipping into her shoulders each time she advanced forward. All the grass was worn down to dirt most places, trod over with tire marks. This girl was pretty, her vulnerability made her pretty. Bubblegum heavy metal overhead, from speakers scattered throughout the grounds. She disappeared into the door of a trailer set on cinderblocks and plywood.

It had come up only a moment earlier when this girl with the aluminum braces had said, You look like someone, don't you? Curtis realized the dealer hadn't told her, Mike hadn't said anything about his past. And so he didn't push it, didn't say, *maybe you heard me on the radio*. But she insisted. What was he supposed to say? And she said:

—Oh my God. Wow. Yes.

And then he saw her eyes, saw her spirit fall a little. He and Hanna waited. Outside the trailer every machine around them looked as if it was one gyration from catastrophic failure. The calliope music piping and tinkling from the different rides drifted in and out of the breeze, occasionally penetrating, breaking up, the heavy metal pop from overhead. A few feet away: one of those rides that spun for too long before you were let off. Beyond: a bumper car lot, one enormous man, driving around in circles like a demented idiot, slamming into empty cars. There was a carousel, whose beauty ached inside Curtis, the horses there like memory, like an oasis of color amidst the smell of burning peanuts and machine oil, the recall of barkers and colored balloons.

The girl emerged from the trailer:

—He gave you a little more, a nickel at least. On the house. Said to tell you he saw you guys in Chicago, in '91. He says, thanks for getting him through his teenage years.

And Curtis thought, *through to what? This, here?* He saw the blinds of a small window in the trailer flicker open, the dim face of a man. A teenager no longer. The guy raised his hand. Curtis raised his hand; it could have meant whatever the guy wanted. But Curtis remembered certain shows. He remembered each of the Chicago venues, the converted old theaters. They were beautiful. He remembered that show in '91.

And then they were in a tent, in the dark, and they'd found a place to hit up. The girl with the crutches had led them there:

—Be quick, she said, then left them. A bench behind a canvas flap in the tent wall. They sat and finished off the bag, then Curtis licked the spoon, tucked it into his back pocket. They stepped from the tent into blinding daylight. Two young, skinny girls in halter tops stood in a short line outside. One of them saw Curtis, did a double-take. Her hand rose and covered her gasp. The girl beside her glanced over. It took a moment, but her eyes widened. He saw the flash of recognition. He recognized it for what it was. If the drugs had given him some physical relief, this gave him a deep and true joy. As if the cheap tar they'd just shot had found in these two girls—in that look of theirs—a natural amphetamine. He recalled many years ago being handed a note from a girl in the audience. It was innocent, it said she loved him. He knew it wasn't true, but he knew she believed it. And this alone made his whole life feel real.

Later he could see the Ferris wheel, a little pinwheel in the distance, behind Hanna's shoulders, her body on top of him, her thighs straddling him. The Ferris wheel, the red and white striped roofs of the tents, some trucks pulled off to the side of the horizon. All the colors flooding around behind her. A stray balloon the color of gold leaf rose into the blue of the sky and he could hear a barker announcing something far off. Lost keys, a special prize, some forthcoming attraction, a discount of some kind, static from the mouth of a small god. Curtis and his Hanna in a field of feed corn, soybean, whatever it had been cleared and burned down, fallowed for another season's planting. There had been a clear space where they lay down. And as they made love she talked about a baby again. She had said it while they made love. I want to have your baby. Like dirty talk. I want you to fuck me and I want to have your baby. Then they drifted off.

He dreamt that they had that baby, it had her eyes but it had him in most other ways. And in the dream the baby turned into a child quickly, and the baby lived in Curtis' childhood home, and if Curtis was, in some kind of dream-morph, that child with Hanna's eyes, he was also the child's father and Hanna was his mother. And in this dream these parents were clean. In the dream, he came with them to an amusement park. A cone of cotton candy was leaning like a tower of clouds from his hand. The events were floating in space, untethered, timeless. He was here and he was there. He was a father and a child, both. And then the father-Curtis and the mother-Hanna left the dream, and this child-Curtis, he was thirteen. The adult Curtis, dreaming himself back in a park in Matteson, Illinois, drinking beer for the first time. Fallen asleep in the park. Back when he knew nothing of the future. Nothing of a career in music, the peaking, the

David Ryan

afterwards. He'd only just started to fool around on a cheap guitar. The dream was all prehistory, this lovely time when nothing had happened yet. And in the dream, this thirteen-year-old Curtis woke the next morning, hungover, covered in dew. In the dream he woke and vomited just past a water fountain's concrete pedestal, near the tall chain link fence surrounding tennis courts. The dream park, empty and silent. Him, swearing he'd never drink another beer.

Curtis woke in the field. Hanna was asleep beside him, her coat spread out beneath her like a mattress. She'd said she wanted to have a baby. He could not imagine that her body, just now, would sustain a child. Her eyes shut, sleeping, they were beautiful: peaceful, untroubled. The carnival, too, was still asleep. It looked old and abandoned. He began walking toward the Ferris wheel. All was quiet. He smelled farms everywhere. The diesel generators had been shut off for the evening.

He had his first cigarette of the morning underneath a staircase that could be moved about, near a platform set up hovering over a bank of generators. He sat beneath the stairs on a crate and smoked. He fished in his pocket for yesterday's baggie and dipped his tongue in it. A woman, someone from the carnival passed, gave him a glare, which he returned. The woman kept walking.

He could see where they'd slept in the distance, see Hanna sleeping there still, a little bright speck on a fallow black field. The sun was rising. To his other side, opposite, the road ran from the fairgrounds, and he saw where they had parked yesterday, the car there by the side of the road, another silent machine. He finished his cigarette and began walking toward the road.

When he reached the car, he set the keys on the seat and closed the door, left the car unlocked. There was some gas in the tank. She would come to the car eventually, probably after she circled the fairgrounds, looking for him. She would find the door unlocked, the keys sitting there. He heard a generator cough, then roar to life. A wafer of orange and yellow and red stars lit on the Ferris wheel.

Later, he will remember her eyes. He will see the little dream child with her eyes. He will recall her eyes from when they were beautiful. He'll remember them months from now, when he sees her at the methadone clinic back in the city, waiting in line with all the others. He'll wonder if she's still staying at their old place, if she still leaves the television on all day and night. If she's found someone else. In the methadone line he'll stand there and know that she knows he's standing there not far off, but that neither of them will acknowledge this. There, waiting in that line, he'll feel as if he left her all over again.

He will remember those eyes, on and off. When he's finally clean he'll occasionally feel a pang, the tightening in his chest, wondering how she is. He'll think, yes, she's likely still sick, and then he'll wonder if she's still alive. He'll feel pity for this person in his imagination, an aching, longing pity. On and off. He'll draw a little comfort imagining her asleep again, that peace in her eyes. She said she wanted to have a baby. He'd proposed to her. He'd asked her to marry him. He's better now. He hopes she's okay.

The eyes come and go, but they don't go away. Years later he sees her one final time. Spots her on Pill Hill, walking out of an art gallery, well-dressed, a white boutique shopping bag, a new one, hanging from one hand: healthy. She's put on some weight. Not too much. She looks good. She's alone. He could just go up to her. Ask how she is. But he wouldn't need to ask. She looks like a woman who's had children, who eats regularly, good food. Whose metabolism has stabilized. She is clean, it's obvious she has been clean for a while—she has that safely recovered look. Not heavy, not at all. Just not so terribly thin.

It's mid-summer, and quite hot on the street where Curtis stands. Even from this distance her makeup is flawless, expensive. *You look so good,* he thinks, and his heart lifts. She had wanted kids, remember? She was always too thin. Even in her prime, before the drugs. Curtis feels himself lift at the sight of her. The relief of knowing she's all right.

Sometimes he hears a song and can't tell—can't tell if it's actually playing anywhere other than inside his head. He hears the band, hears himself singing.

When she stops at the corner and looks across the street, Curtis catches another glimpse of her eyes—even from this far off they are striking. She's getting away. Did she see him? She's gotten her

David Ryan

eyes back. He can't help himself, couldn't explain, but he hasn't felt this good in so long. He lowers his face. The waxed cup at the top, the rim of the trash receptacle. The bin is filled, spilling over one side, the lid on the cup, a straw sticking out. Cup still perspiring.

Those eyes. My god those eyes. He can imagine her children, what they look like. It didn't matter who she married—those kids would be beautiful. There's still a little ice in the wax cup—he sets it down on the top of the overfilled bin. He ticks at a small scab in the crook of his arm with a short, sharp violence. His arms, lined and dotted like staff paper, a palimpsest of musical notation faded up and down them. Some of the older wounds have begun to heal. Good times.

He walks away from the bin, sloshing the cup. He follows her. Maybe he'll tell her: that he remembers now. Not only that he'd proposed. That sometime between the last time he had seen her and now he had found the marriage certificate. *Justice of the Peace, City of New York.* At first he thought maybe it was a warrant, or some paper debt he'd forgotten about.

But then, the paper brought the memory back, slowly. They'd waited at the City Clerk's office. It looked like a high school classroom, it had a chalkboard. They'd taken a number. There was a Latino couple before them. Decked out in front of the podium and the chalkboard, whole family there. A strong bay rum smell of aftershave.

Then Curtis and Hanna's number was called and they rose, approached the small podium. He wants to tell her he remembers kissing her. Remembered turning, walking out. Some of the Latinos were outside and applauded as Curtis and Hanna passed. Sweat had thickened the creases in the folds of the certificate. When he found it, he thought maybe he'd show it to her some time. If he ever saw her again. And now, here she was.

But now: two blocks behind, he'll never catch up. And he just wants to watch her walk anyway. Even the walk, her walk, healed now. No more bones bound in lace. It's like an old friend. Just the way her legs move. Smooth now, extraordinary. He takes a sip of watered-down cola. Still some sugar—the water, cool. She was always too thin. He follows a little more. His hips—well, something is going wrong with them, it is getting worse. Sometimes it's hard to make it up the hill to the clinic. He'll never catch up. Not like this, but he doesn't ever want to stop. He feels good, feels good for her. Seeing her walk ahead like this is the best feeling. The best feeling he's had for as long as he can remember.

David Ryan

Aama, 1978

Bhimi Gurung Collection, Nepal Picture Library

MUNA GURUNG

"I could read my nonexistence in the clothes my mother had worn before I can remember her. There is a kind of stupefaction in seeing a familiar being dressed differently." Roland Barthes, <u>Camera Lucida</u>

" IF WE DIDN'T WEAR a *sari*, word would reach the main office that 'so and so's wife was not wearing a *sari* today,'" Aama says to me between fits of laughter over the phone. "Then they would call our husbands to the office."

She's laughing now because she doesn't have to be afraid anymore. She isn't in Singapore, living in an all-Nepali camp, one of the hundreds of women taking care of their homes and children while their military husbands served the country as Gurkhas.

She's told me this story before, but never with such lightness. Aama and I don't often laugh together. It's not like we are serious all the time, but laughing together requires that we let ourselves be a little soft, a little silly.

"Later, the newer *chyamas* started wearing pants. To think that I used to be so shy in a maxi!"

A maxi is exactly what Aama is wearing in the photo, taken in their kitchen in Block A in 1978. The maxi wraps around the waist and stretches all the way to the ankles, sometimes even kissing the floor. Aama says she was probably making rice in the photo. She imagines it's 9am and that Baba is waiting for his packed meal for the day. When I ask her who took the photo, she shrugs and says, "I don't know." And then after a long pause, "Maybe your father?"

Aama is quick to start every answer with "I don't know" or "I forget." It is her way to keep me at a distance, to buy herself time so she can figure out just how much of the story she wants to allow. Of course the photographer is Baba. But the fact that Aama has to pretend to think, or pretend not to know irritates me. As a younger person, an exchange like this would be enough to set me off. I would storm past her while she reasoned with astrology: "Your planet and my planet, Muna, they just don't align."

Writer Marianne Hirsch once said, "To look is also, always, to be seen." And I sometimes wonder if Aama's pretend-uncertainty about who the photographer is comes from a place of vulnerability. Maybe she can't bear to justify to her grown daughter the way she is looking at the photographer. Her mouth slightly open starting or ending her protest of not wanting to be captured on film in the kitchen, in the middle of cooking, looking like that. But in this soft protest there is pleasure budding in her right cheek; a dimple is waiting to cave in.

It's not like Aama is unable to love. She is just careful about her loving—whom to love and how much. She doesn't show it in the way Baba and I do: with wide smiles, high-pitched voices and touch.

I have only seen Aama and Baba share affection—in the way I understand it—once. I was 12 and we had already moved back to Kathmandu from Singapore. It was late afternoon and I was coming home from school. I walked in through the door calling out "Aama!" as I always did. They groaned from their bedroom to tell me where to find them: Aama and Baba were lying in bed, fully clothed, arms around each other, sleep still lingering in the distance between his nose and her hair. They didn't get up when I walked in. I don't know how our conversation led to this, but as I was standing over them in my school uniform and they were talking to me with their eyes still closed, I remember asking them if theirs was an arranged or love marriage. Baba said, "Love, of course." To which Aama opened her eyes, got up to retie her hair and said to Baba, "What nonsense!" Then turning to face me, she said to me, more as a reminder than anything, "We will always have arranged marriages. We are not those white people you see in movies who wear shoes to bed and marry whomever they want only to get divorced."

Years later, Aama and I will battle over love and whom you choose to be with, why and how.

§

"In the camp, the women got together and taught each other how to sew or knit sweaters," Aama says. When I ask her who in the Singapore heat would wear sweaters, she says, "It wasn't ever for Singapore, silly. It was for Nepal. We would knit sweaters so that we could take them home as presents." I don't push. I don't tell her that if I were on the receiving end, I would much rather enjoy something made and bought in that foreign magical land than something handmade. Before I can say anything, Aama reminds me, "Singapore was always temporary. Everything we did, we did it with Nepal on our minds."

But by the time Baba retires in 1994, my parents have saved up enough to return home in style. They buy a fridge, rice cookers, fans, foldable beds, mattresses, radio, TV, plates, forks, knives, spoons, pots and pans. She clicks her tongue in regret when she thinks about it now. "We didn't have minds. We were like mules," she says. "We never thought Nepal would ever have any of these things. We should have saved up the money. You can get everything here now!" Aama gently taps her forehead. "But—maybe also, we never thought we would travel back to Singapore or visit any other place after we came back."

As a 12-year-old moving back to Kathmandu, I remember being really excited about one piece of cargo. It was a sky blue foldable picnic table and bench. We even had a rainbow coloured parasol for it. There was no green space in the first apartment we moved into, so I would ask Baba to take it out and place it in the garage so that I could do my homework. Aama would hear me and scream: "Don't do it! It'll get dirty! It's for when we build our home with a garden!"

We have a garden in our Kathmandu house now, but they still don't use that plastic table and bench. "It looks so small and cheap," Aama says.

§

"In the early days though, I always asked myself: *Why Singapore? Why are we here?* There was nothing in the rooms they gave us: just a rusty spring bed with a flimsy wooden board. We had to buy everything. It took us years to put things together. Can you believe it, I would wash out the milk cans and use them as flower vases," Aama remembers. When I tell Aama that new hip restaurants in New York use milk cans as vases, there is a silence on the other end and then a "But why?"

The milk cans along with rice, daal, sugar, salt, pepper, bread, biscuits, tea, milk, veggies and meat were all a part of our ration bag that appeared once every 15 days. It was red and chubby. All the kids whose parents could buy them soft Gardenia bread ate that bread instead of ration bread. For the longest time, until Baba got promoted to Inspector, we ate ration bread. But Aama would cut off the edges and say, "See, ration or Gardenia? No one will ever know."

But kids always know.

Aama was a repurposer like that.

The Milo tins and Johnnie Walker bottle on the shelf in the photo are familiar childhood objects. We reused those square Johnnie Walker bottles to chill drinking water in the fridge. But Aama always made sure to set aside one or two bottles; she would make black tea in the perfect whisky hue, pour it in these bottles, and with labels still intact, close the caps and place them in the display case next to the TV. She wanted visitors to see that we had a fine line of drinks.

But Aama is a restless decorator. The sofa in the living room will be facing south one day, and just when we have grown comfortable in the way the light from the balcony hits our legs but not our faces, Aama will change it up on us and move the sofa elsewhere. "I get bored fast," she reasons.

"I can't stand that about you," I tell her.

"I don't like it either," Aama says, and her agreement surprises me. With me, Aama has always found a way to disagree, even if we might be saying the same things, her words come from a place of *but*. "Nowadays, I can't find anything in this house," she says referring to our Kathmandu home where she moves items from one cabinet to another and then forgets where she's moved them. "I'm getting old."

Her "boredom" also has made her get into the habit of throwing away things that are old or just sitting around harmless. "She is possessed on some days. She doesn't listen to me," Baba says. In his small complaint, you can tell that he's not trying to change her ways. If there is a photo she doesn't like, she cuts them into little pieces and throws them away. It's no secret that the photos in our family album only tell the stories that Aama wants to narrate; she doesn't think that anyone in the family would or should object.

"Do you have anything that is dear to you that you keep?" I ask her.

She shows me a coral piece strung in a red thread. "This one here's originally from my sister's necklace. Our mother gave it to her. There aren't corals anymore they say, is that true?" She asks me with a look that translates vaguely into *you should know, I sent you to school.*

"And your blue slippers," she says, pulling them out from a trunk where she has spread two bags full of mothballs. They are fuzzy blue closed-toes house slippers with a panda on them. "You loved them so much. The soles are still good. I'll give them to your child."

It's cute, sure, but also arbitrary. Why the coral, the fuzzy slippers, and not that famous necklace Baba bought for her? "Oh, that! I loved that!" She exclaims. "Your Baba would buy a lottery ticket every Saturday and once he won $75! We were so happy we couldn't feel the ground, but when he won $4,000...I don't think I've felt richer."

I remember this story because my brother said that the day Baba won that ticket, he didn't sleep the entire night. "So with that money, he bought me the necklace I am wearing here," she says pointing to another photograph where she is seated with a friend wearing matching black sleeveless tops, printed maxis, long necklaces, hair parted in the middle with a baby boy each on their side. "I don't know where it is. Probably sold it and ate it."

When I ask her why they are wearing identical clothes, she says that when a friend in the camp bought something they liked, they would ask her where she bought it and then all of them would go to that place and buy the same thing.

"Well, that's annoying," I tell her.

I am a hypocrite, of course. Because I don't tell her about the matching tattoos I got with my girlfriends. Or the way we "accidentally" buy the same shoes. Or how we begin to listen to the same bands, like the same songs. Or how we eat the same things, like the same restaurants. Repeat the same expressions in the same manner. And sometimes how we fall in love with the same kinds of people, or long to be each other and have each other's lives.

"But there were other women in the camp who weren't like us," Aama says. "They were educated and gave private tuition lessons to our children if we could afford to send them there." Most of these women that Aama refers to were Nepalis born and educated in Darjeeling. "They used to call us *pahadhiyas,* mountain people. To them, we were villagers who we had no sense of taste and didn't know how to wear clothes. Maybe they were right."

She speaks about them not in disgust, but in admiration. She tells me how beautiful these women were, how perfectly their hair was made, how their homes looked like sets on Hindi films, and how they walked—straight with their chins up.

"In my next life, I want to be educated like them."

§

Today at 64, Aama rests her reading glasses on her nose, and with a pen clutched tightly like chance between her index finger and thumb, she writes down the following sentences from her first English lesson: "I am a woman. I am Nepali. I am a mother."

I get out of bed. With eyes barely open, I follow the sound of Aama's voice and find her in the prayer room seated on the floor with her notebook on a small stool in front of her. I curl up beside her, my head lightly touching her leg. It's 6am. Aama is doing her homework.

As I listen to her sound out each English word in the sentences, I wonder if she has ever had these thoughts in Nepali. She surely has never said them out loud. These sentences are protests. They are highly political. Only intellectuals and poets speak this way. But here she is with her first lesson where she identifies the "I" in her, and owns the "am." Softly, she translates to me in Nepali: "So Muna, listen: I am a woman, I am Nepali, I am a mother."

It is suddenly clear to me that for the most part of my life, I have failed to see Aama as a woman. I have never tried to see that young woman in the photo who was shy to wrap herself in a maxi, who left her village to go to a country where she didn't complain about how scary it was to turn on the gas stove, or how she didn't know what to wear, how to wear it, where she lived in fear of being watched and seen, where she raised three children who have now made homes far away from her.

"Yes, you are a woman, you are Nepali, and you are my mother," I say back to her.

"You my daughter," she says in English, giggling. Then in Nepali: "Uffff, I don't know. I am so old. What am I doing learning a new language at this age?"

§

As a child, I remember only wanting to be carried by Aama. Her skin was soft and always cool; she never sweat. But she was always sick and always weak and she'd tell me to go with Baba. "But Baba feels hot," I would complain. Eventually, he'd grab me, I'd protest and squirm and cry, finally placating myself by fiddling with the sharply folded tip of his collar. My birth gave her *gastric*, she claims. Somedays, the *gastric* makes her legs boil, sometimes, it sends sharp pains like cold marbles rolling down her spine, and sometimes it causes her to burp fire. A mysterious disease that, to my knowledge, only plagues Gurung women in our family where their stomachs ache but when they go to the doctor, there is nothing there.

"It's easy to remember how long I've had *gastric* for," she says, "It's as old as you are."

A Real Mother

MADELEINE MAILLET

WHEN HIS MOTHER CAME in, she said, *"Y fait crissement chaud dehors."* Christ, it's hot out there. Then she sighed and looked around the condo, "So this is it, nice." She walked past us in the galley kitchen, and around the glass table that indicated the dining area, and out onto the balcony. She rested her ribs on the bannister like a girl.

"The cops are gone," she said, loud enough for us to hear it, and came back inside and stood facing us in the kitchen that was too narrow to feel like a room but too wide to be a hallway. "Outside, there were two black guys, *deux nègres*, yelling at this big fat lady and trying to get inside her bra, and she was trying to hold in her tits," she laughed nervously and looked at me, "They must've been pimps, and she must've been hiding money, or something?" And I nodded, and she nodded, and stared at me, her neck stretching, her chin jutting, and she turned her head to look out the window, "The cops are here. Those negroes are gone," and I followed her gaze to the stoop in question, I knew which one it was already, the one closest to the convenience store, where there was always a fat white lady in bicycle shorts sitting on the concrete, not waiting, just sitting. Then his mother looked at me, "So this is your girlfriend, she's pretty."

Ghislain grinned.

"Annette," she said, to see what it sounded like.

I thought to shake her hand and thought, too formal, and smiled and said, "Nice to meet you." I was thinking, negro! It was like that scene from that avant-garde movie with the razor and the eye, the eye and the razor, that I saw for a month every time I closed my eyes. It was always another eye and my eye, another hand and my hand. Did I want to do it or have it done to me? I thought, negro negro negro, until the word was just noise, while he and his mother talked about his brother and his brother's girlfriend. Her dad was African American, she looked like a tan white lady with a wet look perm, but it was up to her, I guess, if she wanted to say that word. Ghislain's body was stiff, his head was cocked and hearing her. He didn't look quite white. He was a white guy with a black guy's square hairline and deep set eyes. He'd told me she was a real mother, and I wondered what that was.

"Do you like my necklace?" she asked, smiling with her eyes, her mouth open in concentration, pulling it away from her chest so I could see it better. It was a silver Chinese symbol pendant on a necklace like a shoelace. There were matching earrings and a matching bracelet. I nodded. "My friend bought it for me," she said. She gave the word the weight of the masculine. It reminded me of a necklace I bought in Chinatown with my own money when I was a kid. I picked out the pendant and the hemp necklace from separate bins. It only cost me three dollars and I felt so rich, to have something so precious for so little. But, by the time I was a teenager I had a tin of necklaces, some had whales and dolphin pendants, one said, DIVA, another, SWEETHEART. They were all a nest of tangled polyester, and nickel plated metal, and I sat there trying to detangle it for as long as it took me to realize that I would never wear any of it again. I threw it out and felt guilty, and now I felt guilty again. But she didn't see my guilt, her smiling eyes looked down at the symbol in her open palm. I was waiting for her to tell me what it was supposed to represent, but she didn't, so I smiled. And she smiled, maybe pleased with me, maybe trying to be.

"My purse is falling apart," she said, and pulled on the petals of a black pleather flower with a grommet-pistil that drooped from her bag, "I want a new one, a white one, for summer, you should buy one, for your mother." Her commas piled on the way they did in French, dramatically. Her small face fell back to look up to her tall son.

"Let's go, I'm hungry," my boyfriend said. I bent over to pull on my shoes and he kneeled down to tie my laces. When I blushed she smiled at me, like, That's my son.

"Are you hungry?" she asked.

"I'm so sorry," I said. I felt my head unsteady on my neck and tilted it sympathetically, explaining that I had plans to meet my friend. That it was too late to cancel. She looked at me like she didn't hear me with darkly frantic eyes. "Don't worry. She's just stopping by," Ghislain assured me. I thought she'd be offended at that but she laughed. She was always stopping by, her sons were a joy, and she was a joyful woman. You could tell because she laughed at gravity as we rushed down the stairs, humouring her, because she was afraid of the elevator.

"Fancy," she said at the huge print of a woman's lips in the lobby. It had that Lichtenstein type pixelation. My boyfriend grinned, happy that she'd noticed.

It was hot out. Ghislain told his mother they would walk me to my bus stop, it was a block from Jean Luc's corner and Ghislain needed to get his money and give Jean Luc more cocaine. Drake was blaring from a car window, *everyday, everyday, we be sitting on the bench, but we don't really play, everyday, everyday.* And there were people yelling on the street because it was one of those blocks where people loitered and when the tedium of loitering became too much, they'd yell. We crossed the empty parking lot, hopping over the parking curbs.

"Did I tell you, my friend, Marie-Lynne, *elle s'est suicidée,* she hung herself?" she asked. She told us she had depression, she told us what was in the letter, but I don't remember, I do remember, *I want to be with God,* and that it was so hot and that the line in the ice cream parlour was spilling out onto the sidewalk. I had to step into the street. I thought about how suicide is always a reflexive verb in French, like remembering. She went on, about her dead friend's dead husband's cancer, and how that did it to her. Ghislain was holding my hand and I felt intention go from his grip. His face was my face: masking his disapproval at the spectacle of sadness his mother was making.

The Saturday shopping crowd on the sidewalk kept coming at us and past us, couples with postures heavy with heat and happiness, a girl walking fast all by herself with her arms swinging, mothers and fathers grabbing their kids in the crush. At the crosswalk his mother shifted her weight from one foot to the other, like it hurt to stand, and she looked at her son and his hand in mine, and she told us, "I get lonely, I do, *Je me sens seule! Je m'ennuie...* I've got children, thank God." I wanted to let go of his hand. More reflexive verbs for sad and lonesome, even if our conjugations said we did it to ourselves, I could tell she didn't believe it. Her pathos commanded my attention, made me not let go of his hand. If I'd let go, I'd have felt small in the face of her big feelings. But such an outburst, it made me embarrassed for her. So, I looked at the intersection, Ste. Catherine and St. Laurent. Blind green glass on this side, and the friendly cursive of a snack bar sign facing us, the cartoon hotdogs on the streaky glass smiling, too many people waiting to walk.

"How's work?" she asked Ghislain.

"*Ça roule,*" he said. He told her Francois sold ten bags to some guy from Chicago last night, here for the Jazz festival, and that Formula One had been his best week yet.

"*T'es dans la ouate en face de Place des Arts,*" she said, like, location, location, location, this is easy street. Ghislain had been given the best corner in the city by the Hell's Angels, the Opera was across the street.

"*Mais, y'en a qui s'habillent comme des clochards pire qu'à Hochelaga, les pooky, y'en a partout,*" he drawled. There are sorry looking junkies everywhere, even here.

She nodded and looked at me with a laughing mouth and asked, "Did he tell you I used to keep him company on his corner in St. Henri?"

I nodded. I could tell she wanted to tell me about it. I thought of questions to ask, What was that like? Did you get nervous? Were the customers friendly? Stupid, stupid, stupid. I smiled.

Ghislain was waving, I saw Jean Luc's caved in shoulders and fitted cap on a park bench. Everything about his posture was waiting for something. Ghislain told us, "Sit tight." We looked up at him and blinked *yes* in the sun. His mother was pulling her cotton minidress down and her knees were a bit bulbous and old but her ankles were very slight and pretty, her legs would've been called "pins" at some point.

"How'd you learn French?"

"My mom."

"No kidding?"

"She's from Lac St. Jean, originally," I said. It was a lie. My mother studied French in University. But I didn't feel up to talking about my father, how he'd left his mom in Québec and never looked back, called the nationalist spiel *la cassette* but refused to speak English with his kids.

"You should hear my daughter in law. She says, *le garbage,* like that's what it's called." The way she was staring at nothing, with her shoulders back and her face relaxed, you could tell she loved her daughter in law. "All my sons like the Anglo girls, Anglo girls and Haitians."

"You're a waitress, right, where do you work?" I asked. She told me she worked at a Greek diner, she'd worked there for years. I asked her how many, she said, *years,* and told me she'd been a waitress for twenty-two years. Her eyebrows were thin, aggressively penciled. The hairs made the line look blurred, but her eyes were dark and startling and shining. Talk, talk, make talk. "Do you have lots of regulars?"

"Lots of old people! I love old people!"

"I love old people, too."

"Where do you work, Annette?" she asked. Why did she say my name like that? So politely? It seemed too deliberate.

"I'm a stripper," I said in a normal way. She looked at me, looked at my body.

"What's that like?"

"The money's good," I said. She stared at my waist and I watched her, and there were the numbers in her mind's eye, 35-25-35. I crossed and uncrossed my arms.

"Who goes there?" She asked, ardently. "Who are the men?"

"Oh, I dunno. Everybody." I said. "Teenagers and you know, single men, businessmen, married men. Sometimes women, with their men."

"Taxi drivers? Are there lots of taxi drivers?"

"Not really."

"Italians? Italian taxi drivers."

"No, no Italian taxi drivers."

"My friend is a taxi driver," she said. Her eyes were proud and young. Her face was used to waiting. Lips open, so I could see her small teeth, the pallor of her tongue in its darker chamber. It made me feel tender.

"No Italian taxi drivers, no," I said. I thought I should qualify, that I didn't remember, I wanted to be specific and sincere, but I didn't know how.

"I bet." She said, laughing. "I bet you make a bundle." And we both laughed nervously and then broadly and the sun bled all over us and we stood there sweating, waiting for Ghislain to get his money.

He didn't hurry across the street, he never hurried, and when he was before us he kissed the top of my head with a kindness that shamed me. How was he so pleased with me when I was so baffled by his whole family. His mother and his little brother Maxim who was in the gang and also his girlfriend who'd borrowed ten thousand for a car from his shylock father and wasn't making her payments on time.

"What shall we eat?" his mother asked.

"I want a hot dog," Ghislain said.

"Take me somewhere good," she said, kicking at a pebble when he looked at her.

"Let me pay for your taxi," he said.

"The bus stop's just there," I begged.

Then the 85A was turning the corner and I waved, cringing.

"Tention à toi," he said, like, take care, but also watch your back. I ran across the street and down the block to the stop. I was blinking in the noon brightness, the cityscape stuttering like film at the end of the reel.

I met my friend Lester at a coffee shop and told him some anecdotes I felt he was fishing for. How the strippers are always eating hot dogs in the changing room. The Québec celebrities I'd danced for, the ones I'd never heard of. That guy's from a pop punk band called Sum 41, or, That guy's from that action movie, Bumrush, the other strippers had told me afterwards—things I'd have to pretend to be impressed by, because they were. We worked on our Charlie Chaplin presentation. Lester used to be a clown so he wrote most of it. Now he was a waiter at a fancy place and he asked what I made during Formula One. He said he made seven hundred on the Friday, and I told him, twelve hundred, but I was naked, so.

At work it was better than an average Sunday. The Jazz Festival customers were mostly middle aged and polite. One man I danced for told me he hadn't been to a strip club in twenty years. His wife was a feminist, but he was divorced, and now he was here, in Montreal. When I told him I was feminist he gave me the briefest smile and said, "Of course, of course." That made me angry, but when he paid me with a shrug, and grasped my hand a little desperately, saying, instead of goodbye, "You're beautiful," I got to say, "Of course, of course," and it felt like we were square.

After work I walked across the street to Ghislain's. He was sitting on his balcony, four floors up, this was our routine, at three he'd sit outside and wait. In the elevator mirror, I smiled at my lids heavy with false lashes, all the tiny red veins in my eyes looking remarkable with so much makeup around them. All the strippers did smoky eyes, because if lips were the sexy part, our eyes made us engaging. I closed them, and when the chime sounded and the doors slid open I was thinking those careening end of the day thoughts of a hot shower and a soft bed.

He was in the hall waiting for me, his eyes were dark and brimming like his mother's. Crushing my shoulders into his torso, he sighed, and I felt the alertness with which I'd held my body all night melt away. With his hand on the back of my head, with my face against his solar plexus, I smelled soap, cigarettes, and warm cotton.

Ghislain had made his father's macaroni and cheese casserole for us, and now he warmed it in the oven.

"Did your mother cook?" I asked.

"She's a waitress, she wasn't home for dinner. My father cooked," he said. I never asked him about his father because he was a shylock with a side business selling Native cigarettes and my interest in him felt voyeuristic. Ghislain poured me a glass of Pepsi and sat facing me at the kitchen table with that calm and sated gaze of his. He lit a joint he'd rolled for me.

"How did your parents meet?" I asked.

"My father was married when they met, to one of the Dubois brothers' sisters."

"Who?"

"You never heard the name Dubois? That was the *pure laine* Mafia."

"What?"

"They owned all the strip clubs, even the ones for homos, they ran everything in the 80's, the drugs, the numbers…"

"He stepped out on their sister?"

Ghislain smirked. The buzzer sounded. Modesto was downstairs, finished with the night shift. His name was a cosmic joke, he was a braggart. The second time I met him he told me he had a ten inch dick, that he liked to make a lady's vagina bleed a little. I asked if he had cervical anger. He asked, is that what that skin is called, I can feel it sometimes? I didn't correct him, I only nodded, thinking, it's not skin it's an *organ*. The other runners called him The Martian, because he had three Marvin the Martian tattoos, which he always bragged he'd had done before the craze for loony toons tattoos. But he was Ghislain's runner, even after ten years in the streets, so Ghislain called him by his name. Modesto spoke to me in English, he acted like he was extending himself for my benefit, since none of the other runners spoke English. I hated having to act pleased to be speaking English, like it was better because it was easier.

"Ghislain told you they busted me?" Modesto asked, grinning like a fool.

"No," I said. I'm sure I looked shocked.

"How did it happen?" Ghislain asked, his features as still as ever. He knew what happened, this was for my benefit.

"They were behind the bench, foot patrol."

"You didn't look?" Ghislain asked, but he wasn't looking at Modesto, he was looking at me. He wanted me to feel the cynicism of waiting for it, Modesto's grin flagged a little.

"Were you arrested?" I asked.

Ghislain scoffed, "It wasn't worth it, you had what, seven bags?"

"They weren't even gonna confiscate it. The cop was like, is someone gonna hurt you if you lose this?" Modesto droned, imitating the super enunciated question of a concerned officer. Ghislain laughed. His laughter for things he disdained was a high pitched bark, grating and vain. I hated it, it degraded his true laughter which was also high pitched, a boyish trill.

"I was like, what, I can walk away with this? Then the cop saw I was hesitating..." Now that Modesto had told me the anecdote, his eyes darted at the dirty plates and packs of cigarettes and plastic Slurpee cups and prepaid phone cards and the bag of weed on the table. He started rolling a joint. Normally, Modesto would make small talk with us for ten or twenty minutes while we smoked and Ghislain counted his take and gave him his share. I was excited that Ghislain wasn't talking and that I got to be aloof too. When he lit the joint and passed it, it was as if his eyes were inhaling, wanting something from us as necessary as air. I waved the joint away. Ghislain looked at Modesto evenly and Modesto took the cash from the pocket of his hoodie, *four eighty,* he told us and sucked on the joint, holding it in that claw-fisted way Marlon Brando holds a cigarette. Ghislain separated the new plastic money from the old paper money, piled the bills in different denominations and counted, four hundred and eighty dollars. He gave Modesto one hundred dollars. The split was supposed to be fifty-fifty.

Modesto looked baffled and held it delicately as though it was the cash that was flawed. I was waiting for him to say something when Ghislain cleared his throat.

"T'as même pas checker," he said flatly. One hundred and forty was the street value of the seven bags he'd lost. It was embarrassing, that he had to pay the inflated street price. The timer sounded on the oven. Ghislain donned his oven mitts, and the macaroni and cheese casserole smell filled the condo. He made up three plates for us and brought us our supper and cutlery. Ghislain smiled the demure smile of a person putting food on a table. I got up to get paper towels, to be able to bustle in the silence, and Modesto complimented me on my Bart Simpson shorts. *Dope,* he said, and talked about how Anglo girls have better style than those *pitounes* who think they're hot shit, with their fake tits and fake tans and fake nails and hair extensions. Modesto ate with his elbows on the table, his whole posture hunched towards us, his eyes laughing, scapegoating all the French Canadian girls who tried too hard, asking me to take the compliment. I shrugged a thank you. When he asked me where I shopped, my eyes darted at Ghislain.

"Where do those Bart shorts come from?" He prompted me.

"Korea, I said, a Korean store near the nail place I go to."

"You don't shop at the mall do you? The stores all the girls go to."

I shrugged and ate my dinner, ignoring him. The macaroni was better than my mother's so I groaned happily at Ghislain. His smile was preening. It was early weeks, so we were obsessed with each other. Every little animal consideration, every bite of food, every sigh and snore, felt like some keen observation into the goodness of being. He was so happy to be feeding me. I was happy to be fed. Modesto was still sitting there. He told again how they were both on the news at sixteen, soliciting in the street, *Les vendeurs de drogues de la rue St. Denis,* how his mother was so angry. Ghislain said his mother was always at the diner when the news was on, but she didn't mind, she'd known her boys had been working for scalpers since the third grade. We ate in silence again and this time it was relaxed.

"You meet his mother yet?" Modesto asked.

"This morning."

"She's a trip, right?"

"She's sweet."

"She'd visit him on his corner, when we were working in St. Henri." Modesto said, nodding approvingly of Ghislain's mother, how ride or die she was.

"I know. She has a man now, right?"

"He doesn't respect her." Ghislain said.

"She asked me if I'd seen him at work."

"What?"

"She described him to me, said he was Italian, a taxi driver." Modesto was laughing, a disbelieving honk that was so crass. Ghislain's face was open, his expression as still as ever, his eyes cast sparks of humiliation at me, it made me feel like a man, to be the one to make them appreciate how pathetic she was. "When I told her I was a stripper, she went on and on, describing his face, his hair, he's about sixty, dark and handsome, she said." I had no idea why I was making this up. Ghislain's face was contorted and his words were choked in his throat. And I knew I didn't belong here with these boys, whose only loyalties were to themselves, the gang. They were bonded together by those sad animals on the streets they'd tamed together, the junkies, who nodded at Ghislain like royalty when we walked down the street, like I was proof of his power. They called them *pookies*, which was the pet name my mother had for mine and my sister's privates, some nonsense word, she'd say, *girls, wash your pookies.* The coincidence was so perverse. I was laughing. Ghislain was staring off at something. Modesto was laughing, like laughter was a mantra.

"She deserves better." Ghislain said feebly.

She did.

@nature, how well do you know amerika?

WO CHAN

have you met. ever

her, the androgynous here&now
—as in Time & Space—
facefucking

rhythmless, interrupted hacks & wet Chins

                    it was cosmic

on a hill / blasted with wi-fi

          I chased monarchs
          through a field of violet thyme

telling you this, my docu-self

huffs a red sharpie and carves on you an X

                 YOU ARE HERE
                 YOU ARE HERE TOO

against awkward space&time
              voyeur—stunted & schlaffed
out in crud, your fingers swell like angel

cake in my mouth / Sputum River plays

          I learn not to gag, and the tears
          I cry, "im sew happy bb :)))" gd bless

we have, at least, each other's / company ("alimony" sp?)

your Jeep parked outside my barn, the Port & crustacean in your hands / you shouldn't
          have…you shouldn't have…

—Earlier

I said field of thyme / with an "h"
as in yew-man & yew-bris & yew-mid
as in yewman yewbris in the yewmid afterrain heat

dilates the mind

a door swelling shut into its jamb

like an ingrown toenail

it should hurt you

it should hurt you

Afloat a Leaky Vessel

CHRIS AMES

MY WIFE IS A leak. I mean, she's leaking. Halfway through the early bird special, Mabel doubles over and spills clear, tasteless fluid from her nose all over her leafy greens. Granted, we're not exactly brimming with piss and vinegar like we used to, but we still have our faculties about us. I say, "Honeybee, get a hold of yourself." She pinches her nose with her index and thumb, hobbles down the hall to the ladies room and yells, "Don't start without me." People! Always got to wash them at their ends. Just out of nowhere, and still.

For the gossips, it's the talk of the town. A real barnburner. Have you heard about Luce's wife? Incontinent woman near drown the bus boy. Needed mouth-to-mouth just to revive him.

With tissue dangling from her nostrils, Mabel asks, "You still think I'm pretty?"

I turn to Mabel, I say, "Those chicken shits don't know a thing."

But still, the leak. In her youth, Mabel used to model high contrast women's clothes on TV, before it made the jump to color. Brightest outfits you've ever seen. I'd joke, "I'll never lose you in that, ha, ha." She was commercial; she was beautiful. Now we're fiddling in the tool kit for a C-clamp to plug her nose.

"Did you take your allergy pills today?" I ask.

"They make my tongue feel fuzzy like velcro."

"Doc says they'll help with the constant drip."

"That limp dick, and his five dollar words. Shoving his degree in my face. Talking about my un-control. My material expressiveness."

"What did you eat today?"

"Plums, candied walnuts, a beet salad. Tin of sardines. A finger or two of brandy."

"Are those allowed?"

"Doc says women consume in excess. That's why they gotta flush themselves out all the time—this clamp is killing me."

"C'mere." I gently pull off the clamp and bring her close, letting her wipe her nose on my shoulder. "We'll fall asleep, tomorrow will come regardless."

In the morning, a wet blanket. Oh.

"Mabel, what happened?"

"My body's embarrassing itself. I'm losing it."

"You make breakfast. I'll change the sheets."

In the washroom, wringing urine out into the basin. Is this love? I read once that when a woman soils herself, not only does she lose control, she also releases many of the virtues she possessed prior to her looseness. A gossip of the bladder. What's that skip rope rhyme?

> with barely hood
> she pyst where she stood
> than she began to weep

I don't know about all that. But the nasal drip. And now the bed wetting. Dignity's a funny thing. I need to hold her up through all this. Dig her out. Keep her state of quality exhumed from the corporeal waste of the female body. Like separating yolk and egg. She's still my girl.

In the kitchen, Mabel is sautéing diced onions, peeled garlic, and shallots. She's crying.

"I swear it's just the fry-up," she says.

"I got you something. It's your nose clip from when you used to swim. Should be softer than the clamp."

"I miss the water."

"You were incredible. You looked so at home—and those neon bathers. Just a flash of color."

"How do I look?"

"Fast."

"I can't keep anything in. I'm a sieve. I've got too many sluices to let it all out."

"You're full of life. You always have been." I put one hand gently on her stomach, the other on the small of her back. "You're making breakfast. You've made me a husband. You've made us a home. You've made a daughter. You've got little planets growing in here. You can make it all." Between my hands, water sloshes back and forth. Her solar plexus, and all the functioning viscera, hums along to some grand maneuver. She teems.

Chris Ames

In the parking lot of the market, I run into Nance, Mabel's friend from bridge.

"Luce!"

"Nancy."

"Just devastated to hear about Mabel. Gruesome, really."

"I'd prefer to keep this in the family."

"Oh, yes, yes, I agree. I think we're all doing our best to contain her …" cupping her leather-gloved hand around her mouth, "… embarrassing humours." Nancy cracks a smile so sharp it splits a line in her make-up. "And my, how are *you* doing through all this misfortune?"

"This really isn't about me."

"Oh dear, but it is. The things we love are always a reflection of ourselves. And the ones we love, even more revealing. Certainly you must hear what they say down at the lodge."

"I'm not interested in the squabbling of the hen house."

"Well. If that's how you feel. But you know what they say, 'the whore is the leakiest of all female vessels.' I'd just hate for Mabel's good name to be thought of as something unchaste, and hyper-effluent. Such a sweet, simple girl."

When I get home, Mabel is reclining in the armchair, with the TV playing for no one, everyone.

"Can you even see at that angle?" I ask.

"It helps the drip. Plus, I know this Jeopardy by heart. It's those two handsome boys versus the IBM computer."

"Who wins?"

"Oh, the computer. By a long shot. I remember reading in the paper, something about 'soft filtering.' Or distilling natural language. It takes the whole world in, and leaves with the answer. Isn't that something?"

In front of the computer, I start to type *how to love someone* and then the internet suggests *with depression, with anxiety, with attention deficit disorder,* but I think I was really looking for: *again.* I find a quote by someone named Shannon L. Alder: "If you're going to love someone or something then don't be a slow leaking faucet—be a hurricane." Then I find an article titled 'How to Recover from Leaked Nude

Photographs.' How would the supercomputer answer this? In the form of a question. I move the cursor over the prompt that says *sleep*, and then the computer asks, *are you sure you want to go to sleep?* and I click *yes, yes, yes* until the screen goes dark.

"Luce. Are you awake?"
"What is it?"
"I'm bleeding."
"Where?"
"I need you to go to the store."

I haven't had to buy tampons in twenty years. The boy who rings me up says something like, 'Getting these for your granddaughter?' and I say, 'Fetch me the key to your bathroom,' because nothing is lower than being in charge of a toilet. In the stall, some gibberish is etched into the partition.

her nose somedele hoked
and camously croked
never stoppynge
but ever dropyynge

Another brazen act of vandalism. This town is dissolving.

I wake up to the swish and gargle of the washing machine. We're always cleaning now. It's not so bad. The nice thing about laundry is that it's a non-activity. You can be doing laundry while you, say, slow dance with your wife to the radio. The laundry is still doing itself while you gently dip her head back, and still going while Modern English croons *you've seen the difference and it's getting better all the time,* and even still while you sway together, knowing yes, we're delicate, but also yes, we're powerful. It's very different than doing the dishes, which requires all of your body but almost none of your mind. Which is to say nothing of scrubbing the tub, which asks everything of you.

"Luce. Do you remember when we first brought Sarah home?"
"I do."
"We were so worried. We couldn't get her to eat for days."

"She wouldn't latch."

"And then the thrush."

"Look at me now. I'm overflowing."

With the swimming clip, the adult diapers, and the tampons, Mabel's been joking that's she's more machine than woman now.

"According to the Greeks, all this blood and phlegm means you're just too sanguine. Too courageous. Too playful."

"I feel choleric."

"How's your liver?"

"Full of yellow bile."

"I knew it."

"Luce. What if this doesn't stop? I don't know how much more I have left."

"Come now."

"Listen. If I die, you must bury me in my prom dress."

"Why's that?"

"Because Nance thinks I can't fit into it any more—and I can."

I need to learn how to love like a hurricane but I don't know how because I'm so goddamn tired. Mabel isn't the only one falling apart. That's not what I meant to say. I mean, I too wake up with desperate bones. Everything's thinning, the hair, the skin, the vision. Even the skin of my teeth is getting thinner. It will never be said because it's the thing we both know, and the things we know to be true aren't worth saying aloud. I can't get sick. Together, we're a person at best. A ship needs one good man rowing. Clean forget the tempest. Above all, we need good weather.

Mabel's been drinking a strange concoction she calls a 'drain plug.' After I've already made the morning coffee, she'll take the leftover grounds and twice-boil them in a pot with two tablespoons of chicken grease and a pinch of cornstarch. Washes the whole thing down with a bowl of porridge and some saltine crackers.

She says "If it chokes up the sink, why not me?"

We need to get out of the house. I call the receptionist down at the lodge to see if the pool is open.

"Unfortunately, we do not have any senior swim openings right now."

"And tomorrow?"

"No."

"That's impossible."

"Listen, Luce. We've been made aware of Mabel's *condition*. In an effort to keep things sanitary for our other members, we think it's in everyone's best interest that ..."

Click.

In the living room, Mabel is playing a card game called Concentration. You lay all the cards in four rows of thirteen cards. You flip two cards face-up at a time—if they are of the same number and color, then you win the pair. It's a memory game. She's solves the whole thing in under a minute. Her hands fly in between flipping cards, and licking her fingers for grip. From the next room, all you hear is the gentle rattle of her jewelry.

"Mabel."

"Not yet."

"Get your things together."

"One second."

"Now."

"Jesus, what is it?"

"We're going to the beach."

Her eyes haven't shone like that in a long, long time. She was all movement, stuffing extra napkins, pads, and allergy pills into a fanny pack. Before you know it we're in bathing suits, in sunscreen, in sun glasses, in sandals, in the car.

"Can you believe it, Luce? A day at the beach. After everything—"

"We're long overdue for a—"

"Little fun—"

"Distraction."

"Well, yes. Just know that I realize how—watch the road."

"I am. What with my license registration coming up, and us getting older. Who knows how many more times we'll be able to do this."

"How do you mean?"

"You know, care taking takes time. We gotta—"

"You're riding the median. Let's not forget who is actually going through—"

"Enjoy today."

"Okay. Easy on the gas."

"Who's steering this thing, you or me?"

Mabel fiddles with the radio and suddenly The Paris Sisters are singing *I love how your eyes close / whenever you kiss me.* She hums along for a moment, readjusts her nose clip, wipes spittle from her chin, then asks, "Luce, do you think I'm a burden?"

"What's gotten into you? Don't sour today—"

"Answer me."

"That's what love is, you—"

"Slow down."

"Bear one another's burdens."

As I'm pulling into the parking lot, the radio is fading out. We gather our stuff and trudge through the sand in silence. Maybe we haven't been out in a while, but the sun seems to be tearing a hole in the sky. Quick beads of sweat run down Mabel's arms as she drags her folding chair behind her. Sweat crawls into her eyes, the backs of her knees, between her toes, points of her elbows, ridge of her nose, crest of her ear, ends of her hair, nape of her neck, and across the blonde gossamer hair of her upper lip. She glistens. When we reach the shore, she sheds her outerwear, clip and all.

"I'm going in," she says.

"Already?"

She nods.

"I might just rest my eyes here for one moment."

Mabel walks down to the shore, slick with sweat, nose dribbling, tugging on the ends of her neon bathers. She's almost skipping. It's nice to see her like this. Bright and awake. I'm so tired. And the sun's burning heavy on my eyes. Watching Mabel slip into the glassy stream. And those trunks—what color. Rest for a spell. My mermaid, at a distance. Head bobbing, by the buoy. Ingress and egress. So drowsy. Too much of water. Mabel, further still. Brilliant and unpolluted. Clean and invisible to the naked eye. Shimmering, out. Warm sea glint, out. A flash, out, out.

Chris Ames

NEW YORK, N
DEC 4
2 3u PM
1933

Failure: A Writer's Manual

K.A. MAJOR

1. THE FIRST THING I REMEMBER

Watching the Vietnam War on TV in my diapers. A black and green speckled carpet. The sound of the bombs. Pounding and ceaseless. I kept waiting for the sound and the action to stop but it didn't. So I kept watching.

4. BEFORE MY EYES

Braces, swimming at the Jewish Community Center, Lake Michigan, custard ice cream, Hubbard Park, mixers with boys' schools, the first time I saw boys in college. Watching the World Trade Center from Brooklyn when I couldn't sleep at night. Looking at the windows with lights still on, wondering what the people in there were doing.

7. WHAT I WOULD SAY ABOUT MYSELF

That I died of boredom.

That I liked holding babies.

That people made my way in life easier,
and I hoped I paid it forward.

That Christmas disappointed and depressed me.

That I loved walking in light rain.

That for the rest of my life, I appreciated the hours and hours I spent playing outdoors in cold weather.

That I was an excellent seer and feeler,
and a developing storyteller.

8. WATCHING MYSELF

Kirsten Major is on a train.

A woman near one of the subway car entrances is wearing a midriff-baring top, fringed with pink lace at the bottom. Below the lace is a healthy-sized, normal-looking belly button and down below that, just to the left of the center line that Kirsten can't remember the name of, is a dot of a brown mole. Kirsten finds herself glad that this bare stomach fashion is mostly over; and then, helplessly, she slides into considering this woman in a sexual light, engaged with a pretend man gazing upon this lower belly. Very quickly, this thought slides into the obscene. She is plunged into this, and then just as quickly is horrified at her turpitude, and how easy it is. Oh, she thinks for the first time, this is why scantily-clad people make us all nervous: we barge into our own sexuality in a public place. Why had it taken her so long to figure this out? And she realizes this must be some gift of a changing, aging body, one's own sex drive slowing down enough to finally be able to have some insights. When she was in college, her sex drive felt like a set of facts, the way that physicists say that light is not ephemeral but an actual substance like pudding. Pudding: tumid, soft, wet, quivery. Kirsten shifts. I don't want to think about this. I am going to Ikea. On the ferry. *You love the ferry!* she shrieks inside her brain, trying to scatter the naked thoughts away.

Then Kirsten Major realizes she is having these experiences and narrating them to herself. *Don't,* she thinks. *Don't narrate this moment like it is in the novel you just read, and then pronounce your thoughts to be just as interesting and competent, and why don't you have the same success as the author you are reading.*

10. SPEAK YOUR MIND, BUT

There are times when a friend will say something to you so messed up and callously shocking that instead of speaking, you sit there and wonder. Lately I have been reading old journals and I'm struck by how often I blunted myself. Not just in speaking, but also in seeing—I was always expecting disappointment, not love, and I averted my radar to seize some small crumb of attachment. This is my great mistake in life.

This morning, before I could wake up too much and overthink it, I opened an old diary and read about being at a wedding reception when an acquaintance from college casually confessed that he was equally in love with his girlfriend's best friend. "I love them both equally. It's just that things worked out with C—." These two women were my closest friends at the time.

I lay in bed wondering why I didn't say anything. At first, it seemed part and parcel of my fear of intimacy. But then I realized, no: this time, I was silenced by the road of utter devastation he was laying down. Those words, uttered to the girlfriend, would not only just about kill her, but dash their imminent plans to leave the country together and move to Russia, where they both had wangled jobs and were only able to go because of working as a team. He had just handed me means to destroy her life, his life, by using my voice.

I could have gone up to her in a panic and told her. But sometimes the maw of destruction that someone turns on you is too much. I just sat there, awestruck that he'd risk his own life like that. In fact, I could not speak. I did not tell the truth.

13. MAYBE THIS IS A GOOD TIME TO ACCOUNT FOR THE ESSENTIAL FAKENESS OF BIOGRAPHY AND MEMOIR?

After work I rambled to the used bookstore on Hudson, the one with the signed first editions. I found a memoir by an author who lived in such adoration of Ernest Hemingway, I find myself frequently holding the book back to look at it with my nostrils flared in disbelief.

The beginning is pretty thrilling. About 38 years after this appreciation of Hemingway was first published, the author writes a new foreword for a reissue on the eve of Papa's 100th birthday. Now that Mary, his last wife, has passed away, he lets us know that in fact Hemingway's final years and life with Mary were misery, with fighting as vicious as I've ever heard recounted. Two people so disgusted and weary of each other that his use of the word "shitty" during a dinner party causes her to rail at his ability to write at all. His response calls into question her mental competence and she accuses him of being a fraud, and he accuses her of sleeping around…in front of the mortified author. It struck him then that Ernest and Mary had stopped being intimate. They had nothing more than a bitter coexistence.

I am very glad that the author spoke about this fight, these details, as he seems glad to tell the truth at last about a relationship that was making a dear friend so miserable. This is the new foreword, written in 1999.

And then we turn to the book itself, written shortly after Hemingway's suicide in the 1960s, when Mary was very much alive. How warmly their marriage is described! They are cast as gentle balances of each other. Hemingway will get a little too colorful in mentioning a past sexy escapade, Mary charmingly will steer him back towards the discussion of sport. Mary wants to spend time in New York; Hemingway hates the town but obliges her. Hemingway speaks reverently of "Miss Mary."

The point is, the truth changes. They were described one way at a certain point in time, and then a completely different way at a different point in time. *By the same eyewitness.*

So whatever I say here, even as much as it feels like the truth, even though I have the sense of being honest, it is all, to some extent, a needed invention. Years from now, I will tell my story differently. How disappointing.

14. THE COUPLE WHO HATED RUNNING A STATIONERY STORE

In the West Village, on Hudson. It was called Typewriters and Things. The couple stood in silence shoulder-to-shoulder at the register. You'd think it would have made being there unpleasant, but over the years, and unintentionally, the place had turned into a museum. They had the old gummed reinforcements for three-hole paper. I was so glad to see them and remember their bitter taste when licking them to my math notes in high school as I reviewed quadratic equations over and over. There were varying lengths of brass tacks that we called railroad spikes at Price Waterhouse—it was how we kept track of receipts. There were hole punchers, plastic protractors and metal compasses with small pens. In the folder section, there were drab-colored folders with thick, Kelly-green fabric tape reinforcing them.

The couple had signs that said do not touch, and about teenagers being in there unescorted (no!) and about cell phones. You could tell that they had weathered the worst of the NYC 1980s with kids coming in in a group, screaming and upending things; being mugged on the way out with the daily till. Their dislike of retail and the general public had grown deep and abiding. Buying stuff, which I always did, did not even make them happy. They stood there, unhappily watching, while I wandered the two aisles marveling at the delicious appurtenances that belonged in desks in olden times.

It was the end days of Typewriters and Things. Every time I needed a boost of inspiration, I'd go in and treat myself to a notebook and pen. And then there was one day I went there and it was gone. I was sad and a little relieved. I hoped the couple retired and were happy not to go there and worry.

18. SUMMER

The season of the dashed ambitions of the undergraduate for a brilliant year that ended up being just, in fact, another year; the season where *my article, at last!* awakens in the heart of the professor. Graduate students and adjuncts feel their own false promise of summer break; there will be a week or two before summer classes (*not that long, it's only one* they reason), the July long weekend, and then a week or two at the end for focus, both glorious and then sad (so little real useful time, so little money).

For myself, there are two distinct phases. June is the month where the days grow as long as they ever will be on this planet. There is something about daylight stretching beyond the dinner hour that makes me feel wise and patient. It's all the babies I've held, the babies of friends, as a babysitter, putting them to bed in the still-blue light. Yes, June is partly that for me: the face of a sleeping infant under a glowing blue sky, the miracle of patience and the pain of birth and then feeding and sleeping and just being here. The smell of white milk and the softness of bird-delicate bald heads.

There is something else to be said about life on June evenings: in my mind we are all on porches, silently looking at our neighborhoods and then opening our mouths to express it, identify that thing that we are reaching for. And it doesn't come out easily or sometimes at all.

And then the rest of the summer is black, humid, dark night. I speak exclusively of the summer of the child; the weather of childhood is really the stage setting for the rest of life. The sweltering days don't even make an impression on me; the next point at which the world becomes possible for thought or feeling is the black night—that's when you get out the bikes and permission from your parents. I rode hard just for the feel of the air moving. For a shiver. And then it seems we'd bike and bike around the village until we ended up on someone's front lawn, just outside the pool of the porch light, and the sweat and heat would close around us and sweat would suddenly be everywhere, streaming out of our hair, our necks, down our backs. It was the 1970s, era of synthetic foods; someone served artificially flavored Country Time lemonade or Kool-Aid or something horrible called bug juice. That segment of the summer was deep, black, hot and hopeless and exciting. Those endless dark nights when it seemed all we could hope for was that the next day wouldn't be so hot and boring. And then the queer rumble in your stomach when these rides continued into August; on TV suddenly a back-to-school commercial would appear and then I was reaching for the summer to do something for me: heal me, rest me, repair me while riding through the night, the rides now errands into the black macadam streets with the lamps and silence. I'd whiz through the night and pray, let there be something about this I can take into school with me. So the first day will be less frightening. So it will be better than last year. I will have an epiphany on this night journey that will finally protect me from all the cruelty kids inflict on each other, the names and the bottom on the social order. On these last few bike rides before there are no more night bike rides because it is a school night, let the world underneath these spinning wheels give me something to take into the fall.

20. THE NIGHT BEFORE LAST, I THREW OUT OLD COSMETICS, A MONOGRAMMED TOWEL I WAS SO PROUD TO GET FROM BLOOMINGDALE'S IN 1992.

22. YESTERDAY I TOOK MY REMAINING BOOKS, PUT THEM INTO A SUITCASE AND LEFT MY APARTMENT.

We're having humid days and I was wearing a navy-blue tank top. The suitcase was heavy—it had my big fat picture book on Archaic Greek Art, my beloved book on Medieval history with the prim drawings of pop-eyed Carolingians, battle formations, and the maps of movements of tribes like the Jutes and the Ostrogoths and the Franks, popping in and then out of history. A picturebook of Freud's apartment. I walked to 181st Street and turned left and went uphill, crossed Broadway, to the nice part of the Heights, the part that people compliment me on when I say where I live. I arrived at the Starbucks and as the woman had promised on the phone, there was the community bookshelf outside. It was cool and little plops of rainwater kept landing on my skin. Looking like a crazy person or at least a performance artist, I stopped, unzipped my suitcase there on the street, and took my books out and started unloading them.

The worst moment was leaving the one book I had set aside, thinking I would save it. It is *A Room Made of Windows* by Eleanor Cameron and it is about a 12-year-old girl, Julia Redfern, who is determined to be a writer. I reread the ending for probably the 200th time, standing there. It is after Julia realizes she has to let go of her perfect room and free her mother to get married again. Her brother said, *There are chess masters who are able to see ahead move after move so that they know how the game will turn out. I wonder if there are life masters. If there are, I wouldn't want to be one. I wouldn't want to know how everything is going to turn out before it happens.*

She is getting ready to leave her room and she's thinking about how she's going to have to keep seeing things and feeling things and having new experiences all the time to be a good writer. *I wonder if that is how life is going to be!* She thinks with excitement. Then she leaves her room made of windows.
I have loved this book and kept it close for 30 years. Reading the ending for the last time, it occurred to me that the final message of this book and any book is the same: this happened; now it is over. Now you will have to move on.

I thought, this is the central point of everything about being alive. I should bring the book back home with me and type up these last pages, so I will always have them.

But I'm not a cheater.

I closed the book. I put it on the public shelf and zipped up my empty suitcase. I walked away.

24. ON DEPARTING FOR ANOTHER COUNTRY

I have accomplished what I set out to do: I filed two years of back taxes and now have the summer clear. I am canceling the trip to Ireland (for reasons). And now, there is nothing between me and writing. Other than: doubt, love, failure, warning and fear. Once I start I finish; I know that about myself. So I am being deliberate about starting. I know starting is right because I feel mournful and sad about leaving land. It's the kind of thing where I envision a harbormaster saying *may God save you* as I start the journey.

27. EVERYTHING ANNIE DILLARD SAID ABOUT DOSING COFFEE AND WRITING WAS RIGHT.

I've experienced two miracles of sleep in my life. The first in which I had gone to bed at 10 and had a dream that I was exploring this large castle that was just like boarding school, only big, big, bigger. This architect whom I was in love with was there—outside the castle we were kissing, and he was supposed to meet me inside. There were security guards and I remember they were apologizing for either not letting him in, or losing him. I was confident and happy. Don't worry, I told the guards, when he wants to find me, he will.

I woke up for the only time in my life naturally at 6 a.m., well rested and with my heart floating. The happy sun was doing its work and I walked to work with an uncharacteristic appetite for the day. The dream, I understood, was true. It was true that when my love wanted to find me, he would and that I was fine. I still remember that castle and the guards who were friendly men and what I really knew.

28. HAIR PART 1

The whole first part of my life, people asked about my hair. How I could be half black and have the hair I had?

29. HAIR

Letting my hair grow out from this blonde dye job feels like some sort of important gradual transformation back to me. The bleaching and cutting off of my hair feels like a separation—everything happened to another person. I stepped out from under my scalp and walked away. And it has been something to see brown hair surface and start taking over my head again.

I'm two people: the person who is confident being very formally dressed and made up. Who likes attention and handles it well.

The other person is the floppy slobby writer, who wears comfortable clothing and feels a bit shy. Who is unassuming, the "who me?" Diane Keaton type. I like both people. Both people have my own real hair.

30. THE BALL OF THE UNIVERSE

I went out to dinner with a friend and in the pink neon light of the restaurant sign and pleasant hubbub, I got one of those moments when companionship and a good meal whet the tumor of anxiety, causing it to grow slippery and release from my guts. Then for a few shimmering minutes I could see—it's all fine and it's all a miracle. Early evening in mid-spring in New York, I had walked a mile or so to the restaurant just to enjoy the day; my friend was telling old, comfortable jokes that still worked. The pop-eyed anxiety and sorrow was swimming like a wet ball in a pond, and as I spoke and ate I had the sense of being able to observe it and it being small.

31. THE WORST TIMES TO BE SINGLE ARE FRIDAY NIGHTS AND WEEKEND MORNINGS.

33. THE BIGGEST JOURNEY OF WOMEN IN THE FIRST WORLD

I know that men have their own struggles. I think that one lifelong journey of a woman in the United States is the struggle to feed herself. I remember stuffing myself to excess, and I remember when I realized I was profoundly sad and food was just a proxy. I also remember entering the strange and delightful world of eating until I recognized that I was just satisfied. This happened in college. I was astonished that food was so indifferent to me; instead of calling *eat me*, food was impersonally just sitting there—on plates, at the college bookstore, at receptions.

Around this time, Margaret Atwood came to campus. I stood in line for her to sign my book. Her book ended with a detailed description of a woman who had been starving herself going out to the grocery store and buying all the ingredients for a cake, baking it from scratch, decorating it as herself and presenting it to her selfish fiancé. He recoiled. The woman then gave it to her lover, who ate it. Duncan.

"Ms. Atwood," I said, "could I ask: what was the significance of Duncan eating the cake at the end?"

"Sometimes," she answered, "a cake is just a cake."

34. EXEGI MONUMENTUM AERE PERENNIUS

You realize that even after you die, you are still, present tense, the author of your book? "Jane Smith is the author of *Space Ship from Hell, Love on Mars,* and *The Party Blast.*" You don't say, she *was* the author, even after she's dead because death doesn't change anything about having written a book.

36. POSSIBLY

I've set myself up for loss. Possibly it's all my fault.

37. MY DAUGHTER

When I was younger I would get ready for Saturday night dates by listening to Garrison Keillor's "A Prairie Home Companion." While I was in a towel, eating, getting dressed, putting on make-up, he would run through his homey stories and folk music as I went through rituals in New York, where I had my very own midtown apartment, a single young woman in a *New Yorker* story. After I was done getting ready, and still listening to the radio, I would tidy up the apartment, and then, as a grand gesture of affection for myself, I would set out pajamas on the bed and fold the covers down. I knew I would arrive late and tipsy home in a cab, just like young pretty women with good jobs who are out on the town do. I told myself that someday I would have a daughter and I'd tell her about evenings as a young woman before I met her father, and when she was old enough, she'd do the same thing and think of me.

38. THE 'RENTS

Some people have a habit of finding surrogate parents; I'm the opposite. I am terrified of the verisimilitude of that life force. Only once it came as a comfort. I was in high school and it was after classes and I was wearing a kilt with a gold pin of which I was proud and a blue turtleneck and loafers with no socks. I had stopped by to see Mrs. Simms in the basement of Kellas and I was standing at a distance from her, near the bike stands, and she asked me a question and I said, "No, it's all a façade!" Only I actually cried "fa-kade" with a hard c. Mrs. Simms laughed in a pleased, astonished way and said, "It's fa-sad." The quality of her laughter I remember was unlike anything I'd ever experienced before; it was amused laughter that didn't make fun of me. Then a thought jumped into my head completely unbidden: *I have a mother.* I was entirely unprepared to see her that way, but the thought floated and beamed, light and pleasing in a way I never associated with love.

40. SADLY, NOTHING GOOD HAS EVER COME FROM MY ASKING A MAN ON A DATE.

41. I FLEW FIRST CLASS

I asked the flight attendant for blankets, which annoyed her. I asked her if we were flying over Lake Michigan and she haughtily said that she couldn't tell me because of 9/11 and security precautions, which caused everyone to glare at me (ten minutes later the captain got on the loudspeaker and said he'd like to point out that we were on the western side of Lake Michigan).

I do remember this: I was given a cup of coffee in an American Airlines china cup. The china was good, heavy and had painted in gold the American Airlines logo and a golden matching rim on the saucer and cup. The coffee was full-bodied and aromatic and the heavy cream made it rich; it was delicious.

43. FIREWORKS AT THE JCC BALCONY IN MILWAUKEE

I didn't watch. I was scared of the noise. I sat on my father's lap, hiding in his jacket. He had his arms around me.

46. THE WORST MOMENT OF MY LIFE, IF I HAD LET IT

I buried my high school biology teacher. No, I mean, I didn't bury him, like myself with a shovel. I went to his burial. He had been our hall associate. He and his wife. She wore cardigans and they had mid-Atlantic accents. You know, the kind where you sound like you are from England. They came to our teas and talked about their courtship at a country club in Newport, Rhode Island. She was the faculty wife who had driven me back when I had teeth pulled for braces. She had driven me back from the maxillary surgeon, after she had sat with me. She had. Not my mother. She had made it okay for me not to have a mother.

It did not occur to me not to go to his funeral. He had phoned a classmate when his wife died. We were in our thirties then. He wanted to talk. I was so surprised, the classmate said. Surely, she said, there must be someone with whom he was close, a friend. I didn't think that. Our teachers worked impossible hours for low pay and sacrificed friends and family life. It was too much; I knew it then. Only my way of knowing things…not dependable, private, at odds with reason. While desperation and loneliness in adults with family and connection frightened me, I believed it.

They wanted to be buried together, and she went first, years ago, and had been cremated and was in a box. And he had been cremated and was in a box. And we stood there and watched while his box, wooden, and hers, white and plaster, were handed out of wheelbarrows and lowered into the ground. Just as they were sitting at our hall tea. Just as she was telling us about her grandfather's desk with stock quotes scratched on it. They had the legs sawed off and used it as a coffee table. They sat next to each other at our tea, laughing, that clump of hair that forever boyishly flopped on his forehead. And there they were in square little boxes being lowered into the ground.

And I thought: this is it. If I let this in, if I really feel what is happening, this will be the worst moment of my life. It was clear that I needed to save them—we should save them. My junior year suitemate, Tina, stood next to me, crying bitterly. They had done so much for us and now we just stood here and watched this? We had to stop this. There was obviously some way to stop this and they were waiting for us to do it.

I pulled back. Tina was married and had young children at home. I wanted to meet a man too and kiss his bare shoulder and if I let this moment in, if I really accepted this as the realistic ending, I would not. I let myself attach to her crying and I pulled back.

47. THE TRAIN RIDES

There was a year when I worked for my boarding school, and I took the train from New York City to Albany frequently. I will always remember a summer ride when we paused before Poughkeepsie and a family was busy re-hitching their boat to the trailer in the golden sunset. They had spent a day on the Hudson. There was a little boy, and he looked about ten, with an orange life preserver, face in shadows, hair tall and stiff from wind. Sunlight winked off them, their boat, and this was silent as I watched from the stopped train. *The golden silence throbs*—a line from a forgotten poem from 1895. I stared at the Hudson, thrilled at the sight of an occasional egret, and pondered my romantic life and the romantic lives of all my roommates in boarding school. I knew I should have had a notebook open. About twenty of the best short stories I will never write were born and died on that afternoon train.

The trip up always meant being picked up by a beloved faculty member, now retired. It meant joining the world of every preppy novel and every keen and earnest hope I ever had, and every sense that I should be thoughtful and smart, and promising. There is such a wonderful quiet available around every human life: I basked in it during these special hours.

One thing I must relate that also occurred to me over and over was how different life would have been if my trip to school had been a simple train ride. I arrived on a plane from Wisconsin, on scholarship, poor and brave; dropped off at the airport to fend for myself. I flew hundreds of miles and it was the end of a part of my life, not a gliding continuation. I would not give that up now, the feeling of departing on a rocket ship to a new world. But what would my life have been if boarding school had been all of a piece?

48. IN WHICH I QUIT BALLET

Sometimes dance just finds the right body, and there is no terrible fight. Sometimes dance finds the right soul, a pure and obsessive one, in the wrong body: then the battle is on. Like the girl with the back acne and thick legs who was good but whose body was tight and bottom heavy. She trained herself to move and she was in demand as a performer.

Once freed from the academic requirements of school, this girl turned all of her drive on her body size. Her body was always going to seek thickness, but by God she lost so much weight her face didn't look the same. If you knew her face from before this weight loss, you would realize she was starving.

I could not write and dance. A dance class is 1.5 hours, and it probably takes an extra hour to 1.5 hours to travel to class, check in, get changed and warm up, then cool down and change again and go back home. You can't blow three hours of after-work hours and write. I had been fighting that battle for years.

I remember the class when I realized it was over. I had taken a class after work at the American Ballet Theater—it was fun right then because Mikhail Baryshnikov was taking a class and I could steal a glimpse on my way out. He was doing his own private barre as the class went on, which is common for older dancers. You know what your body needs and no one requires your obedience anymore. I wanted to stay but I knew if I was caught gawking, I'd be asked to leave. I let myself have one lingering glance and I made myself break away. Outside, it was a sunny warm day. I remember the strong summer sunset beaming into the windows as I walked by my office, where people were still toiling. New York: The City Where It Is Never Over. I knew that I wasn't going to be able to do anything as a writer if I was pushing myself to go to dance class three to five nights a week. And I was bored. I had peaked and I wasn't ever going to get any better. The teacher made us turn off the air-conditioning and the class sweltered to the point where I felt nauseated at times and I was sick of all the grandiosity, putting up with nutty teachers and *la reverence* for them. Walking to Union Square I felt both calm and disgruntled, shoved back into my work clothes for the train ride back to Brooklyn. That night I gave myself permission to stop taking class and see how it felt. A week became a month, and a month became another month.

During this time, I offered myself dance classes: *Would you like to go tonight?* I'd ask, packing my bag for the day or waking up on a week-end. *You can always go back,* I told myself. The answer came back as a polite, *No, thank you.* Eventually my friends noticed. I was so ferocious about it for a long time, I think they initially worried.

But I had writing to tackle in the way people had a family to raise. I turned to my writer's desk and didn't dwell on not dancing. I did not gain weight. I put on a few pounds a year later and I was amazed that it was not the crisis of cosmic maladjustment with which I had always regarded weight gain. I lost interest in watching dance, and then I actively did not want to see it. I think that was when I realized I had moved to retirement. I remembered Arthur Ashe saying once he had retired from tennis he didn't want to play anymore or go to matches. There was no pleasure in it for him.

50. ONCE

Now, ten years on from having made the decision to stop, I sometimes do like watching dance. I even went back to the Joyce Theater to see a couple of shows. They had all my old information, my address in midtown, from my subscription days. I can watch dance now without my knees aching in sympathy. And years of ballet gave me a tolerance of aches and pains and a rock-solid belief in my resilience that serve me well. My interest remains fleeting, though. I am not a benefactor, or a fan. I was a practitioner.

Husbandly Things

CAROLINE BELLE STEWART

THE MORE SHE EXPRESSES doubt about her husband, the more I fall in love with him. She tells me things he would not want me to know.

I have learned of his regrets and accidents, the swirls of too-thick hair in hidden places, the dust and residue around the house that only she sees.

He disappears up to his attic studio the way a falcon would, swift and mean. There, he writes alone by hand for hours. Then he swoops back down, unexpected, wanting sex. But she's asleep by then.

Of course she is conflicted, still in love and aware of his merits. I, too, am in love and aware of his merits, and so I let her doubt.

I did not try to be her friend. It is that way with me and wives. But I have given in, would like to be a better woman, united with her as I am in my doubt for my own husband.

Her husband spends more time apart from her now.

She asks husbandly things of me now.

I have removed spiders, millipedes and roaches from her drains and corners. I have braided her hair.

But as she and I sit on her porch beneath the orb-weaving spider, who unfastens its web each day and builds a new one each night, I do not tell her of the husbandly things her husband asks of me.

I have helped him move writing desks and bookcases, heavy and sharp-cornered, up his attic stairs.

I have taken him on long drives down secret dirt roads, roads my husband showed to me, leaving golden wakes of dust.

In red pen, in loops of cursive, letters endlessly admiring, I have marked his drafts of prose.

And in my car, in the woods, as small birds have flown near and broken his thoughts, I have heard him doubt his wife.

She has no need for books, plans her life by the planets and suns. Her worries spread about the house like vines, creeping up into his attic. From the doorway she accuses him of tinkering, as though his craft has no ends.

She talks through problems.

Always out loud. For she is not a writer, does not write.

And as I drive with him, flushing birds from thickets, he cannot know I think of him, alone behind my book at night, wishing he was with me, waiting for my husband to come to me.

He cannot know that I encourage her to leave him, under the premise that all men should be left.

I want to believe that if it were me in her important wifely role, I would not linger in his doorway. I would not interrupt or ask. I would be diligent and distant, out of sight.

And if I were in her place I'd be awake when he came down, my books piled up around me, the words I'd say to him only brief and only smart.

Then in the morning I'd be out of bed before him, locked up tight and writing somewhere.

Writing so hard I would hardly exist.

But I think of my own wifely impulse, gravitating towards my husband when he is most withdrawn, the things I say growing more urgent the more he backs away. How I talk across our distance. Talk and yell.

A writer wouldn't do such things, her husband says.

But a woman would.

I have been watching the spider on her porch grow all summer, planet-shaped and larger than the rings we wear. Dead center in a swaying web above her door, it is not quite a protector, not quite an intruder.

Each night, her husband passes beneath the web with wine, pretty bottles with feathers on the labels, to briefly drink with her before he goes upstairs. These gifts are one of his merits.

She cannot know the care I give to insects.

I trap them alive in her husband's wineglasses, and leave the glasses tipped in the grass outside.

Clients

EVAN REHILL

CHAUNCEY MALONE ARRIVED UNEXPECTED, singing through our cemetery gates. A terrycloth bathrobe flapped around his coveted Judas Priest t-shirt and knee-busted jeans. From the top of the hill we watched with eyes glazed from the joint passing between us. His first escape from the madhouse took half a year, the second eight weeks, and this last time he'd been locked up all summer and most of fall already.

The moonlit graves separated the quiet avenue in the distance from the woods at our backs. We had arrived through the trees, riding our bikes on a winding dirt path. Before Chauncey's surprise appearance the scene had stayed quiet except for one of us coughing smoke, another's laughter in response, or a car rushing by with the passengers holding those breaths, never turning their heads in our direction. A white-barked ash held its stripped arms out over us where we leaned against the frigid tombstones. It was easy in November to pretend we were shaking off the cold, because as a teenager you want to believe the dark is nothing to be afraid of. For a long time we can live that lie. But later we learn we were right. If the stars blew their fuses? And then darkness? Who knows what would come for us then?

The song in his throat was a medieval elegy. He discovered it in an a cappella music book that hadn't been taken out of our town library in a million years. Endless in verses, the scroll of lyrics spoke to him. Chauncey chanted the words in some minor key dirge down in his basement room on Roosevelt Turnpike, holding court before Anthony Giacombossi, Remy Slesinger, Warren Chlebek, and me.

Above the shuffling of our poker cards and banshee vocals from the cassettes in the boom box, we could hear the boots of Chauncey's stepfather creaking overhead and, late at night after our tapes played themselves out, the flick of a lighter as Chauncey's mom—*Maureen,* we called her—settled in with a cigarette at the kitchen table for the first in a series of sighs as her smoke drifted to the ceiling fan, spinning with the blades to get shot out once again, continuing to rise with gained momentum into the ventilation shaft; through the house's thin walls, drifting past the insulation, rusted pipes, loose wiring, spiders and their webs, the smoke would travel until it entered the attic room, lingering there, suspended over the sleeping bodies of the state's cast away retarded girls.

Beatrice, Anastasia, Rose, Claire, Janette—they were freshmen in the Special Ed program at our school. When they saw us in the halls they waved; we always looked the other way. Otherwise they became blurred faces behind the windows of a small yellow bus shuttling them to and from Maureen's. On those rides home after school they must have looked forward to dinner, where it wasn't Maureen's cooking that stirred them into a frenzy, but the attention from their permanent guest at the table: Chauncey's stepdad.

Everyone called him Lucky. His white eyebrows and blonde mustache made him an easy target in the WANTED posters of his past. At the collision shop his boss had a habit of saying he'd hire criminals but never trust them, and Lucky would slither under a smashed up Indian low rider, a spark plug gripped between his teeth. Once a month he unlocked his cabinet of illegal guns in the garage to polish the weapons that were now his souvenirs of a life he'd left behind. Every night he sat down at the head of the kitchen table in his moth-eaten undershirt, surrounded by the attic girls' beetle brows, crooked ears, wall-eyes, clawed cheeks, hung jaws.

After the dropped forks and spilt milk of their evening meal together, Lucky ran a comb through his mustache, lifting the tattoo of a serpent that curled around his forearm. Getting to his feet, he took his flannel shirt from where it hung on the back of his chair and filled its sleeves, fastening buttons with callused fingers (his hands were stained black with grease; not even the industrial soap he used could return them to pink) and said, *Who's in for repairs?* The girls shrieked, each struggling to raise her hand the highest. Wintertime meant a Thursday night ritual, when they would flock around the workshop in the garage as Lucky tinkered with his motorcycle. Lining the shelves, labelled coffee cans held nails, screws, washers, bolts, spark plugs. One unmarked can overflowed in crumpled dollar bills Lucky no longer spent on cigarettes—a fund he called his wishing well.

Three photographs tacked to the garage wall:

1) Maureen in the middle of a blizzard wearing dark sunglasses.

2) Stan Deridoorian—Lucky's best friend and former partner in crime—seated on a motorcycle in undershirt and jeans, arms

across his chest, looking away. (A month after this was taken, fleeing a flower store robbery Lucky had refused to go on, Stan lost control of his handlebars, broke through a guardrail, jack-knifed into a ditch he never came out of alive).

3) Lucky kneeling with the girls outside a movie theater with posters behind them for *Return Of the Jedi*. Beatrice and Claire grasp his hands. The others hug him. Lucky's mustache rises above his cheekbones in a smile as he yells something at the camera.

I knew from all the awful horror movies Chauncey had dragged me to that zombies did not return to the world singing. They came back for revenge. The low moaning notes rumbled through his voice as he ascended the hill, grappling for breath. Remy Slesinger spooked when an ash branch tapped his head. Balancing on the limb, a squirrel settled its glassy eyes on every one of us before it leapt to the ground and darted off down the slope, veering out of Chauncey's path. *'Twas a haunting between/Did smash up our dream/We'd now only glean/In the jagged-edged gleam/Of shards*, he chanted from a face obscured in shadows. I imagined phantom arms reaching out of the ground to drag him under. One blink and he was gone. I rubbed my eyes and he was back. Shaking my head at Anthony Giacombossi I said, *I'm seeing things.*

Anthony stared down, following the path of his leather jacket's zipper to where it disappeared over the bulge of his stomach. *I'm scared*, he said, taking a Jawbreaker from a pocket and popping it from the wrapper into his mouth. Warren Chlebek stabbed the joint out on a gravestone and whispered, *Play dead.*

I'd be pushing up dandelions by now if I hadn't buried the habit! Lucky yelled to Maureen through the door that separated the garage and the kitchen. *But I won't become one of those people who preaches.* Maureen exhaled over her crossword puzzle. She smoked alone after he quit. His forsaken Winstons had become her brand, and she lit one after another while he worked on his motorcycle. Maureen listened to him talking to the girls through the shut door and pictured him on his knees beside the engine, pointing a screwdriver into the air. She heard him ask, *Who wants a job? Lucky needs a beer.* When the door flung open, Maureen did not turn around to see the clumsy bodies scrambling to the refrigerator before hurrying back to him, each bringing a can. With her back to the closing door, she stared at the clue under her pen (DOWN 7: Person or thing past saving) then the empty boxes waiting to be filled. 5 letters. The word was on the tip of her tongue when she heard Lucky pop the tab of a beer, and imagined him drinking from the can. She closed her eyes on the blurring newspaper and saw Lucky watching thick flakes fall past the high windows lining the garage door; he licked foam from his blonde mustache, and she tasted snow.

Through the woods came a blast of wind to our backs. We braced ourselves. Fallen leaves brushed past, chased by a white plastic bag that took flight down the hill, flying over Chauncey's approaching figure. Clouds crept in, extinguishing the moon. In his natural range—the middle register—he sang now about goblins and saints, witches and angels, the specters of this world and the next who deliver prophecy. No wonder the spine of that music book hadn't been cracked in so long. Who wanted to hear songs like this? Chauncey crooned, snapping his neck as he threw back his head.

The date he picked wasn't a mistake. My sixteenth birthday hadn't felt any different from all the others. The same cards from my aunts had come along with the same phone calls from my two remaining grandparents, followed by the same sit-down with my mom where she told me the same story of my birth that always began, *You almost killed me.* At home a Carvel cake would be in the freezer, and a box of candles would yawn beside a note that said to rouse my parents when I got home from the library. They'd have had my head examined if they knew where I spent most of my nights. In the graveyard we had the vantage point, overlooking the whole town. A patrol car's misery lights could be spotted with plenty of time to make a getaway. Not that any of us felt important enough to get chased after, except for Chauncey, who demanded it, becoming our undisputed leader by default.

Did he mean the song as a present to me? If so, it proved a bad one. On November 13th—nine days after this night—Chauncey Malone would turn eighteen. Almost two years before that, on *his* sweet sixteen, I rode for hours in the passenger seat beside him in his jeep, heading into upstate New York to visit his real father, Patrick "Bones" Malone, whom Chauncey hadn't seen for six years, since Bones chased him out a second story window, a fall that broke both Chauncey's arms and got him sent down to live with Maureen in Jersey. Upstate there are more woods than any place, and in autumn the trees burn reds and oranges for miles along the single-lane roads. Insects splattered against the windshield as we wound the tight curves. I prayed we wouldn't run out of gas while Chauncey talked: *I had to call my dad this morning and REMIND him it's my birthday.* He pushed in the car lighter (which had never and would never work), tucking a cigarette between his lips. *Yours is November 7th,* he said. His hand in the air between us mimed a pistol, the hammer of his thumb dropping, barrel of the index finger pointed toward the roof. *See, I know that,* he said. *I'll ALWAYS know that.*

> *My birthday's the 4th.*

He pulled the car lighter from the dash and stared at its rusted spiral.

There were no streamers, no presents, no cake. The three of us sat around Bones' kitchenette with instant coffee while Bones strummed an out of tune acoustic guitar. The bathroom door opened to a girl in food-stained sweatpants who could have walked right out of Maureen's attic. Her eyes looked too close together in a massive head. The thermal arms of her shirt had to be pushed above the elbows to free her hands, which she stood wringing in the doorway.

> *That's Candace,* Bones said.

Chauncey turned to her and said, *Today's my birthday.*

She smiled, revealing the whitest, straightest teeth I had ever seen. My own were growing in on top of one another. Bones leaned the guitar face-first against the wall. *Wasn't for the clients we'd be starving up here,* he said. *Union's been on strike since Labor Day.*

The work Lucky did all winter geared up for spring, when he could return to his night rides. On *those* evenings Maureen missed the deep freeze, the blizzards, the haled backstreets and iced traffic lights that kept everyone indoors. But once the weather shifted, Lucky opened the garage door to the driveway, corralling the girls into lawn chairs at the threshold as he wheeled out his Triumph.

He gave them gloves, earplugs, protective glasses, a child's helmet. As the motorcycle revved he'd bungee-cord the first sputtering passenger to his body then call over his shoulder, *Rosy don't do like last time and choke on the wind so I have to pull over and carry you home again. When your mouth fills up with air, press it into the back of my shirt and breathe through the nose, understand?*

Storming through the kitchen door into the garage, Maureen jabbed the air with her cigarette and said, *The clients don't have any business on that motorcycle!* The girls puckered shut their eyes as Maureen passed them and stepped onto the driveway, smoke pouring out her nostrils. *It's their time for bed.*

Lucky said, *The girls can't stay cooped up in that attic.*

What if the state people…what if they…Lucky, huh? What if I lose those monthly checks from the state, and then I lose the mortgage on this house, and then we have no place to live, then what do we do? Tell me, what do we do then?

The girls want to fly, he said, knuckles grazing her cheek until she shook him off. Behind him, Rose lipped his shoulder, a trail of drool leaking from her lopsided grin as Lucky cleared the kickstand with a boot, tearing into the night. In the basement, we could hear the motorcycle roaring up Roosevelt Turnpike. I said to Chauncey, *Where's he take them, anyway?*

He lit a joint and inhaled, counting off with his fingers one, two, three, four and a half before the smoke danced out of his lungs. *He rides out along Marlingale Avenue and back,* he said. *Takes about five minutes but they think they've been gone a week.*

Outside the garage in her frayed bathrobe, Maureen crossed her arms under her breasts. You could tell she'd been a real knockout once, with that red hair and porcelain skin. When she'd married Lucky she told him no more kids; she was through with all that. But as the motorcycle reappeared in the driveway her frown lifted into a smirk, and her eyes lit up when applause erupted from the folding chairs.

Where they came from none of us knew. Their mothers sent coloring books, Easter candy, makeup kits, glossy magazines, knickknacks from tropical islands—things Maureen had to keep from them. *What are the clients going to do with a makeup kit?* Maureen said. *Make a filthy mess out of the attic, that's what. I can't give them candy, are you kidding me? I'll have them bouncing off the walls they're already bouncing off. Here, you kids eat it, you, all of you look stoned out of your minds. Have any of you eaten anything today?*

The parents never visited, but the State people did, and those days Maureen locked us out of the house, yelling through the screen door, *Stiffs coming today, boys!*

Calendars full of X's—we've flipped through them, trying to pin-point when everything went wrong. By the fifth month Chauncey had become someone who smashed windows with a fist. The seventh month he couldn't pass a fire alarm without pulling it. During the tenth month he assembled a bomb in the park out of a tin can, broken glass, and gunpowder, which exploded before he could finish building it. He walked home, bleeding, his face and arms black, into the kitchen where Maureen finished wiping one of the clients' mouths with a paper towel, turning to him, unshocked. *What the devil happened to you?* she said. He poured himself a glass of water, blood on his hands, in the sink, a bright red streak across the glass he was about to drink from. *I blew up*, he said. Weeknights of the eleventh month he went out to the tracks alone, where he could throw Molotov cocktails at passing trains. On the twelfth month he would hold up a convenience store with a toy gun, two days before his 17th birthday. On this Sunday night the place looked empty. A security camera recorded the entire episode:

The woman working the counter has frosted hair and chipped nail polish. The last thing she ever imagined doing on a Sunday night in her forties was working at the 7-11 in our town. Chauncey Malone enters dressed in black. The woman reads a tabloid magazine at the counter, which she looks up from as Malone approaches the register and laughs, which we can see but not hear. He falls to his knees, disappearing from the camera. The woman closes her magazine and watches Chauncey perform what we have speculated is a backwards somersault. Landing on his feet, he reappears on the screen, wild-eyed. He twirls a realistic-looking pistol, cowboy-style, on one finger, pointing with his free hand at the cigarette racks over her head. Does the woman on the screen recognize Chauncey Malone? We don't know. But she does not step back or raise her hands above her head. Instead she gives him a long, hard look—a stare like a slap that says: *I have already wasted my life on men like the one you will become, and you don't scare me, not at all.* Chauncey lowers his head as she throws a pack of Marlboroughs to the counter, flicking a matchbook behind. He pauses with a parted mouth he decides to shut, jamming the cap gun into the waistline of his jeans before snatching up the cigarettes to tap the pack against his leather wristband. Walking through the glass doors, he exits the video. With her palms flat on the counter the woman stares after him, then picks up the phone. We do not see Chauncey Malone sit down on the curb outside, although the woman does. Chauncey listening to the sound of his stolen cigarette as it burns out between his fingers, waiting. We watch the woman on the video watching him. She is our witness. She sees Chauncey flick the cigarette away as the lights of a police car approach: red, blue then blackness again. No sirens. Chauncey lights a match from the book and holds it before his eyes. Beyond the flame the flashing lights, our town, the whole world disappears.

The thirteenth month they sent him away.

When Chauncey forgot to take out the trash a second week in a row, Lucky ripped open the basement door and shouted from the top of the stairs, *You make a mess, you live with it!* A black bag landed at the bottom step with a thud. Then another came rolling down, leaking a trail of grease. The four of us stood, our red eyes widening. Chauncey kept guard at the sheet that was his bedroom door. Lucky called, *A loser—that's you. LOSER!* before the door slammed, shaking the walls. The only light came from a lava lamp Anthony Giacombossi found on a curb during Big Trash Night. He had carried the lava lamp down the basement stairs cradled in his doughy arms, plugging it in on his hands and knees. *Sorry,* he'd said. *This may take a few minutes to warm up. Sorry.* From a pocket he pulled loose a Twizzler whip and devoured it with his eyes closed. Remy Slesinger, embracing the boom box to his chest, pressed STOP then REWIND as he said, *You don't have to apologize for every—*

I'm sorry, Anthony said.

The lava lamp was tacky, ridiculous, and all of us loved and wanted to own it. So it went to Chauncey's, where we spent the most time together indoors. Already we had brought things of our own to the room. Remy's Iron Maiden cassettes shared the same space with Warren's Heavy Metal comic books. The boom box was mine. Now Anthony's offering completed the pact. Plumes of fog swirled in a purple storm, pin-wheeling a tornado of smoke against the glass to mesmerize us all.

That's not me, Chauncey spoke out from the silence that had descended. *It isn't. You guys think I'm a loser?* Remy Slesinger pressed PLAY on the boom box, and a slaying guitar solo lifted our spirits. Remy could not stand at full height in the basement room. To be over six and a half feet tall at fifteen, his parents worried he would end up a giant. He rolled his shoulders forward, even sitting down. Blonde ringlets framed his face and fell over his chest. *Why listen to anything your jerk-off stepfather says?* he asked. Beside the lava lamp Warren Chlebek sat drawing skulls on his forearm with a ballpoint pen. His thin mane was tied into a ponytail. He hated Remy's hair and height, knowing he himself would be bald before twenty five—a tradition among men in his family—and he would always be five inches shorter than he thought was fair. He said, *Lucky's the loser. That retard belongs in the attic anyway.* A big round of laughter erupted, followed by a sudden hush.

Turn up the music, I said.

Chauncey stood and said, *Turn it up alright,* staring at the basement's low ceiling. *Wake the dead.* He walked to me in the corner, throwing an open hand I met, our palms smacking together. Then he cradled his arms around Anthony's gaining weight and hugged, hoisting the boy off his feet. Anthony struggled as Chauncey yelled, *I may be half-crazy but at least I'm alive!*

Somewhere in the haze of those fourth, fifth, sixth, seventh months of trouble, we sat in the school cafeteria above our gray lumps of food on neon orange trays, drinking soda from paper cups without straws or lids. Chauncey's hair hung to his shoulders. A fake diamond earring pierced his left lobe. Holding the cup, his hands were sheathed in gun-metal-gray, fingerless gloves. He sucked up ice and spit it back into the cup, one cube flying from his lips towards the face of Steve Fretano, a hulking presence passing by, heading for a table near the windows where other football players in Polo shirts laughed with blonde girls wearing push-up bras and Jordache jeans. The ice cube whizzed by Fretano's profile, just missing his nose. His eyes opened wide, one hand leaving his own cafeteria tray to point a finger at Chauncey. *Go bang your mother, Malone*, he said. Chauncey's leap across the cafeteria table looked anything but graceful. Like a doomed superhero, he punched Fretano in the lips with a fist still clutching the paper cup. Ice cubes spilled to the floor. Fretano, although twice Chauncey's size, looked terrified. Because you never know what somebody who gets called a lunatic might do in the name of his mom's honor, like grasping your ears and rolling you across tables with him as kids finishing last minute math homework gasp and foods go flying, Chauncey still turning with you, off the table, where you land on your back, smack against the cold floor, and spinning on, the way as a kid you descended those long hills until the world turned too fast, but Chauncey with you now, above then below and on top again as you roll past the feet of the five girls from Maureen's attic who sit at an end table, girls who stand, dragging untied shoelaces with them, swooning when they recognize Malone. He pulls you to your feet, taking you in his arms as though about to dance, and slams you both into the concrete wall. It all lasts until two gym teachers enter the cafeteria blowing whistles to pull him off you, Chauncey still spitting in your face.

Sitting in the principal's office half an hour later with his clothes full of ketchup, milk, mayonnaise, sauerkraut, grease stains, Chauncey appeared as if ready for a talk show, himself the guest of honor with one leg crossing another and his fingers laced together over a kneecap. The rest of us waited outside, watching and listening through the left-open door. The Principal, a bachelor who wore funereal suits with loud ties, shook his head behind the desk that was too large for him. *Tell me, Mr. Malone, why are you sitting in that seat?* he said. *Did I not tell you last week I didn't want to see you in here again? Am I dreaming, Mr. Malone? Are you a ghost?*

The madhouse would keep him out of jail, they said, although it wouldn't, not once he'd slipped off for good. Maybe they figured: if he *is* insane then he's going to the right place. And if he isn't, he'll come back. The problem was he *did* come back, acting crazier than ever.

On the day of his first return I sat in my room thumbing through an issue of Playboy I'd found in the woods. Water damage to the pages meant I had to peel them apart. The long strands of my brown hair, so greasy it turned black, kept falling into my face. Just as I was prying loose the folds of Miss April 1984, an emerald field with a Centerfold's doe legs appearing before my eyes, my mother yelled out my name from the bottom of the stairs. Dropping the magazine and kicking it under the bed, my face blushed and erection died. *I'm doing my Biology homework!* I yelled, cracking open the door.

Malone on the phone, she sing-songed back. Her shoes squeaked off toward the sound of water running in the kitchen sink. Tearing down the stairs, I rushed to the receiver.

You're out, I said.

I'm back. His words got swallowed in a garble of static.

Back where?

In the tomb, he said. The earpiece crackled. *Reception's hell down here on the cordless.*

You're fading out.

My mother hummed over the faucet, washing last night's dishes.

The graveyard, his voice said from far off. *Fifteen minutes.*

Burial grounds turn a different place in the daylight, when there's nowhere to hide. I strolled the aisles of headstones—*Saracci, O'Cullen, Valagopolous, Mazza, Daniels, Zarokovsky, Garmo, Erikson, Shambelon*—until I came to an empty hole. At its side stood a mountain of dirt with an abandoned shovel jabbed in. Over the edge? Only blackness. Lowering myself beside the rim, I smoked half the joint I'd rolled to celebrate Chauncey's release and, angry at him two hours later for never showing up, I finished the rest and spat into the grave, looking over both shoulders as I pedalled off.

We have since theorized that the phone call to me came after he'd escaped, gone home, and been trapped—when he knew there was no secret passageway to corkscrew him from his fate. Following this thread, it's easy to imagine Lucky entering the kitchen, surprised to hear Chauncey downstairs. This is the part we don't like to think about, but has to be true: Lucky turning the skeleton key on the lock of the basement door to seal Chauncey inside. With

Chauncey on the phone below him, Lucky rode his motorcycle to the police station, five minutes away. When Lucky approached the front desk, a man in uniform asked, *What's your trouble?* Lucky sneezed. This happened when he got nervous. A shotgun blast—*Wah-chooo!* A glaze settled over his eyes. Under his boots, the floor shifted. *Wah-choo…wah-choo!* He'd never been inside a police station without handcuffs on. Gripping his nose, he held his breath before exhaling: *A loon's trapped in my basement.*

That was in May. The police came and dragged him back to the madhouse, but he broke out again by the end of June. At that time I was down the shore with my family. A tradition. All the uncles and all the aunts and all the cousins got together in the big house the adults rented every year, which would be overflowing at the finish of those two weeks with sand, flip flops, half-eaten cheese sandwiches, soggy towels, a million cigarettes, after-hours laughter, off-key warbling, arguments, empty bottles. I cloaked myself in black shorts and t-shirts, spending most of my time in the arcade (a cave full of smoke and neon lights) obsessed with Donkey Kong and Q-Bert. Sometimes I'd put on my mirrored sunglasses to walk the boardwalk among older boys with sunlight reflecting off the tin badges pinned to their wet swimming trunks. They whistled at girls who were probably my age but looking much older in their bikinis and summer tans. Afternoons, swimming in the cold ocean, I heard the white-nosed lifeguard from his tower of a wooden chair blowing a whistle, screaming at someone to come back. There wasn't a jelly-fish or hypodermic needle epidemic that year. One happened earlier—waves of them, jellyfish everywhere; my mother cursed the sea, wept in the sand, red sting marks covering her arms, legs, the palms of her hands. The other would come later. After hundreds of needles washed up along the Jersey shoreline, we stayed away for years. My father refused to ever swim in the ocean again, a decision he would later admit had broken his heart. On the beach at night I smoked grass with other loner kids. They, like me, were just visiting. When we exhaled over the sand dunes, listening to the sound of crashing surf, we could almost forget fall and the lives we would return to.

Chauncey Malone woke Anthony by shouting his name in the Giacombossi's front yard. His voice had woven into Anthony's dream. Anthony opened his eyes, happy, then scared. Chauncey was both in his dream and outside his window. Anthony wanted to go back to the dream. A voice, his name. *Anthony! Anthony!* He did not go to the window. The blinds remained closed, but Anthony, lying on his back, breathing through his nose, could picture the neighbors already mowing their lawns, some retrieving newspapers from doorsteps as they arrived back from trips to Main Street with brown bags full of hot bagels or pink boxes stuffed with donuts. Before he could imagine biting into a powdered jelly himself, he saw the neighbors turning to stare at his house, his window, as Chauncey yelled, *Anthony! I'm outside! Come to the window! It's me!* Anthony rolled onto his stomach and buried his face in a pillow until the dream scattered, and the voice went away.

Chauncey walked to Remy Slesinger's house, which looked tiny when considering the boy's unstoppable height. Calling Remy's name, Chauncey stomped through the flowerbeds. The Slesingers (people of average size) were en route to Maine, taking Remy to basketball camp. Mr. Slesinger had had it with his tall shadow of a son, *the gloom stooping over you at fifteen years old! It's summer,* he said. *This is fun I'm talking about. You'll love camp. Remy Slesinger did not love camp.* Humiliated in bright basketball jerseys and gym shorts, even in the middle of nowhere Maine, he stood out among kids intimidated by his height, his golden curls, his acne-scarred shoulders. Walk to the basket; watch for the ball. Even there, with his enormous hands waiting, he looked tragic. Remy Slesinger never touched another basketball after that summer. He kept growing and his parents continued shaking their heads. Later, none of them saw the footprints Chauncey Malone left over the chrysanthemums, where he had pressed his face to the Slesingers' living room window. He curled a fist, half-threw it then bit his knuckles, heading to Warren's.

When he got there he pulled clumps of grass out of the manicured lawn. A neighbor, hidden behind a curtain, dialled the authorities. Chauncey's voice, hoarse by then, coughed out Warren's name. *Kleb-ek! Kleb-ek!* With soiled hands he unscrewed the Chlebek's garden hose from the sprinkler and sprayed Warren's bedroom window. Warren raised the blinds and stood behind the spray with his hands to the glass as the police cruiser arrived. Later, Warren would tell us,

I almost didn't recognize him. They cut off all his hair.

Another time, during a party at his house when Maureen and Lucky were away, Chauncey picked the lock to the gun cabinet. In the kitchen we sat drinking whiskey on the rocks, betting cigarettes on our game of blackjack. Beside a pyramid of Camels, Remy Slesinger fanned the cards one-handed and said, *You're in or you're out. Last chances.* Smoke curtained the air while the stereo blared a Van Halen LP in the living room. Don't ask me where the clients were that night. I don't remember. I'll never forget Chauncey's stepsister Ashley showing up. Ashley at twenty-two years old, an age we couldn't even imagine; Ashley who sold grass grown somewhere upstate with her prison guard boyfriend; Ashley who always wore miniskirts, even in winter, when she accessorized with leg warmers; Ashley chain-smoking Parliaments in Maureen's bedroom; plastic bags lined with fresh green across the baby-blue pillowcases. A secret knock got you inside the room to Ashley crossing her legs on the edge of the bed, her tight black sweater crushing all our lungs. We emptied our wallets with haste to feel her fingertips brushing our own as she passed over the bags, taking our cash and tucking it away inside her bra. We lingered there, hands in pockets. We could not stand to watch her waving goodbye as she pulled a purse strap over her shoulder and walked out the front door to her rusted emerald Camaro. We wanted to yell, *Wait! Take us with you!* But she was already gone. I still wished she wasn't, hoping she'd let me ride shotgun as Chauncey handed me a pistol at the kitchen table. Kids poured in the front door—faces from the halls. In a town our size, a party didn't mean you waited for an invitation; you heard about one and you went. Beside me, Warren Chlebek said, *David Lee Roth is such a fag* as he folded his cards. The music rose from the living room until the kitchen table vibrated the half-empty cups, rolling papers, plastic motel ashtrays, stolen lighters, a bag of Doritos, a National Enquirer. I was not in the kitchen hearing Alex Van Halen's double-kick drums thunder through the house but listening to the same song from the cassette deck of Ashley's Camaro. I saw her twisting the volume knob all the way up as she shifted into fifth gear, cut the headlights, and we were gone when I raised my hand and pointed

Evan Rehill

the gun at Jessica Rosenthal.

Why Jessica Rosenthal? The richest girl in town? I didn't even know her. She wore red lipstick, a white t-shirt with a black bra, acid-wash jeans; her blonde, feathered hair looked soft at her narrow shoulders, and her long-fingered, pretty hands worked on a Rubik's cube across the table. Why her? It could have been anyone. She didn't look up, not even when Chauncey smacked me in the face and took the gun out of my hand.

The foundations of our houses had sunk in the deep valley. I could see this from the graveyard when the cloud cover rolled off and the moon reappeared in slivers. Then the streets caught the glare and shimmered, snaking our direction until the rust of the cemetery gates looked as clear as the cracked-up path that led into the tall grass, where all up the line the glowing headstones had become the color of polished bone. Shouldering free of his bathrobe, Chauncey's ragged clothes swung loose over his chiselled frame. His face rose to the moon's spotlight, illuminated. A buzzed skull. Those sunken eyes. Like a real maniac now, he held that look of the departed, the fallen, the missing, the already gone. When his voice went falsetto the song cracked but continued in broken notes forming a soundtrack for the earth to spit coffins into the sky, a scene fit only for Chauncey Malone, the star of what this had become: the worst horror movie ever—a musical!

No one sang in the freezing morgue of our town's Shop Rite. Ruined men with scarves noosed around their throats ran the butcher counter, sighing as they ripped wax paper from huge spools. They never made eye contact, too busy watching the big clock at the wall, not time seeming to pass between the fish and the pork chops and the ground beef and the cold cuts. The women stocking the aisles wore fake lashes over black eyes. They lived out by the tracks and already looked ten years older than they could have been. Blue-lipped from the temperature nobody could figure out how to control, they cocooned themselves under layers of snowflake sweaters. Their favorite thing to do was huddle in the employee lounge upstairs—an airless room boxed in with wood panelling—and chain smoke. They would do this until a manager wearing a ski mask came and found them, demanding they all get back to work.

Chauncey, earmuffed, manned the checkout register five nights a week. He always had his nametag on upside down. The name printed on it was wrong anyway. Everyone there called him Charlie. The Halloween he worked at Shop Rite, they had an employee contest for best costume. Fifty dollars, cash. We stopped by to see him that night, clutching bags full of candy we'd earned by throwing sheets over our heads and walking from house to house with empty pillowcases. Chauncey's powdered face held a trickle of fake blood running lip to jaw line. In his mouth a set of plastic fangs clenched an unlit cigarette as he jumped through the automatic doors. *I won!* he said. *I'm a winner!* his cape flapping in the wind.

That money went toward his prized possession—the reject jeep. The jeep came with a snap-on canvas roof full of rips and tears. The seat belts were a joke; they wouldn't have protected anybody from anything. The car's gas gauge didn't work, and how many times did I have to help push that piece of garbage back to Maureen's? The jeep would die for good out on Marlingale Avenue half a year later. I stood at the side of the road as he destroyed the vehicle with a crowbar. First went the headlights and taillights, followed by the windshield. Glass cascaded over the asphalt. The canvas roof fell away where he slashed it free. Then he dented the hood, the doors, the fenders, and wailed on the bumper until it crashed to the ground. Last went all three rear view mirrors. *Seven years,* I said each time.

Undertakers must go on vacation come October, because the weeds grew as high as the wild blades in the cemetery. Knotted vines climbed out of the soil to strangle the headstones. Maintaining his lead, Chauncey trudged uphill, keening now, *Darkest light/Unholy night/ Tangled frights/And no flight of sleep/Exhumed in the deep,* as the automatic sprinkler system came to life, arcing jets over the graves he crossed.

Warren Chlebek said, *Here comes the client.*

Shut up, I said.

Remy Slesinger bent his knees, jabbing a finger into Warren's small chest. *You're a real bastard, Chlebek,* he said. *You know that?* Raising two middle fingers, Warren yelled, *I was just kidding, you ogre!* Then he dropped his hands and turned. Jesus, Anthony, he said, *why are you crying?* With his damp lashes batting and his blurred vision still focused on Chauncey's advancing face, a spasm shuddered through Anthony's plump body then caught in his throat, so he gagged before spitting out the words, *I'm just so sorry.*

It had already happened by the time I knew it was over. Biking the long way home from the graveyard no-handed, I kept to the backstreets lined in piles of dead leaves, tearing into one heap after another, feet in the air, leaving a mess in my wake. Somewhere a fireplace blazed; its chimney smoke curled into my nostrils, releasing the after-burn image of Chauncey as he had climbed the final slant of the cemetery's hill, his lips in a jagged smile that made me look away. I took a left onto Main Street to glide through the only traffic light, past the already-closed pizza place, the Five and Dime, the Italian deli, the bakery, the magic shop, the single screen movie theater I'd been fired from for refusing to cut my hair. His singing hushed when I turned my back on him, and it wasn't until riding off on the dirt path into the woods, never looking back, that I heard the voices calling after me, his loudest of all. The spokes of my bike tires rattled over the train tracks, where the No Name Bar's window held the shadows of arms wrestling under wreaths of smoke. In my fogged head, I fast-forwarded myself home, where I would enter through the kitchen and climb the stairs to my room. Behind me I would close the door that always screeched from its unoiled hinge. This sound would jerk my father awake downstairs in front of the television, where he would reach for the remote control, pressing buttons. My mother, an insomniac, propped up in bed with a scotch in one hand and a book in the other, would hear the noise and spill her drink over the sheets, then pick up the empty glass, holding it to an ear. The wind was all I could hear now and the only thing left to feel as it flailed my hair into a whirlwind of strands whipping my chin and cheekbones. I pedaled the home stretch to my driveway and ascended to the side of the house, dumping the bike on top of the coiled garden hose.

For Chauncey Malone it would always be trouble: sent to the madhouse again, his voice unanswered again, the police again, locked up again, a life full of train-smashed pennies again, again, again, again, again. A year later we already thought of him as the one who got away, because his next escape would be to New York City, where the state of New Jersey could no longer touch him. We would not know then (how could we? But we would, we would) that he would fall in with criminals, drug addicts, mad and half-mad men, that Chauncey would die early this morning on his twenty-first birthday in a rat-trap apartment among people who were not his friends. Even in solitaire there are double-dealings—cards we'd sooner hide or bury, but we're forced to look, and here's the most crooked hand of all: it should have been him who aimed that revolver on Jessica Rosenthal, but it wasn't. It was me.

Evan Rehill

Rachel in Her Swimsuit

BUD SMITH

on my way to prison
in a gray bus with
NO CHANCE
stenciled on it
my hands shackled together
and fixed to a bolt in the floor
I'm facing a sentence, 75 to life
just up the muddy road
I think in the dream, I've killed
some other dreamer
there's never a feeling like
"I've been framed" or anything
all I have is guilt for my crime
the guard on the other side
of the metal gatew
sits with shotgun on his lap
dozing off, and the other inmates
are wide eyed with dull sorrow
but I always feel like I am
the only one dreaming
we bounce down the muddy road
and the driver gleefully says
"Half way there, fuckers!"
the shotgun guard snores
a man behind me begins to weep
and I set my head against
the sweaty window and almost cry too
but then, outside the window

I see my wife, Rachel, in her swimsuit
and I feel fine, she's waving to me
from the edge of the blue spruce pines
she puts a blowgun to her lips
firing a series of darts
that pop each of the tires of the bus
we skid to a hard stop
and the driver and the guard
get out to look
more darts get them in the neck
they collapse in the mud
and everyone on the bus cheers
as Rachel takes the guard's keys
and comes back on the bus
to free, only me.

This is the Way Things Are Now

KATE DOYLE

1. CATHERINE AND HELEN: In high school, they would sleep over in the same bed on the weekends. Catherine would comment on Helen's sleep-talking in the mornings, and Helen would cover her ears and say, Don't tell me I don't want to know. Now, Catherine has a boyfriend she more or less lives with, and she is saying things like, Thank you for coming for the weekend, Helen, and here is your air mattress on the living room floor.

2. CHRISTMAS, 2014: Every year, this one no exception, their parents give Helen and Evan and Grace each a tree ornament meant to commemorate some life experience in the last year. What will mine be this year, says Helen, Congratulations you've had a meltdown? Evan suggests, Congratulations you work at a coffee shop, as a possible alternative.

3. Early in her meltdown, in a weirdly warm part of November, Helen calls Catherine from Washington Square Park, on a day when it has just stopped raining. She stands oriented to Fifth Avenue with her back to the fountain, at the edge of a puddle, looking down into her reflection which spreads out in a murky wobble. She apologizes. Catherine is glad to hear from her. Catherine appreciates her saying she's sorry for being a shitty, selfish friend; sorry for hating her best friend's boyfriend for no reason other than liking how it feels to have an opinion. Please also tell Alexander I'm sorry, Helen says, Please tell him I'm sure he's actually a nice person.

4. Alexander and Catherine already know that if they have children, they will not raise them in the suburbs. And Helen really hates it, lately, the way she can so readily co-opt facts about other people for her own self-deprecation—e.g. My best friend Catherine lived much of her childhood in Prague; for comparison, I grew up entirely in fucking Westchester—as if this were the whole point of Catherine's life, to stand in contrast. Nevertheless the fact remains: Helen really has no idea where she will raise her children, if she ever has them. She may not even want them.

5. CATHERINE, STANDING IN CONTRAST, SEEMS POSSESSED OF A STRIKING CERTAINTY WITH REGARDS TO HER THEORETICAL CHILDREN, ESPECIALLY FOR SOMEONE WHO USED TO SAY IN HIGH SCHOOL: I mostly just hope I have many, many affairs.

6. FOR COMPARISON: Catherine says, age fifteen and twirling the spoon around her coffee mug, In at least one of them, I'll throw a glass of water in his face, and that will be it, the end, I'll be gone. Helen makes an expression to suggest that this sounds silly. Catherine looks out the window and adds, I think I'd also like one to happen somewhere on the Mediterranean Sea.

7. In Westchester, Rye to be exact, there are sprinklers on timers on the athletic fields behind the public high school. It is Catherine who suggests they run through them, on a night in May when they are 17, and it is Catherine who wants to do it again seven years later. It is Helen who says from the passenger seat, seven years later, No way definitely not, because this is the first time they have seen each other in more than six months, and Catherine in the car has just said the thing about wanting to have eventual babies with Alexander, and Helen is not at all interested in acting out some pretense of frolic on a football field at night. Anyway, then it starts to rain.

8. What Helen's mother says about her: You were always very set in your ways.

9. What Helen's mother says about Evan: Why does it matter that we always said Evan was a better actor than you were? Couldn't we let him have one thing to be better at?

10. Evan and Grace and Helen's tree ornaments, respectively: The Eiffel Tower for studying abroad; a squash racquet, self-explanatory; and a paintbrush for taking that one extension school course at The New School last spring.

11. Catherine's bed, in high school, is worn and beautiful like an old

cloth doll. Her sheets have a pattern of blanched pink vines, and she keeps black and white postcards taped to her wall. When she shuts off the lamp, the light through the window from the house next door falls over both Catherine and Helen's long hair on their pillows. In the mornings, they eat toast in Catherine's bed.

12. On a napkin during a slow day at Caffeine in December: Helen writes, the tension between the past and the present will ruin you. Then she throws it away, because how prosaic. She doesn't know what else to do, so she cleans the espresso machine.

13. ON THE WAY HOME FROM CAFFEINE: She always cries. This is a main feature of the meltdown she's had, is having, along with this bombed-out sensation in her chest all the time.

14. I am a very bad person, she says. (You're being far too hard on yourself, says her father.)

15. While the Gilmore Girls are fighting on television: Helen says, Grace, I'm sorry I have been a horrible, aloof sister. It is Grace's first night back and they are watching Netflix with the volume up too high. Grace says, I think you haven't really been horrible per se but thank you. She says, I really hate to see you this way. Helen turns her face into the cushions of the couch and starts crying, again. Can you move over please, says Grace.

16. ADJUSTMENT DISORDER: It does sound like something you would have, the whole family agrees.

17. GRACE'S EX-BOYFRIEND: Grace says, while they are making Christmas cookies, I called him yesterday. Helen looks up from frosting a reindeer to ask, Why? Grace says, shaking green sprinkles onto her wreath, Because while you were crying on the couch the other night I was thinking about how difficult it is for me to be here for you. And that made me feel like I needed to thank him, for being there for me when I was going through my thing. Helen says, Wait what thing? Casually she replies, Oh, after we left Rye. After we moved to the city I was always

walking around campus, just crying and crying. I was really crazy.

18. WHAT CATHERINE SAYS OVER THE PHONE ABOUT THAT: Poor Grace.

19. WHAT THEIR MOTHER SAYS ABOUT THAT: I always liked him. (Thanks, we know, says Grace.)

20. WHAT HELEN SAYS ABOUT THAT: Grace, why didn't you tell me?

21. CATHERINE'S BED NOW: Is it as comfortable as the old one? Helen has no way of knowing.

22. TERRIBLE FIGHT ON CHRISTMAS: You are always paddling against the fucking stream, says Evan, not even looking at her, and he throws the wooden spoon into the sink and huffs off to the living room. If this family doesn't stop fighting, says their father, sadly, and doesn't finish the sentence.

23. Evan is only going to be home for twelve days of his winter break anyway, after which he is going back to Middlebury to be in a play. Before the terrible fight, he and Helen both agree he should spend the whole time at Caffeine, learning his lines and letting her ply him with espresso drinks. One day he actually shows up. She makes him a macchiato, and then another.

24. MEET-CUTE: Catherine drops her commuter pass getting off the T. Alexander chases after her, up the stairs and down the block and into the stationary store in Harvard Square, where she is looking for a birthday card. They go out for a glass of wine. He asks for her phone number.

25. WHAT HELEN NEVER GOT THAT YEAR: A birthday card. But how petulant to hold that particular grudge.

26. BIRTHDAYS: Catherine's is October 3 and Helen's is May 14. When Catherine turns seventeen Helen brings cupcakes, and they sit on the steps at lunch in their sweaters and jumpers and slip-

ping-down school socks, and around them the air is just slightly too brisk. They drink coffee from the cafeteria, the sun warming the stone steps, the wind making the leaves bristle down the driveway. One day this will all seem very far away, says Catherine, while Helen is trying to light a candle and not succeeding. Helen smirks because how misty and all-knowing Catherine can make herself sound. In the end they leave a dozen dead matches piled on the steps and go back to class, Helen carrying their leftover cupcakes and Catherine bestowing them on passing classmates in the halls, the ones she likes. Actually, I just liked that last one's earrings, she confides as they walk into English class, I don't even I know her at all.

27. Twelfth Night, Evan replies. I don't know why I didn't ask you earlier, Helen says, feeling sheepish. They are drinking beer on Christmas Eve with most of the lights off, after their parents have gone upstairs. Across the room, Grace has fallen asleep, hair streaming down over the side of her face, falling over the edge of the couch, very nearly touching the floor. Evan says, And what about you? I mean, are you enjoying your life here?

28. CATHERINE'S TEXT: Feeling spontaneous... A and I are going to come down to NYC next week for New Year's... let's meet up?

29. CONTRITION: And Helen really is very sorry for being the way she's been about Alexander. But the fact remains that she doesn't like him, and as soon as she reads the text she realizes the problem hasn't gone away. She isn't going to be mean about it any more, isn't going to be vocal about it, but it doesn't change the fact that she doesn't really want to see him, not at all. Not a bit. And this is maybe the way it will always be.

30. Evan says, Helen what could possibly be in that text message that is making you cry.

31. PRAGUE, WASTED ON CATHERINE: She always says, Honestly I can't say I remember that much about it.

32. HELEN'S TEXT: Yes! Let's do New Year's.

33. In Rye, if their parents are fighting, they go to Evan's room and Helen and Grace sit on the floor. Then Evan climbs up on the bed and performs the argument with extraordinary flourish. He has a pair of glasses he wears to be their mother and an Oxford shirt he wears to be their father. Evan is going to be famous famous famous, Helen says, and Grace says, Now be me! When Evan is being Grace, he wears pink, and when he's being Helen, he wears a headband. If things get especially loud downstairs, he sings pop songs at the top of his lungs, or if that fails they just say, Grace, cover your ears, and Grace will put her head down in Helen's lap.

34. Their mother says, One day you will be married and you will see, you will see, this is simply how it is, couples fight, they simply do.

35. BEGINNING OF THE TERRIBLE FIGHT: Evan says, while they are doing the dishes after Christmas dinner, Look don't be offended, but as for me I never intend to move back in with Mom and Dad.

36. Grace re-activates her membership at the Park Avenue and 23rd Street New York Health & Racquet Club. Grace does not want to go to the movies with Helen and Evan and their parents on the day after Christmas because she needs to practice. Helen and Evan go to the movies with their parents but do not speak to each other, because of the fight.

37. Evan paces around the living room doing this one monologue over and over and over and over again, always messing up in the same place and then swearing. And Helen knows the line herself actually, but she just keeps sitting there on the couch with her knees crossed, eating her bowl of cereal, not looking up.

38. Helen is getting to be very skillful with her latte art. (You're becoming very glib about yourself, says her father.)

39. ADJUSTMENT DISORDER: For paperwork purposes you know

we need to say something, says the psychiatrist, whom her parents send her to see in the weeks before Christmas, because the melt-down is seeming less and less likely to resolve itself, and they are concerned. The psychiatrist clarifies, It just means you're having an intense emotional reaction. And in a way that's just how being human can be.

40. THE PSYCHIATRIST SAYS: It's okay to miss her. Why don't we just take a moment and miss her?

41. HELEN SAYS: I think I have significantly over-shared.

41. THEIR FATHER SAYS: I never wanted to go to therapy myself.

43. THEIR MOTHER SAYS: Nor did I.

44. GRACE SAYS: At school they give you all the sessions you want, for free. I think it's great.

45. EVAN SAYS: I don't need therapy, I'm a performer and I'm perilously in touch with my own emotions; there is nothing a therapist could reveal to me that I don't know; my heart is on my sleeve.

46. CATHERINE SAYS, ON THE PHONE: Seriously I'm glad to know you're taking care of yourself, it's important.

47. When Helen turns 17, Catherine calls up to say, Wear a bathing suit under your school uniform, don't forget. Helen makes some insinuation that this sounds a little juvenile, but in the end she promises, she will. What a memory, too: She's on the landline and Grace is in the background saying, Can I use that now can you please get off right now? The next day after school Catherine says, Okay so did you ever know about the sprinklers? Then, with a faintly glamorous smile, Oh just you wait. After play rehearsal, the pair of them sit together on the bleachers until dusk settles in, until the lawn goes up, all at once, in rows of long and waving plumes. Later, out there in her bathing suit under the darkening swoop of sky, bare feet in wet grass,

Helen tips her head back to watch this one particular spout reach its height and start to fall.

48. CATHERINE, FROM SEVERAL SPRINKLERS AWAY: You're supposed to run through them, Helen, not stand there considering them. Run! Frolic!

49. NEW YEAR'S EVE: Shit I love your earrings, says Catherine. Alexander says, Hey how's it going.

50. HELEN, DRUNK, LATER: I'm sorry Alexander, did Catherine even tell you that, I'm sorry I'm sorry I'm sorry. It's only this is the thing: I have never wanted to lose her.

51. Their father says, Sit here on the couch, and so they do—Evan in his ratty Middlebury College sweatshirt, not looking at Helen. He displays a careful expression of defiance. She is terrifically hungover. Their father before them is looking from one to the other and back again; he says something about new year, new leaf, let's resolve to get along. And then Grace comes clattering from upstairs, long-legged, springy, but dragging the squash racquet dully at her side so that it thunks down and down and down and down the stairs, the thunks reverberating in Helen's fuzzy skull, thunk thunk thunk. Can you not, she snarls. I thought you were turning over a new leaf on the spiteful front, Grace says, and with showy indolence drops the squash racquet to the floor. From the kitchen their mother says, Grace for God's sake you will break that squash racquet and then you'll be sorry—and Evan snorts, because for as long as any of them can remember their mother has been telling them that X is going to break and it's going to be your fault, you were careless, you were trying to make a point, and it will be broken and then you'll be sorry. In this moment, Helen catches Evan's eye.

52. IN RYE, THE STORY HAS IT: Helen is seven and Evan is five and Grace is three, and because of the sandwiches, which Helen and Evan insist they've finished but have actually conspired to throw away, their father shuts the trash can abruptly and says, Come into

the living room right now please, I want to have a talk with both of you. Interlude: a stern seminar, somewhere offstage, on the topic of how lying is wrong. Eventually, glumly, they rejoin Grace at the kitchen table. She looks up brightly from her half-eaten sandwich. She asks, Dad? He says, Yes? She says, Do you think you could also talk to me in the living room? Could I also get to do that?

53. Their mother imposes herself on the terrible fight. You have always been this way, the two of you, I mean really. Always coming home after school, complaining to me about your day, and bickering with each other, I mean when are you ever going to start pointing out what's going well instead of what's going wrong? And Grace, quiet until now, just drying the dishes and saying nothing, flares up from nowhere, slams a saucepan to the countertop. She hisses, Don't you think we might all ask the same of you?

54. THIS THE YEAR IT FINALLY OCCURS TO HELEN TO ASK: What did you even talk about in the living room? Their father says, I asked her how her day was going. She said it was going pretty well.

55. HELEN, DRUNK, STILL: She seizes Catherine lovingly by the wrist and leans in close to her ear. On the television, blurry in the background, the Times Square Ball shimmers and descends. Take my glass of water, Helen murmurs. Look at Alexander. Remember what you always used to say?

56. CONSIDER THE EMPHASIS: Helen says, You're meant to say crownèd, not crowned, you know. Evan says, Of course I know I just sometimes forget. There is no one else there, and they regard each other from either side of this impasse, and in the silence between them the espresso machine hums. Finally she says, More? But he pushes the empty cups towards her; he says, I've already had far too much.

57. BECAUSE I AM YOUR MOTHER: Grace, age eight, starts to cry. She says, But all three of us really want popcorn. We really just want it so much. So you're just making us really sad right now. Don't you

care that we're so sad because of you?

58. MOMENT OF CRISIS: Catherine says, You exhaust me, and twists her arm away from Helen's fingers.

59. THREE, TWO, ONE, HAPPY: 2015 arrives, and as it does, Helen swings at the glass of water with the back of her hand so that it spills all over the tabletop and the floor, spills into Catherine's purse, spills over her stockings and the knees of Alexander's stupid-looking pants, spills everywhere. I can't believe I came here tonight with just the two of you, says Helen, rising. She says, I must be insane. Catherine is saying, Jesus Christ, Helen, and shaking the contents of her purse out on the bar. And all around them everyone is singing, while Alexander is putting his hand on the sequined back of Catherine's dress.

60. When she lets herself into the apartment in the early hours of this year, still wearing her celebratory paper hat and crying freely (as she figures must just go without saying by now), she finds her father sitting up. Remember, she says sadly from the doorway, and he looks up from his book, Remember how angry I used to get if you waited up for me in high school? How childish and over-supervised it made me feel? Do you remember the way it made me feel like I was your science experiment and not your child? Do you remember the way I used to scream at you? He says, Are you all right? Can I get you a drink?

61. Evan packs up to go back to school. Before he leaves the two of them spend a morning in the living room running his lines, the sun falling in through the apartment windows. When he reaches the problem monologue, he gets up on the couch and delivers the whole thing with extraordinary flourish. Impeccable, says Helen, sitting on the floor, except remember: always crownèd, never crowned. He says, Stop it, stop, I know. Then Grace, from the top of the stairs, rubbing her eyes, says, Some of us were trying to sleep you know. Cover your ears Grace, they say together. And Grace, showing a small, shy smile, plodding down the stairs, says solemnly, You are going to break that couch, Evan.

62. GOING AWAY DINNER: Their father raises his drink. He says, To me it is a delight in every way to have us all together. And he takes a quick, deep breath. Anyway, cheers. Break a leg, Evan, and we will see you at your play. And their five wine glasses, making contact, chime. Their mother drinks, looks at her napkin and back up again, a little teary, maybe. She says, Evan I hope you've remembered to pack everything and did you print your ticket yet like I asked you to do?

63. SQUASH: You can come with me, says Grace, but I'm not going to go easy on you. I'm going to destroy you. And do you even know where your goggles are? I don't have a second pair to lend you.

64. HELEN'S TEXT: I'm sorry and I don't know what to do anymore.

65. CATHERINE'S RESPONSE:

66. ACT II SCENE III: "I was adored once, too."

67. PRAGUE: Catherine says, One day we'll go together. They are sixteen and lying on a blanket in Catherine's backyard, eating pizza, looking at the sky, and can think of no reason such a thing would fail to come to pass. It seems certain, they have set it in motion just by saying as much. She says, From there we'll go on to Vienna and we'll listen to orchestras. We'll bring nothing more than we can fit in our backpacks. We'll walk beside the Vltava and the Danube and drink beer in cafes. We'll meet numberless men in Prague and Vienna, she says. Helen laughs, Will we?

68. On his way to the 3:32 out of Penn Station, Evan stops by for a final espresso. He says, I hope to see you at the play next month, by which point I'll have learnèd all my lines. She bursts out laughing. He says, Wait stop don't cry. She says, It's just I'm very moved and also I don't know.

69. Grace says, flung out on the couch, Lucky you, lucky you, you still get me for two more weeks. Do you want to watch the next episode? Move over please, move over. You are, as always, completely

crowding my space.

70. ALWAYS: The air is light and sweet; a thin cloud slips quickly over the sun and keeps moving on. Everything shadows, then lightens: the backyard, the side of the house, Catherine's long bright hair. She turns her face to rest towards Helen's, leans it on the crook of her own bent arm. She says, We will, we will. Helen giggles. Catherine lets her forehead touch Helen's shoulder. She says, It won't end well. They'll always miss us. Always, always. They'll think of us often, and wonder how it happened like it did.

FORGET-ME-NOT

D. A. POWELL

AIR MAIL

PASSED BY CENSOR.

you're a hard flower to
                take anywhere.
In the grove where we go
                to forget, you are patiently
waiting to be spotted
                by the sepia moth or needle blue
flies near the alpine buttercups, but unlike
                those heliotropic faces
you take the cooler side
and do not send your fragrance out
                in the day. Let's hope
they don't discover a cure
for forgetting. I remember you fondly
                you pale blue flower
                        and then not at all.

CHRIS AMES is a writer who also draws. His work has been featured in *Big Lucks, Eleven Eleven, Fourteen Hills,* and elsewhere. He lives in Oakland, and can be reached @_chrisames or CHRISAMES.NET

JASMINE AN is a queer, third generation Chinese-American who comes from the Midwest. A recent graduate of Kalamazoo College, she has also lived in New York City and Chiang Mai, Thailand, studying poetry, urban development, and blacksmithing. Her chapbook, *Naming the No-Name Woman,* was selected as the winner of the Two Sylvias Press Chapbook Prize and is forthcoming in February 2016. Her poetry has recently appeared or is forthcoming in *HEArt Online, Stirring, Heavy Feather Review,* and *Southern Humanities Review.* As of 2016, she can be found in Chiang Mai continuing her study of the Thai language.

CINDY BERNARD'S career spans three decades and she is best known for the widely exhibited series *Ask the Dust* (1988-92), which is in the collections of the Museum of Modern Art, the Museum of Contemporary Art, Los Angeles and the Pompidou. She is a recipient of numerous grants and fellowships including a Guggenheim. She has exhibited in museums and galleries in the US, Canada, Mexico, Europe, and Japan, and her work has been included in the Whitney and Lyon Biennials. She is currently working on *Vinland,* a meditation on the shifting relationships between spaces, social and economic structures, and personal and collective histories and on a episodic visual history of social nudism. Bernard was appointed the inaugural Ruffin Distinguished Artist-In-Residence at the University of Virginia in 2013/2014 and is a 2016 MacDowell Fellow.

KATHERINE BOWLING moved to NY soon after this letter was written. She has exhibited her paintings for over 25 years and lives and works in NYC and Upstate NY. KATHERINEBOWLING.COM

BRIDGET BREWER is a writer, artist, and performer living in Providence, Rhode Island. Her work has been published in *Paragraphiti, Awst,* and *Caketrain,* among others. Currently she is completing an MFA and teaching fiction to undergraduates at Brown University.

WO CHAN is a queer Fujianese poet and drag performer. A recipient of fellowships from the Asian American Writers Workshop, Poets House, Kundiman, and Lambda Literary, Wo's work has been published in *cream city review, Cortland Review, VYM Magazine,* and elsewhere. Wo is a member of the Brooklyn-based drag alliance, Switch n' Play, and has performed at venues including Brooklyn Pride, The Trevor Project, and the Architectural Digest Expo.

NICK CRISCUOLO graduated from Montserrat College of Art with a BFA in painting. He currently works in video, animation, and ink painting, and likes to mix the three elements. His paintings, animations, and illustrations have been featured on fimmakermagazine. com, animalnewyork.com, boingboing.net, engadget.com, lifehacker. com, laughingsquid.com, trendhunter.com, cartoonbrew.com, radio. com and others. He has attended artists colonies including MacDowell, Yaddo, VCCA, and I-Park.

KATE DOYLE'S writing has been featured in *Meridian,* the Franklin Electric Reading Series, and the NYU Emerging Writers Reading Series. She is completing her MFA at NYU this year.

TONY Y. FU is presently biking between Mt. Pyre and Lilycove City. They are working toward the Rain badge and training a team strong enough to challenge the Elite Four. On weekends, they attend pilates mat classes at the Lab, a cozy fitness studio in DUMBO with complimentary towels and two gender-neutral changing rooms that always smell of flowers. We might as well start somewhere. Tonight perhaps rain and in two seasons the Perseids will arrive, meteors dragging across the sky like the finger movements of a promise made with clumsy sincerity.

MARY GAITSKILL published the story collection *Bad Behavior* in 1988; since then she's written two more collections of stories (*Because They Wanted To* and *Don't Cry*), and three novels, *Two Girls, Fat and Thin, Veronica* and most recently *The Mare.*

Originally from south Louisiana, DANIEL GRAMMER is an MFA candidate at UMass - Amherst, where he writes fiction and poetry, and works with *The Massachusetts Review.* His stories and poems have appeared in *smoking glue gun, plain china, If&When,* and *Delta Journal.*

KELLE GROOM is the author of a memoir, *I Wore the Ocean in the Shape of a Girl* (Simon & Schuster) and three poetry collections, *Five Kingdoms* and *Luckily* (both from Anhinga Press) and *Underwater City* (University Press of Florida). Her work has appeared or is forthcoming in *AGNI, American Poetry Review, Best American Poetry, The New Yorker, New York Times, Ploughshares,* and *Poetry.* Her awards include a 2014 NEA Literature Fellowship. She is on the faculty of the low-residency MFA Program at Sierra Nevada College, Lake Tahoe, and is Director of the Summer Workshops at the Fine Arts Work Center in Provincetown.

MUNA GURUNG splits her time between Kathmandu and NYC. Her fiction and translated works have appeared in *Words Without Borders, The Margins, HimanSouthasian, VelaMag* and *Lalit.* She received her MFA from Columbia University, where she was a teaching fellow. Muna currently directs a high school writing center in NYC, where her students help her discover America through activities such as eating an entire packet of "Sour Patch Kids" while writing about the flavour blue. Muna also founded KathaSatha, an organisation that fosters a public writing and storytelling culture in Nepal.

YEJI HAM is a Korean-Canadian writer in Providence, Rhode Island. Currently, she is an MFA candidate in the Literary Arts program in fiction and an undergraduate instructor at Brown University. She is working on a collection of short stories tentatively titled *Doraesol.*

GENEVIEVE HUDSON is an American writer living in Amsterdam. After earning an MFA in writing from Portland State University, she moved to the Netherlands as a Fulbright fiction fellow. Her work has been published by *Tin House* (online), *Bitch, Portland Monthly Magazine, The Believer Logger, The Rumpus, Word Riot, Bookslut* and others. She's currently working on a novel about queer love and coming of age.

CHRISTINE IMPERIAL is currently finishing up her BFA Creative Writing (poetry) degree from Ateneo de Manila University. She resides in the Philippines.

LAURA LARK is an artist and writer living in Houston, Texas.

MOHD AZLAN MOHD LATIB was born in Balik Pulau, Penang in 1974. Latib graduated in Medical Imaging (1996, University of Malaya Medical Centre), majoring in interventional Radiological and Cardiac Imaging procedures. HTTP://WWW.AZLANMAM08.COM

DIANA KEREN LEE has lived in Austin, New York, and Los Angeles. Her poems have appeared in *Painted Bride Quarterly, TINGE,* and *Asian Collections,* and she has received fellowships from NYU and The MacDowell Colony.

REBECCA LEVI is a musician, teacher, writer and translator living in Medellín, Colombia. As an educator, she has worked in Peru and Venezuela with El Sistema, a model for music education for social change, and in 2010 she founded an orchestra program in a public charter school in Boston. Her work as a translator has appeared in *Carlos Chávez and His World,* Saavedra, L., ed. She currently performs folk music of the Americas with her group, De Barro, in Medellín, where she also teaches.

MADELEINE MAILLET is a writer and translator living in Montréal. Her work has appeared in *Matrix, Hobart* and *Joyland* and has been anthologized in the 2015 *Journey Prize Stories.* She is also the fiction editor of *Cosmonauts Avenue.*

KIRSTEN MAJOR has had fiction and essays appear in *Crannog, The Rake, Chelsea,* and *Berkeley Fiction Review,* and the podcast series The

Other Stories. She holds an MFA from Cornell University and has recently completed a short story collection. She was born in Milwaukee, Wisconsin, and currently resides in New York City.

JAC MARTINEZ spends her time packing a suitcase of film and cameras, chasing light around the world. With a background in commercial and fashion work, Jac hopes to continue her career in Documentary and Fine Art Photography.

Born in Lagos, Nigeria, TOCHUKWU EMMANUEL OKAFOR'S work has appeared, or is forthcoming, in *Southern Pacific Review, Aerodrome, Bakwa Magazine, Flash Fiction Online,* and elsewhere. An MTN and Etisalat scholar, he won the Comptroller Charles Edike Prize for Outstanding Essays (2014), and two Festus Iyayi Awards for Excellence for Prose and Playwriting (2015). He is currently at work on a full-length debut novel.

AWUOR ONYANGO is a writer and visual artist who lives in the pagan citadel of Nairobi in neocolonial Kenya. She is a queer womanist and former reader of laws who embraces existential depression, delusions of united Africanities and extreme curiosity about humanity as her preferred catalysts to call for change in society through various art forms. Her first memory of writing is that of using charcoal on walls to tell the story of the quick brown fox that jumped over the lazy dog. From about the age of nine, she went on to write poetry and plays that were performed by the various schools she attended up to national competition levels and even attempted to revolutionize the high school romance circuit by writing novels with African characters in them on exercise books and distributing them throughout the school "To combat the notion that romance only happened to women with rose-coloured nipples in the ranches of Arizona". She is a writer, a fine artist, a photographer and a budding filmmaker. She struggles with wide interests in different media exploring themes that include gender, art, cultures and cultural histories as well as individualities and their survival in the hyper-globalized world we live in. She's had a few essays and short stories published (Brainstorm, Jalada, Storymoja, Manure Fresh etc) and most recently can be found trying to revolutionize the structures of the East African Art scene as an undercover researcher cum Gallerist.

SHELLY ORIA was born in Los Angeles and grew up in Israel. Her fiction has appeared in *McSweeney's* and *The Paris Review* among many other places, and has won a number of awards, including the Indiana Review Fiction Prize. Her short story collection, *New York 1, Tel Aviv 0* (FSG and Random House Canada, 2014) earned nominations for a Lambda Literary Award, a Goldie Award, and the Edmund White Award for Debut Fiction. A MacDowell Fellow in 2012 and 2014, Shelly teaches fiction at Pratt Institute, where she co-directed the Writers' Forum from 2011 to 2014. *New York 1, Tel Aviv 0* was recently translated into Hebrew and published in Israel by Keter Publishing.

D. A. POWELL'S books include *Repast* (Graywolf, 2014) and *Useless Landscape, or A Guide for Boys* (Graywolf, 2012). He lives in San Francisco.

ALICIA JO RABINS is a poet, composer, musician and Torah teacher. Her book, *Divinity School,* was selected by C.D. Wright for the 2015 American Poetry Review/Honickman First Book Prize. She lives in Portland, Oregon.

EVAN REHILL'S work has been published in *American Short Fiction, Open City, Little Star,* and *Lumina.* He is a founding curator of Picasso Machinery.

NELLY REIFLER is the author of a story collection, *See Through,* and a novel, *Elect H. Mouse State Judge.* Her stories have appeared in *McSweeney's, BOMB, jubilat, Story,* and *Lucky Peach,* among others, and anthologized in books such as *Lost Tribe: Jewish Fiction from the Edge* and *Found Magazine's Requiem for a Paper Bag.* A Recommendations editor at Post Road, she teaches at Sarah Lawrence College and lives in Saugerties, New York.

ROBIN RICHARDSON is the author of *Knife Throwing Through Self-Hypnosis* and *Grunt of The Minotaur.* Her work has been shortlisted for the Walrus Poetry Prize, CBC Poetry Award, Lemon Hound

Poetry Prize, and ReLit Award and has won the John B. Santorini Award and the Joan T. Baldwin Award. Her work has appeared in many journals including *Tin House, Arc, The North American Review,* and *Hazlitt of Random House* and is being interpreted into song by composer Andrew Staniland for the Brooklyn Art Song Society in New York. She holds an MFA in Poetry from Sarah Lawrence College and BA in Design from OCAD University. Richardson's latest collection, *Sit How You Want,* is forthcoming with Signal Poetry.

DAVID RYAN is the author of *Animals in Motion* (Roundabout Press). His fiction has appeared in *Esquire, Fence, Tin House, Electric Literature, BOMB, the Mississippi Review, Denver Quarterly, Alaska Quarterly Review, Booth,* WW Norton's *Flash Fiction Forward,* and elsewhere. You can read more about him at WWW.DAVIDWRYAN.COM.

TATIANA RYCKMAN was born in Cleveland, Ohio. She is the author of the chapbook *Twenty-Something* and Assistant Editor at sunnyoutside press. Her work has been published with *Tin House, Everyday Genius,* and *Hobart.* More at TATIANARYCKMAN.COM.

JOSEPH SCAPELLATO was born in the suburbs of Chicago and earned his MFA in Fiction at New Mexico State University. His work appears in *Kenyon Review Online, Post Road, Unsaid,* and other places, and his debut story collection, *Big Lonesome,* will be published in 2017 (Houghton Mifflin Harcourt). He teaches at Bucknell University in Lewisburg, PA.

MICHAEL SHARICK holds an MFA from Warren Wilson College. His fiction has appeared in *Conveyor* and *Lumina.* He serves as Technical Director for the Picasso Machinery performing arts series in Williamsburg. Sometimes, Michael tells people that he'd rather be fishing, but that's not true. Also, the nanobots are coming to get you. Michael lives in Prospect Heights with his wife and son.

CHAD SIMPSON is the author of *Tell Everyone I Said Hi,* which won the 2012 John Simmons Short Fiction Award and was published by the University of Iowa Press. His work has appeared in many print and online publications, including *McSweeney's Quarterly, Esquire, American Short Fiction,* and *The Sun.* He lives in Monmouth, Illinois, and is an Associate Professor of English at Knox College.

BUD SMITH is the author of the novels *F 250* and *I'm From Electric Peak,* among others. He works heavy construction in refineries and power plants. He lives in NYC. WWW.BUDSMITHWRITES.COM

SOFIA STAMBOLIEVA won the first prize in fiction in 2015 SLS Disquiet literary contest. She was a finalist in the *American Short Fiction* contest. She has a Master's degree in Literature from Sofia University St. K. Ohridski, Bulgaria and was a graduate student in Literature at City College New York. Sofi Stambo had been published by *Promethean, Ep;phany, The Kenyon Review, The MacGuffin, New Letters, Fourteen Hills, New England Review, Stand, American Short Fiction, Guernica* and *AGNI.* Two more of her stories are pending publication by *The Lifted Brow* and *The Avalon Review.*

CAROLINE BELLE STEWART'S work has appeared in *Black Warrior Review, Quarterly West, Hobart, Mistress, Big Big Wednesday,* and elsewhere. She lives in Northampton, MA.

KARA VERNOR'S fiction has appeared in *Monkeybicycle, [PANK], The Los Angeles Review,* and elsewhere. She is an Elizabeth George Foundation Scholar at the Northwest Institute for Literary Arts.